VOLUME 2
2006 | 2022

SOCCEROOS
A WORLD CUP ODYSSEY

VOLUME 2
2006 | 2022

Emeritus Professor
JOHN MAYNARD

FAIRPLAY
PUBLISHING

First published in 2023 by Fair Play Publishing
PO Box 4101, Balgowlah Heights, NSW 2093, Australia

www.fairplaypublishing.com.au

ISBN: 978-1-925914-50-4 (Volume 1)
978-1-925914-51-1 (Volume 2)
ISBN: 978-1-925914-86-3 (ePub)

© Emeritus Professor John Maynard 2023
The moral rights of the author have been asserted.

All rights reserved. Except as permitted under the *Australian Copyright Act 1968* (for example, a fair dealing for the purposes of study, research, criticism or review), no part of this book may be reproduced, stored in a retrieval system, communicated or transmitted in any form or by any means without prior written permission from the Publisher.

Cover design and typsetting by Leslie Priestley.
Photographs via Alamy, Jason Goldsmith, Texi Smith
and John Maynard's personal collection.

All inquiries should be made to the Publisher via hello@fairplaypublishing.com.au

A catalogue record of this book is available from the National Library of Australia.

Contents

Acknowledgements	1
Foreword	2
Introduction	3
WORLD CUP QUALIFICATION AND FINALS 2006	
– Germany	5
WORLD CUP QUALIFICATION AND FINALS 2010	
– South Africa	39
WORLD CUP QUALIFICATION AND FINALS 2014	
– Brazil	67
WORLD CUP QUALIFICATION AND FINALS 2018	
– Russia	103
WORLD CUP QUALIFICATION AND FINALS 2022	
– Qatar	155
Postscript	217
References	219
About the Author	223

DEDICATION

This book is dedicated
to the memory of the "Boss" Rale Rasic OAM.
On being asked a few years ago,
what the Socceroos meant to him he answered:
"Very easy question and I have a
simple answer: the Socceroos and the green
and gold jersey are my life."

ACKNOWLEDGEMENTS

I am so fortunate that I grew up in a suburb like Adamstown in Newcastle, an Australian soccer stronghold dating back to the late 19th century. I lived across the road from the Adamstown junior grounds, and in my young life several pitches with literally hundreds of kids playing the round ball game. School life in Adamstown was the same. There was only one football code played in that suburb; you never sighted a rugby goalpost.

I wish to thank the 'boss', the late Rale Rasic for agreeing to support and write the Foreword to this book. Rale kindly read and made comments and suggestions on the draft manuscript. I will be forever indebted in spending time and conversations with this wonderful man. Rale set the bar as a Socceroo coach carrying the passion, knowledge, and drive to take an Australian team to its first World Cup in 1974. But Rale also knew the importance of history, and in recognising the long journey of Australian teams on the world stage.

I have written this book in celebration of the hundreds of players that have pulled on a green and gold jersey in a World Cup match. The book is in recognition and celebration of them all.

I pay a special thank you to my publisher Bonita Mersiades and Fair Play Publishing for her support and expertise in seeing this book through to publication. Bonita is someone like me who carries a long love and passion for this great game, and I thank her for her ongoing support of not just my book, but the game itself.

I recognise that this book would not have been possible without many, many match reports gleaned from so many publications including the BBC, ABC, Fox Sports, Sky Sports, Guardian, the OzFootball website, and dozens and dozens of newspaper articles.

I take time to thank and acknowledge my beautiful wife Victoria for her love, support, encouragement and advice, and my children Courtney, Ganur, Kaiyu, Kirrin-Yurra and late daughter Candice who have all enriched my life.

FOREWORD

This book, the history of the Socceroos and the World Cup, is something that deserves attention.

John is a true educator—unfortunately we don't have many authors and books of this nature. True football, you could say, is a most powerful weapon for the future. Football (or any sport that is beneficial) is of great worth—there are less problems, less kids on the street, less kids on drugs.

Positive and inspirational stories and history can assist this process and ensure social change for the better. My perception is everything is achievable, but don't just dream. It *starts* with a dream but don't dream *too long*. So that means: 'Wake up baby, start doing!'

When I look back to 1974, Australia was not laughed at—the green and gold was respected. We had superb physical qualities. I still say if someone could encapsulate that 1974 team, we exceeded all expectations through desire, discipline, and pride. We had six different nationalities and an Aboriginal player. When I look back, it was all about pride and honour for our country. Whenever there is the question of education through football, the power of the mind should be respected more than anything. The mind is a funny thing; the mind can rule the world.

I cannot say anything but congratulate John on this book—something so powerful and so strong. The story of the Socceroos on the world stage is a magnificent story across so many decades and campaigns full of incredible joy and heartache. My sincere congratulations and hope that generations of Australians will benefit from this book.

Rale Rasic OAM
Coach of the 1974 Socceroos World Cup team

INTRODUCTION

Australia's fixation on the rollercoaster ride of emotions with the football World Cup is unquestionably one of the country's most exciting and enduring sporting chronicles. No other sport or group of athletes has witnessed the sheer magnitude of events that have unfolded around the 'Socceroos', as the Australian team became known during the 1974 World Cup qualification series. Since 1965, Australia's national soccer team has played in war zones, been subjected to riots, rockets, bans, boycotts, terrorist threats, pandemics and even the spell of a witch doctor. They have travelled like no other Australian sporting team in history to some of the most remote and exotic locations on the planet, enduring blazing heat, humidity, rain, snow and freezing cold. The World Cup odyssey for the Socceroos is unmatched for excitement or global magnitude by any other Australian sporting endeavour.

The football World Cup is the world's biggest sporting event. It is watched by billions of people across the globe—many millions more than the Olympic Games. It represents a four-year cycle for national teams to make the finals, encompassing nearly every country on the planet. Australian participation in the 'world game' has endured on the domestic scene since the late 19th century, battling xenophobia, corruption, media sabotage and blatant obstruction. My own passion for the Socceroos had its beginnings with the tours of Australia in 1966 and 1967 of high-class European and British teams: AS Roma and Manchester United. I had seen Northern NSW take on these brilliant teams, watching the likes of Georgie Best, Bobby Charlton, Fabio Cudicini and Victor Benitez sowing the seeds of my devotion to the game.

In 1969 I listened to all of Australia's early qualifying games for the 1970 World Cup, broadcast by legendary ABC caller, Martin Royal. The final match of that qualifying series and the game that carried Australia's hopes to make the Finals in Mexico was played at the old Sydney Sports Ground. My parents drove me down from Newcastle at the age of 13 to watch the match alongside a crowd of over 32,500. That 1-1 draw was one of the single greatest disappointments of my life in following the Socceroos. I was heartbroken at the final whistle—this brave and courageous team, who had been made by FIFA to circumnavigate the globe in a cruel program of matches, in the final analysis faced too big a hurdle to overcome.

Following this near miss in 1969 I watched Australian qualifying matches for the successful 1974 qualifying for the World Cup in Germany and many other subsequent World Cup campaigns that the green and gold have undertaken, including going to the World Cup Finals in South Africa (2010), Brazil (2014) and Russia (2018). This book is not just the history of Australian World Cup qualification, including games and players, but it additionally examines the (at times) panoramic social and political upheavals and intrigue of both world and football politics that have impacted the game and the Australian teams across those decades.

WORLD CUP QUALIFICATION AND FINALS 2006-GERMANY

The intervening years— The Australian team, 2002-2006

After their exit from the World Cup qualifiers and their Oceania Federations Cup elimination, Australia did not take the field again until early 2003. Looking ahead to the 2006 World Cup Finals, it would mark 32 years since Australia's only appearance back in 1974. Across those years were many disappointments, shocks, and despair. The World Cup in 2006 would in a way carry a sense of déjà vu, as it would, like 1974, be held in Germany ... could this be a sign to break the Socceroos' long drought?

Of course, across those years there were so many near misses against Scotland, Argentina, Uruguay, and the greatest tragedy of all, the elimination by Iran at the MCG in 1997. There were some who still carried the belief that the Socceroos were jinxed, and that it all went back to the curse inflicted by the witch doctor back in Mozambique in 1969, and the failure to pay him for his services.

Former captain Johnny Warren was one who certainly believed in the hex curse that was imposed upon the Australian team. Comedian John Safran, having read Johnny Warren's book *Sheilas, Wogs and Poofters* and then speaking to the former Socceroo captain, decided to do something about it through his show *John Safran vs God*. Safran flew to Africa and Mozambique and found that the original witch doctor had died. Safran persisted and found another witch doctor to lift the curse imposed back in 1969. He went with the witch doctor to the stadium in Mozambique where the Socceroos had played Rhodesia 35 years before. They both sat in the middle of the pitch and the good doctor killed a chicken and splattered the blood over Safran. The second stage of supposedly lifting the curse was invoked when Safran returned to Australia. This involved getting Johnny Warren to accompany him to Telstra Stadium where they both had to anoint themselves in some clay that the witch doctor had prepared for Safran. So theoretically the curse was lifted—all we could do now was to wait for the qualifiers.

Alongside lifting of the curse, the game in Australia was to undergo a cataclysmic upheaval that would bring about great change, success, and interest. In June 2001, Frank Lowy was approached to meet with a group of lobbyists keen to revolutionise the game, including former Socceroos' team manager Bonita Mersiades and former Socceroo Robbie Slater. The lobbyists were concerned that the game was not progressing because it was rife with petty jealousy and greed, including decades where some people were more interested in plundering funds for themselves instead of furthering the game. The group beseeched Lowy to return to the game and lead it to 'the promised land'. Lowy responded in the affirmative but only if the politics of the game were taken care of and people were put in charge to make change. Mersiades said at the time of Lowy: 'He was the obvious choice because he would give the game instant credibility and he had a longstanding love of the game. He simply told us: 'If you can sort out the politics, I will come in'.'

This led the group to lobby the Federal government via the interim Soccer Australia Chairman, Ian Knop, for a review of governance and management of the game, resulting in the Crawford Report. The Howard government inquiry would hand down damning revelations and did not have one positive thing to say about the game. The recommendations called for a complete overhaul, including a new board and chairman.

Prime Minister Howard, after the 2002 World Cup on a visit to Germany, realised that soccer 'has a far greater reach than any other sport'. It took an additional call from John Howard to Frank Lowy to convince him to return and lead soccer out of the wilderness. Lowy had grown tired of the politics and infighting back in the 1980s and had vowed never to return after he withdrew his team from the National Soccer League competition a few games into the 1987 season.

Lowy's vision was conditional that his leadership would not be a democratic approach—if he was coming in, it was to be how he ran his company: from the top down. The game needed to be cleaned up from the boardroom to the change rooms. The big difference in having Lowy was having one of the richest and most powerful men in Australia at the helm. Tycoons and media titans had largely controlled major sport in Australia, and they only funded their areas of interest. Soccer over many, many years was largely starved of funds and media coverage. There was also the influence and open door to politicians that Lowy brought with him. He took soccer onto the front page, so to speak. He was courted by prime ministers and politicians of all persuasions, and it was all about clout, money, and power. Lowy would oversee the greatest revolution soccer in this country has ever seen and initially it would achieve unprecedented success.

The detractors of Frank Lowy may have valid arguments over his style of leadership and decisions, but there is no argument that soccer would not have achieved the phenomenal success it would achieve in the next ten years without him. Sponsorship and backing were immediately witnessed—major brands like Hyundai, Qantas, Coca-Cola and the National Bank of Australia were amongst those beating a path to the newly formed Football Federation Australia door.

Frank Farina's crowning glory as coach of the Socceroos was achieved at Queens Park Rangers' Loftus Road home ground in London in February 2003. The Socceroos were up against a star-studded England team. Despite the match being used by England coach Sven-Göran Eriksson as preparation for their World Cup qualifiers and using eleven substitutes throughout the game, the England team bristled with stars like David James, Sol Campbell, Rio Ferdinand, Gary Neville, David Beckham, Frank Lampard, Paul Scholes, Michael Owen, and making his debut off the bench, Wayne Rooney. Despite the quality of the England team the Australian team that night was also made up of star players, all of them playing at the highest levels in Europe.

Tony Popovic rose high to a Stan Lazaridis free kick to power home a header to put Australia 1-0 up after just 15 minutes. Harry Kewell increased Australia's lead just three minutes before halftime when he played with the English defence before slotting the ball past James for a 2-0 lead. Francis Jeffers, a second-half substitute for England, reduced the deficit after 69 minutes, but Brett Emerton raced through on a ball with only six minutes to go to seal a great victory for the Socceroos. They continued with another match against quality opposition when they were beaten 2-1 by Ireland in Dublin, before following up with a 2-1 win over Jamaica in Reading to round out the year.

The 2004 year rolled around with an opening game against South American opposition Venezuela that resulted with a 1-1 draw. Then another match at Loftus

Road saw Australia down South Africa 1–0. Turkey, a revelation in the 2002 World Cup Finals in winning third place, toured Australia in mid-May for two games, winning both games: 3–1 in Sydney and 1–0 in Melbourne. The Socceroos were then into the Oceania Football Confederation Nations Cup which doubled as the 2006 World Cup qualifiers. The winner of this tournament would also qualify for the Confederations Cup in Germany as a lead-in to the 2006 World Cup Finals.

I was living in Adelaide at the time of this series and attended the games with my son. Hindmarsh is such a great soccer stadium with atmosphere to boot. The opening game of the tournament saw Australia go up against their old enemy, New Zealand.

Australia 1, New Zealand 0
(*Halftime*: 1–0)
Scorer: Bresciano
29 May 2004
Referee: Bruce Grimshaw (Denmark)
Crowd: 12,130
Hindmarsh Stadium, Adelaide

Australia: Zeljko Kalac, Stephen Laybutt (Adrian Madaschi 73), Simon Colosimo (Jade North 54), Tony Vidmar, Brett Emerton, Josip Skoko, John Aloisi, Stan Lazaridis, Vince Grella, Max Vieri (Mile Sterjovski 68), Marco Bresciano
New Zealand: Mark Paston, David Mulligan, Steven Old, Che Bunce, Tony Lochhead, Ivan Vicelich, Noah Hickey (Brent Fisher 51), Leo Bertos (Shane Smeltz 69), Simon Elliott, Vaughan Coveny, Raffaele De Gregorio (Duncan Oughton 78)

There was a clear difference in the class of these two teams. The Socceroos, with a raft of European-based stars like Emerton, Aloisi, Max Vieri,[1] and Bresciano were faster, stronger, and more skilled than the Kiwis.

New Zealand went for a very tight defensive structure and tried their very best to lock Australia out. The Socceroos were badly treated by the linesmen on several occasions early on, particularly with Vieri who simply outpaced his defensive cover

---

[1] Christian Vieri's younger brother who chose to play for Australia over Italy.

and was wrongly judged to be offside.

It would be no exaggeration to say that Australia with an ounce of luck could have been 4-0 up at halftime, such was the difference between the two teams.

John Aloisi should have given the Socceroos the lead after 20 minutes following a sublime through ball from Bresciano, but he shot wide with only Paston to beat. Vieri also had a great chance from an Emerton cross, but his powerful header was well saved by Paston.

The Kiwis were not without chances on their breakouts. Vaughan Coveny forced Zeljko Kalac into a hurried save that gave New Zealand a corner.

It took a brilliant free kick by Bresciano, after he had been fouled by Kiwi defender Tony Lochhead on the edge of the penalty area just before halftime, to give the Socceroos a worthy lead.

After halftime, speedster Stan Lazaridis had a quick interchange of passes with Bresciano and forced Kiwi keeper Paston into a great, diving save to deny the Birmingham winger his first goal for the Socceroos.

New Zealand appeared happy with the low-scoring loss and Kalac in the Australian goal was not seriously threatened in the second half. Second-half substitute Mile Sterjovski should have increased the Socceroos lead late in the game, but he squandered a golden opportunity.

Coach Frank Farina was content with the result: 'I'm happy with the win and with parts of our play. But I know our finishing can be better and should be better.'

The win over New Zealand placed Australia on top of the group after the first round of the World Cup qualifying tournament and in a very positive mindset. New Zealand were regarded as the toughest assignment. Steve Laybutt was in doubt for the second game against Tahiti after rolling his ankle late in the game. Simon Colosimo was also a likely omission after being replaced by Jade North early in the half with an injury.

Australia 9, Tahiti 0
(*Halftime*: 3-0)
Scorers: Cahill (2), Skoko, own goal, Sterjovski (3), Zdrilic, Chipperfield
29 May 2004
Referee: Harry Attison (Vanuatu)
Crowd: 1,200
Hindmarsh Stadium, Adelaide

Australia: Zeljko Kalac, Jade North, Tony Vidmar, Scott Chipperfield, Josip Skoko (Patrick Kisnorbo 46), John Aloisi (Mile Sterjovski 46), Tim Cahill, Stan Lazaridis (Ahmad Elrich 46), Vince Grella, David Zdrilic, Adrian Madaschi
Tahiti: Daniel Tapeta, Angelo Tchen, Pierre Kugogne, Jean-Yves Liwaut (Georges Pittoeff 80), Samuel Garcia, Billy Mataitai, Axel Temataua, Farahia Teuira, Vincent Simon (Larry Marmouyet 61), Felix Tagawa, Hiro Labaste (Taufa Neuffer 58)

The Socceroos dominated this clash from the opening whistle. There were five changes from the team that had beaten New Zealand, including Tim Cahill earning his second cap in this game. There was special significance connected with this game for Cahill. After a long, drawn-out fight, FIFA granted him the right to represent Australia in a competitive match after earlier making his debut against South Africa in a 'friendly'. The issue was that Cahill had played in a youth game for Samoa aged only 14 without realising it might jeopardise his future chance to represent Australia.

Cahill opened the scoring in the 14th minute of the first half. His first goal for his country came from a simple header at the near post after a good cross from Stan Lazaridis.

Tahiti tried but failed to execute a packed defensive system like New Zealand used. Josip Skoko scored the goal of the night in the 43rd minute when he dummied past a defender and crashed a curling left-foot shot past the keeper from the edge of the penalty area. Then in injury time of the first half a Tahitian defender could only deflect a ball into his own net to give the Socceroos a commanding 3-0 lead at halftime.

Tim Cahill, in what would become a feature of his career, was on the spot only two minutes after the restart to steer another header home to make it 4-0. Mile Sterjovski then scored another after 51 minutes; his first attempt, a miskick, was followed by another go and he dispatched the opportunity.

Sterjovski's second after 61 minutes was a superior effort. Latching onto a beautiful cross from Tony Vidmar, he volleyed the ball home. Sterjovski completed his hat-trick after 74 minutes from another comical effort—he connected with a header that the Tahitian keeper Stanley Tien Wah could only parry back to him. Sterjovski, now on the ground, poked the ball into the net.

David Zdrilic added a simple goal in the 85th minute before Scott Chipperfield rounded out the scoring in the 90th minute. It was a comprehensive result.

Australia was now in the box seat in the standings. Coach Farina was again more than happy with the performance: 'I would look at how the players kept up the intensity and the pressure. You can drop off in games like that, but they worked through to the end, no one was stopping, that's the pleasing thing.' Farina also hinted that there would again be a rotation of players for the next game against Fiji.

Australia 6, Fiji 1
(*Halftime*: 2-0)
Scorers: Cahill (3), Madaschi (2), Elrich
2 June 2004
Referee: Pedro Hernandez (Spain)
Crowd: 2,000
Marden Sports Complex, Adelaide

Australia: Zeljko Kalac, Jade North, Tony Vidmar, Scott Chipperfield (Alex Brosque 46), Brett Emerton (Ahmad Elrich 46), Tim Cahill, Vince Grella, Patrick Kisnorbo, Mile Sterjovski, Max Vieri (David Zdrilic 60), Adrian Madaschi
Fiji: Laisenia Tuba (Simione Tamanisau 46), Lorima Dau, Emosi Baleinuku, Jone Vesikula, Malakai Kainihewe (Alvin Avinesh 83), Thomas Vulivuli, Luke Vidovi (Pene Erenio 57), Taniela Waqa, Viliame Toma, Laisiasa Gataurua (sent off 58), Waisake Sabuto

Fiji came to compete, and they gave the Socceroos a scare during the match. Australia took the lead after only six minutes through Madaschi and looked the better side and on track for another easy win.

But Fiji defended well and were capable of springing rapid counterattacks. In the 19th minute, they surprised the home side by equalising through Laisiasa Gataurua. This was the first goal Australia had conceded in the tournament.

Australia regained the lead through a trademark Tim Cahill header after 39 minutes. Madaschi added a third goal five minutes after the restart. The game was sealed in the 69th minute when Gataurua, the goal scorer, was sent off after punching Cahill. Australia capitalised on the sending off and scored three further goals through

Cahill—another two to complete his hat-trick and a late one from Ahmad Elrich.

Farina again was well pleased with the result and the form of Cahill: 'The pleasing thing for me is that we were patient, especially in the second half and we just stuck to it. [Cahill] makes great runs and it's very difficult for defenders to track that.'

Australia 3, Vanuatu 0
(*Halftime:* 1-0)
Scorers: Aloisi (2), Emerton
4 June 2004
Referee: Charles Ariiotima (Tahiti)
Crowd: 2,000
Hindmarsh Stadium, Adelaide

Australia: Zeljko Kalac, Jade North, Tony Vidmar, Brett Emerton, Josip Skoko, John Aloisi, Stan Lazaridis, Alex Brosque (Ahmad Elrich 69), Vince Grella, David Tarka, David Zdrilic (Mile Sterjovski (69)
Vanuatu: David Chilia, Lexa Bule Bibi, Graham Demas, Fedy Vava, Seimata Chilia, Moise Poida (Pita David Maki 43), Lorry Thompson, Alphose Qorig (Etienne Mermer 74), Jean Emanuel Maleb (Richard Iwai 61), Roger Joe, Tom Manses

Australia was pushed by Vanuatu in winning 3-0 to confirm its place in the Oceania Nations Cup Final play-off later in the year. This was not one of the Socceroos' better performances, but they always looked like winning. Vanuatu keeper David Chilia had a 'blinder' in goal and his defenders were courageous in frustrating the Australian attack.

The Socceroos began in a whirlwind fashion and Chilia made a series of great saves from Emerton, Aloisi, Zdrilic and Skoko. One talented save stood out when he charged from goal to deny Aloisi with a diving reflex action.

Spanish Osasuna club striker John Aloisi finally broke through in the 25th minute—after a Stan Lazaridis corner found Tony Vidmar who sent in a powerful half-volley that Chilia could only parry onto the head of Aloisi to nod home.

Despite the Socceroos' overwhelming possession and pressure, Vanuatu was well organised and continued to frustrate Australia. It took Australia until the 81st minute to seal victory when Brett Emerton was on the spot to score his first goal of the tournament, smashing a rebound back past Chilia. Only two minutes later, Aloisi grabbed his second (and Australia's third) goal, after a nice through ball from Emerton left him with a simple chance to place the ball wide of Chilia.

Frank Farina summed up the game: 'We were never in danger and, again, we created so many chances… Obviously their keeper would be man of the match.'

Australia 2, Solomon Islands 2
(*Halftime:* 0–1)
Scorers: Cahill, Emerton
6 June 2004
Referee: Eduardo Gonzales (Spain)
Crowd: 3,500
Hindmarsh Stadium, Adelaide

Australia: Zeljko Kalac, Jade North, Brett Emerton, Josip Skoko, John Aloisi, Tim Cahill, Alex Brosque (Simon Colosimo 46), Patrick Kisnorbo (sent off 56), David Tarka (Ahmad Elrich 46), Max Vieri (Mile Sterjovski 46), Adrian Madaschi
Solomon Islands: Felix Ray Jr, Leslie Leo, Mahlon Houkarawa, Nelson Kilifa, Alick Maemae, Batram Suri, Commins Menapi, Jack Samani (George Lui 63), Henry Fa'Arodo, Paul Kakai Jr (Stanley Waita 63), George Suri

Fifty years to the day after the massive WWII Allies' invasion of Normandy in France in 1944, the Solomon Islands produced their own 'D-Day moment' in producing the greatest performance in their football history to hold the Socceroos to a 2–2 draw.

Frank Farina gambled by selecting a more inexperienced team for this match. The result ensured that the Solomon Islands would face Australia at the end of 2005, instead of New Zealand, with the winner earning the right to play-off against the fifth-placed South American team to qualify for the 2006 World Cup Finals in Germany.

Commins Menapi, who formerly played in the old National Soccer League, was the unquestioned star for the Islanders. He opened the scoring only minutes from halftime when he outmuscled Madaschi for the ball and smashed it past Zeljko Kalac for a 1–0 lead. Australia could not match the intensity of the Solomon Islanders in the first half.

They were playing as if the game was the World Cup Final itself—in a sense, it was for them.

Australia could only fashion one serious first-half chance when Brett Emerton got on the end of a nice Alex Brosque cross to smack at the goal, but it was well saved by keeper Felix Ray Jr.

The second half began with Australia at last running rampant. Tim Cahill made a penetrating run and fired home the equaliser through a crowded goalmouth after 51 minutes. Only two minutes later, it appeared all over for the Islanders when Brett Emerton was on the spot at the far post to crash home a fine cross from Ahmad Elrich.

At 2-1, Australia looked on course for victory but only minutes after Emerton's goal, a crude tackle from Socceroo defender Patrick Kisnorbo saw him dismissed with a red card to deliver a numerical advantage to the Islanders. With 15 minutes left on the clock, it was Menapi again on the spot to smash a shot and equaliser past Kalac for 2-2. The Solomon Islanders were in absolute celebration overload, and they hung on for the draw.

Menapi was chaired off the ground by his team-mates. They had achieved a result that no one had expected. In summing up, coach Farina was philosophical: 'Look, the objective has been achieved, we came here to beat New Zealand and win the tournament and we've done that. I would have preferred a better scoreline. I've been saying to the lads all week about complacency, irrespective of who you're playing, we came up against a team tonight where, really, it was their World Cup Final.'

The two teams would now meet again at the end of the year in a home-and-away final to determine who would be crowned Oceania champions and in 12 months' time would again face off to determine who progressed in the World Cup qualifiers.

It was good to see a final of this tournament feature another team other than just Australia versus New Zealand. Solomon Islander coach Allan Gillett was planning well in advance for the two-game final. The 2-2 draw that the Islanders achieved against the Socceroos had given the 500,000 Islander population an enormous lift and interest in the game. But he hoped that the team kept their feet on the ground as they had been on 'cloud nine' since the draw. The Islanders played a warm-up game against Brisbane Wolves and Gillett felt it was a reality check when they were well beaten 2-0. It was the team's first outing since qualifying for the play-off.

Gillett was adamant that he now had to refocus attention on the games ahead for the Oceania Cup. In the coming weeks- the Solomon Islanders would prepare in a camp in

Singapore and play two games against the Singapore Under-23 and national side. The reality of what faced the Islanders was stark—they were ranked 126th in the world and faced a star-studded Australian XI. The massive gulf in quality was revealed in the two-game Oceania final—the Socceroos were too good for the Islanders in the first game in Honiara, winning 5-1, and in the return clash at Sydney Football Stadium they again demonstrated their class, winning 6-0. It would now be another 12 months before the teams squared off again in the Oceania World Cup qualifier final.

The Socceroos would begin a long preparation for the Confederations Cup opening with a 2-2 draw with Norway at Craven Cottage in London. They then had a return game against South Africa in Durban to start the most critical of years, 2005, with a 1-1 draw. The Socceroos next played games against quality Asian opposition; they defeated Iraq 2-1 in Sydney in front of more than 30,000 people and then were too good for Indonesia, winning 3-0 in Perth. This game was organised by the newly constituted Football Federation Australia, led by Frank Lowy, as a fundraiser following the tragic tsunami that had devastated parts of Asia. In a final lead-up game for the Confederations Cup, Australia played New Zealand at Fulham's home ground of Craven Cottage. The game attracted a crowd of over 9,000, mainly made up of expats from Australia and New Zealand who witnessed the Socceroos win 1-0.

The 2005 FIFA Confederations Cup in Germany was meant to be the build-up and preparation for the 2006 World Cup qualifiers. Instead, it led to a complete change in direction. The Socceroos opened their campaign in Frankfurt and were beaten 4-3 by Germany. Australia displayed a defensive frailty and were left exposed on several occasions. Then the Socceroos were downed in their second match against Argentina 4-2. As in the game against Germany, defensive errors led to their demise. The final game of the tournament was the 'final straw' for Frank Lowy and the FFA. The Socceroos were beaten by Tunisia 2-0 in a poor performance. Coach Frank Farina stepped down as coach by 'mutual consent.' Farina had been under pressure for some time and a clash with a television reporter and ongoing disputes with a television network had not helped his cause.

The news was announced that Farina would be replaced by Dutch super coach Guus Hiddink. This was a major coup. Hiddink had taken Holland to a semi-final of the 1998 World Cup and even more impressively, taken South Korea through to a semi-final in 2002. Hiddink was a hard taskmaster and would run a strict regime. On his appointment, Hiddink stressed the attraction: 'I like to travel and to go into unknown or unstable situations and see what you can manage there.' The first call of duty was to call a training camp to be conducted in Holland with 28 players. The majority were all playing at high levels in Europe, minus Liverpool's Harry Kewell who had torn his adductor 20 minutes into the Champions League Final in Istanbul against AC Milan—a game Liverpool would win after coming back from three down. There were three additions from the new A-League: Archie Thompson, Jade North and Sasho Petrovski all flew in from Australia.

It was noted that Hiddink's first comment after just ten minutes of an organised practice game during their first session was: 'Stop, stop! This is shit!' The boss had taken charge and things were going to change—he wanted the players to relax, assist each other and stop roaring instructions to one another. However, after the session had concluded, Hiddink had a newfound respect that the 'mentality, the attitude, the commitment was more than 100 per cent.' Hiddink realised he had the players and they responded and lifted. He was a strict disciplinarian. Josip Skoko was adamant that compared to being under Frank Farina, this was a 'terror camp'.

In September 2005, in another milestone achievement under the new Lowy-led revolution, came the news that Australia would no longer be a member of Oceania but had joined the Asian Football Confederation instead, a recommendation that had been put to him in June 2001 when visited by the lobbyists wanting change. Things would never be the same again. The Socceroos still had their Oceania commitments for the 2006 World Cup qualifiers against the Solomons Islands and a play-off game against the fifth-placed South American team, but in future they would be charting a World Cup course through Asia.

Hiddink raised some eyebrows over his selection of Mark Viduka as the new captain of the team. It would be an announcement that would lift the big striker. Hiddink was not without criticism of the V-bomber, commenting that he was lazy and needed to lose at least four kilos. The Socceroos first challenge under Hiddink was to overcome the Solomon Islands.

Australia 7, Solomon Islands 0
(*Halftime:* 3–0)
Scorers: Culina, Viduka (2), Cahill, Chipperfield, Thompson, Emerton
3 September 2005
Referee: Subkhiddin Mohd Salleh (Malaysia)

Crowd: 14,000
Sydney Football Stadium

Australia: Mark Schwarzer, Lucas Neill, Tony Popovic (Marco Bresciano 57), Tony Vidmar, Brett Emerton, Josip Skoko (Vincent Grella 72), Mark Viduka, Tim Cahill, Jason Culina, John Aloisi (Archie Thompson 61), Scott Chipperfield
Solomon Islands: Francis Aruwafu, Leslie Leo, Mahlon Houkarawa, Nelson Sale (sent off 54), Alick Maemae (Stanley Waita 46), Kidstone Billy, Batrum Suri (George Suri 43), George Lui, Gideon Omokirio, Henry Fa'arodo, Francis Wasi (Richard Anisua 59)

It was a wet introduction for Guus Hiddink in his new role as coach of the Socceroos in Sydney against the Solomon Islands. Realistically, the gulf in class between the two teams was gigantic and it showed.

Australia applied pressure from the kick-off, but the Islanders were composed at the back and resolute. The Socceroos' opening chance fell to John Aloisi after nine minutes. New captain Mark Viduka laid a ball back to Aloisi to hit from the edge of the area, but it cannoned away off a defender.

After 17 minutes, Solomon Island defender Leslie Leo was forced to clear a ball away off the Islanders' goal line. A few minutes later, the Solomon Islands mounted their first attack, but the move quickly broke down.

On the 20-minute mark, John Aloisi laid a ball back to Jason Culina who had raced forward from midfield, and he smacked the ball from 15 metres out beyond the reach of keeper Francis Aruwafu.

Despite a wealth of possession, Australia wasted a run of good chances through Viduka, Aloisi and Cahill. The Solomon Islands packed their defensive line, and it frustrated the Australian attack.

Finally after 36 minutes, despite the pressure of defenders, Tim Cahill managed to lob a ball to Mark Viduka. With his back to goal, the captain then leapt into an acrobatic overhead kick and the ball was whipped into the top right-hand corner of the net.

Just before halftime, Australia scored a third. Josip Skoko sent over a pinpoint cross that found the head of Viduka who powered the ball past the hapless keeper into the top corner of the net.

After halftime, the Socceroos picked up the tempo. The Solomon Islands were not helped when Nelson Sale Kilifa was given a straight red card for a diabolical tackle on Jason Culina.

In the 56th minute, Tim Cahill was on the spot to head home. Substitute Mark Bresciano then sent a low, skidding shot that skimmed off the wet surface and nearly got under the keeper. Archie Thompson, on as a substitute, also went close as he headed just wide with his first touch.

Scott Chipperfield then sent a 30-metre ground shot that whizzed under the keeper for 5–0. Viduka thought he had secured a hat-trick when he headed home, but he was judged to be just offside. Since coming on Archie Thompson had proved a handful and was looking very sharp. In the 68th minute, he scored a brilliant goal. He controlled a bouncing ball and swivelled to smack it past the keeper from a very acute angle.

The Socceroos were now on the rampage. Thompson hit another effort just over the bar and Bresciano whacked one just wide. Brett Emerton sealed a 7–0 victory when he sent in a 25-metre shot that should have been easily saved.

Guus Hiddink had some reservations about the win: 'Seven goals, that's not bad. I'm not unhappy with that. But against an opponent like the Solomon Islands, you owe it to yourself to win convincingly. There is room for improvement though. A Latin opponent is going to be an altogether different story.'

The return leg in Honiara drew some criticism and disbelief from Hiddink. He was critical of the team bus, accommodation, lack of a mobile phone signal and the state of the pitch. However, his biggest 'bark' was for the team performance. Hiddink recalled the game years later: 'I got very angry at the game—it was so undisciplined, wa crap game.'

The country itself was in turmoil; earlier in the year a younger Socceroos' match was abandoned after a hostile crowd hurled glass bottles, rocks, and other projectiles onto the pitch. The political climate itself was one of simmering tension. International peacekeepers including Australian troops were there to ease the tension. On the day before the game, Australia was in a team meeting in a flimsy fibro shack when a 4.2 magnitude earthquake struck on the ocean floor some 90 kilometres west of Honiara. The ground and building shook—it was an unnerving experience for the Australian players and officials.

Hiddink made five changes to his side and reverted to a back four, with lone-striker Viduka upfront.

Australia 2, Solomon Islands 1
(*Halftime:* 1–0)
Scorers: Thompson, Emerton
7 September 2005
Referee: Shamsul Maidin (Singapore)
Crowd: 15,000
Lawson Tama Stadium, Honiara

Australia: Zeljko Kalac, Lucas Neill, Brett Emerton, Mark Viduka (Ahmad Elrich 45), Tim Cahill (Luke Wilkshire 45), Scott Chipperfield (Stan Lazaridis 71), Vince Grella, Archie Thompson, Jon McKain, Jason Culina, Mark Bresciano
Solomon Islands: Felix Ray Jnr, George Suri, Gideon Omokirio, Lesley Leo (Richard Anisua), Mahlon Houkarawa, Henry Fa'arodo, George Lui (sent off 49), Francis Wasi, Stanley Waita (Jack Samani), Commins Menapi, Batram Suri (Abraham Iniga)

As a match that would mark the end of Australia's presence in the Oceania Confederation, it was hardly a worthy send-off. Australia performed poorly. There were excuses of course: a humid, very hot day, and the pitch was unpredictable in its bounce as it was dry and hard.

The Socceroos from the outset looked disjointed and lacked any rhythm or cohesion. On the sidelines, Guus Hiddink erupted with frustration at the poor showing. The Australian players on the field and on the bench were subjected to a barrage of abuse: 'If this is what they are going to give me, I'm not going to ruin my reputation coaching this shit! I'll leave if this is the crap I have to deal with.'

The Solomon Islands were greatly improved with the addition of Commins Menapi. He had missed the first game in Sydney through suspension and his close control, power and strength made him a constant threat in this match. Bartram Suri and Henry Fa'arodo were also in the mood and menacing.

On the 20-minute mark, Vince Grella split the Islander defence with a pass through to Archie Thompson and he lobbed the ball over the advancing keeper for 1–0 to defuse the tension.

Whilst the Socceroos remained in charge and their defence looked comfortable, this game was no walk in the park.

After the break, Lucas Neill was forced to bring down Fa'arodo and the referee pointed to the spot. This was followed by a series of wild moments. First, Menapi stepped up and took the free kick that was brilliantly saved by Kalac. The save and missed opportunity saw an eruption from the Islander players that resulted in George Lui being sent off. Inexplicably, the referee then ordered the kick to be retaken by Henry Fa'arodo, ruling that Kalac had moved for the first kick. Fa'arodo put this one away and the Solomon Islands were level.

The goal spurred the Islanders on for a few minutes, but down to ten men, it was a big ask. The Socceroos regained their composure and with an extra man were able to find room and space. In the 59th minute, Brett Emerton found himself on the edge of the Islander box to crack home a shot.

The Solomon Islands mounted some pressure in the dying moments but were unable to force a draw. At the final whistle, Australia were through to a meeting with a South American opponent.

A disgusted Hiddink could not hide his disappointment: 'If we play like that in November, then it will be mission impossible.'

At this point, their South American opponent was still 'up in the air'. 2002 opponents, Uruguay, were in fifth place at the time with two rounds remaining, and Chile, Colombia or Ecuador might still gain the spot. In preparation for the November game, Hiddink called for another camp in Holland before a warm-up match against Jamaica in London at Craven Cottage. Although a second-rate opponent, the game against Jamaica saw a welcome return to form after the debacle in Honiara. The Socceroos won in a canter, 5-0.

However, Hiddink was still far from happy and railed at his players during the game—probably still carrying resentment over their poor match against the Solomon Islands. At least to the cameras, he was able to offer some encouragement after the game: 'It's a good victory, the team got confident, there were some very good things defensively, but you have to look a little bit through reality, that it was not the strongest Jamaican team.'

Shortly after the Jamaican game, Uruguay faced Argentina in their final qualifying game. They needed a win to hold down the fifth qualifying spot and secure the play-off match against the Socceroos. The talented Alvaro Recoba scored the winning goal for Uruguay to book their play-off berth against the Socceroos.

Four years before, the Socceroos had flown into a hostile Montevideo. The team came through the normal passenger terminal exit to be jostled, howled at, and there were allegations of spitting. There was none of that this time round. The preparation, with no expense spared, was meticulous. Four years earlier, the Socceroos certainly did not have the clout or power of a boss like Frank Lowy or a coach like Guus Hiddink. The sponsorship of the team had also been taken to another stratosphere under the new FFA regime. It included Qantas—a sponsor who would have a major bearing on (and bonus for) the team, particularly in the lead-up to the return game in Sydney.

This time the team did not fly into Uruguay to prepare. They went to Argentina and spent a week in Buenos Aires in relative peace instead for Hiddink to work his magic. Hiddink selected the training ground in one of the poorest areas of the city, surrounded by slums and despair. The location was meant to toughen up the Australian team. The Socceroos only flew into Montevideo 24 hours before the match, and on arrival were given the protection of 100 policemen and a motorcade that was given the right to skip red lights—it was unprecedented. Hiddink stuck with his 3-4-3 formation and despite the knowledge that Uruguay has a star-studded team with recognised world stars in Alvaro Recoba, Diego Forlan and Dario Silva, there was a quiet confidence in this Australian team.

The 'cloak and dagger' mental games behind the scenes were well and truly ramping up. The time of the kick-off for the first game was a major bone of contention. It all came down to how the two teams would get to Australia. There was only three days and eleven hours between fulltime in Montevideo and kick-off in Sydney, and 24 hours would be spent in the air. The last commercial flight leaving Montevideo would leave late on the night of the first leg. Uruguay had played a sneaky hand and requested that kick-off be delayed from 4pm to 9pm in order to delay Australia's departure until the following day. They had organised a charter flight straight after the game for themselves and clearly held all the aces, or so they thought. But they did not know that the Socceroos already had a Qantas flight organised and waiting on the tarmac to fly them straight to Sydney after the game. Further calamity struck Uruguay when their charter flight arrangements fell through, meaning they would be forced to catch a commercial flight. There was uproar when they discovered that the Socceroos had their own flight locked in.

There was a resulting hue and cry over changing the kick-off time back so that they could catch the late flight out, and after much pleading, they were granted a 6pm kick-off. But this clearly demonstrated the homework and preparation done by the Australian administration—they held the upper hand.

However, Australia had some injury concerns with Moore, Popovic, Bresciano and Kewell. Harry Kewell was on the return from his adductor troubles, whilst the other three were in recovery from injuries in their most recent games.

Australia 0, Uruguay 1
(*Halftime:* 0–1)
12 November 2005
Referee: Claus Bo Larson (Denmark)
Crowd: 55,000
Estadio Centenario, Montevideo

Australia: Mark Schwarzer, Lucas Neill, Scott Chipperfield, Tony Vidmar, Tony Popovic, Brett Emerton, Mark Viduka (John Aloisi 80), Harry Kewell, Vince Grella, Archie Thompson (Marco Bresciano 52), Jason Culina
Uruguay: Fabian Carini, Diego Lopez (Guillermo Rodriguez 63), Paolo Montero, Dario Rodriguez, Carlos Diogo, Pablo Garcia, Diego Perez, Alvaro Recoba, Diego Forlan (Dario Silva 18), Marcelo Zalayeta (Fabian Estoyanof 63), Richard Morales

Uruguay opened with a lot of passion and power and were intent on pressuring and storming over Australia. But this was a very different Australian team to 2002 and the defence settled quickly. They weathered the opening ten minutes with their goal intact. Australia even forced the first two corners of the game and a good Viduka free kick was well saved by Carini.

After 15 minutes, dangerman Recoba took a free kick that bounced off bodies in the penalty area like a pinball machine before falling into Mark Schwarzer's arms. Morales tried his best to convince the referee that he had been impeded in the area, but it was to no avail.

After 18 minutes, Diego Forlan, clearly carrying an injury into the game, suffered a knock and was taken off. Alvaro Recoba was the next Uruguayan to go down like he was shot, and his resulting free kick forced Schwarzer into a fine save. Dario Silva was booked for a foul on Scott Chipperfield soon afterwards.

Uruguay began to up the tempo and Carlos Diogo was free, but his weak header from a perfect Recoba corner was easily saved by Mark Schwarzer. Silva then forced Chipperfield into a foul and a yellow card into the bargain. Another questionable foul by Chipperfield was called soon after when he and Perez were both tangled up. It provided Recoba with the opportunity to showcase his incredible free-kick accuracy to find a running Dario Rodriguez, and he powered a header past Schwarzer. This goal lifted both the Uruguayan team and the crowd that had been silenced by the Australian resistance.

Silva then went on a run down the right and his high cross was palmed away by Schwarzer. Australia repelled further Uruguayan assaults before halftime and going in just 1–0 down was not the 'end of the world'.

Australia began the second half well. Mark Bresciano came on for Archie Thompson after 52 minutes. The game had its moments; both Lopez and Grella needed medical attention. Uruguay claimed a handball against Bresciano that was waved away.

It was that man Recoba again on the 60-minute mark placing another free kick on a dime, but Diego could only lift the ball over the bar. Shortly after, Recoba was through on goal with Schwarzer out of the area. Recoba went down claiming he was contacted by the keeper—but again the referee waved it away.

Vidmar was then forced into conceding another free kick and fortunately, for once, Recoba did not do justice to it. Then another Recoba free kick whizzed across goal only needing a faint touch to score, but the ball evaded all.

In a rare Socceroos' attack, Jason Culina shot wide of the Uruguayan goal. Hard-working Mark Viduka was replaced by John Aloisi with ten minutes to go. The 90 minutes ticked over, and four minutes went up on the clock, but the Socceroos weathered the Uruguayan pressure. Going back home only one down was a great result.

After the game, coach Hiddink offered his insight: 'We dominated the first half completely, but we weren't determined enough to finish it off and we got a sloppy moment on a free kick... We played well, but we had to finish it off because we know they are very dangerous on set pieces.' The big advantage Australia would now capitalise on was the Qantas jet parked at the airport ready and waiting just for them. It was all perfectly planned; they boarded the aircraft in Montevideo and once in the air, their meals were to be served on a Sydney lunchtime schedule to help them acclimatise. They also had massage tables built-in to the cabin, courtesy of Qantas, and had the full and undivided attention of the Qantas cabin crew. And of course, they were set on Australian-time sleep patterns.

Uruguay meanwhile had to catch a flight to Santiago (2.5-hour trip), and then board a normal commercial flight to Australia with many of the team cramped into economy. Frank Lowy brought so many benefits, and his influence across so many spheres was unparalleled as far as the Socceroos were concerned. When Lowy asked for help or made a demand, people jumped to attention. Back in Australia, there was a growing confidence in super coach Guus Hiddink as the man who could break the long drought and qualify Australia for a World Cup Finals' series.

The media coverage and attention given to the game in Sydney was unprecedented. Uruguayan superstar Recoba added 'fuel to the fire' before the match, stating that Uruguay 'had a divine right to be in the World Cup Finals.' It was a sell-out at the Sydney Olympic Stadium.

For sheer excitement, there was nothing to match this game—the atmosphere was electric. Eighty-three thousand fans jammed into the stadium with another 15,000 outside watching the game on a big screen. The stadium was rocking in a sea of green and gold. Fans cheered and roared their support from the outset. A banner was waved proudly in the stadium proclaiming the late, great Socceroo captain Johnny Warren's words 'I told you so!' Sadly, Warren died of lung cancer in 2003 at the age of 61.

Australia 1, Uruguay 0
(*Halftime:* 1–0)
Scorer: Bresciano
16 November 2005
Referee: Luis Medina Cantalejo (Spain)
Crowd: 83,000
Olympic Stadium, Sydney

Australia: Mark Schwarzer, Lucas Neill, Scott Chipperfield, Tony Vidmar, Tony Popovic (Harry Kewell), Tim Cahill, Brett Emerton (Josip Skoko), Mark Viduka, Vince Grella, Jason Culina, Marco Bresciano (John Aloisi)
Uruguay: Fabian Carini, Diego Lugano, Paolo Montero (Marcelo Sosa), Dario Rodriguez, Carlos Diogo, Perez Pablo Garcia, Guillermo Rodriguez, Gustavo Varela, Alvaro Recoba (Marcelo Zalayeta), Richard Morales, Mario Regueiro (Fabian Estoyanoff).

The first 30 minutes of the game seemed to indicate that the South American giants were on their way to another World Cup Finals, whilst Australia would again be heartbroken onlookers to the 'big dance' in Germany. Inter Milan superstar Alvaro Recoba was a bubbling source of danger as Australia gave away repeated fouls that provided the little maestro with opportunities to weave his magic left foot into action. But miraculously, Australia survived.

It was Recoba that provided an early fright when he struck a shot from distance that confused Schwarzer and bounced away off the keeper. Only minutes later, another Recoba pinpoint through ball forced Scott Chipperfield to head it away for a corner, just beating Carlos Diogo. From the resulting pinpoint corner kick from Recoba, Uruguayan fullback Diego Lugano headed wide of the far post with the goal open.

On the 20-minute mark, Fabian Carini's goal kick saw Richard Morales flick the ball on to the racing Recoba, dissecting the Australian defence. All Australian fans held their breath as the little maestro, bearing down on goal, elected to shoot early and for once, his famed left foot missed the target as his shot whizzed past the post.

Only minutes after, another Uruguayan move nearly released Recoba again, but Tony Popovic collared the little master with his left arm and was lucky to only receive a yellow card. This heralded the change on 27 minutes which altered the course of the match: Hiddink replaced Popovic with Harry Kewell.

Jason Culina's well-hit, low drive forced a top fingertip save from Carini soon after. Brett Emerton then smacked a shot over the bar following good work from Viduka. Australia was coming. The mood of the match had shifted. Only four minutes later, a move down the left saw Cahill and Viduka combine to make an opening for Kewell, but he mishit his shot. The ball skewed across to the unmarked Mark Bresciano who smashed it into the roof of the net. Australia was now dominating the game and Kewell was in a menacing and tormenting mood.

The game was still locked at 1–0 at halftime. The Socceroos began as they had left off in the first half, pushing forward for a second goal. Uruguay gave away a free kick and Bresciano's pinpoint delivery found Scott Chipperfield on the far post, but his header whipped across goal.

Then against the run of play, Uruguay very nearly equalised when a Recoba corner found big striker Morales unmarked, but his powerful header, aimed down, went up and over the bar.

The X-factor of Harry Kewell was the dominating factor; his cross found Tim Cahill, but he volleyed wide. Mark Viduka then beautifully knocked a ball down to Bresciano, but he shot over the top.

The threat of Recoba disappeared after 72 minutes when he was replaced by Zalayeta. Uruguay suffered another cruel blow when captain Montero suffered a hamstring injury and was replaced.

The Socceroos were full of running, and Uruguay was wilting under the pressure. The secret Australian flight home from South America and Uruguay's exhausting flight were now showing dividends.

Australia surged forward. Tim Cahill had a diving header whiz just wide of the post. Carini then brought off another top save from a near-post shot from Kewell. A Bresciano corner found Chipperfield soon after, but he did not react quickly enough, and the chance was gone.

Spanish referee Luis Medina Cantalejo blew fulltime, and we were to be subjected to extra time.

Surprisingly, it was Uruguay who found another spark. They lifted to create two great chances. Another Uruguayan corner found the head of Gustavo Rodriguez, but he headed over the bar. This was followed by a Zalayeta flick finding Morales, but his shot flashed just wide of the far post. Zalayeta was left with another chance late, but he headed straight into the arms of the relieved Mark Schwarzer. The referee called time and it was now the pain of a penalty shoot-out.

Guus Hiddink had intended to replace Mark Schwarzer with Zeljko Kalac for the penalty shoot-out, but the late forced substitution of Brett Emerton with Josip Skoko had curtailed those plans (thankfully). This was one of the most tense, exciting, and nail-biting moments in Australian soccer history. Harry Kewell, a more composed and assured player one would be hard pressed to find for the big occasion, stepped up for the first kick. He placed his shot to Carini's right with the keeper diving left, 1–0 Socceroos.

Dario Rodriguez then stepped up for Uruguay. He sent his shot to Schwarzer's left but the big keeper was ready to parry it away! Australia 1–0.

Lucas Neill stepped up for Australia and sent Carini diving in the wrong direction. Australia 2–0!

Varela was faced with a pressure kick, and he again showed nerves as Schwarzer again went the right way. He was a whisker off saving again as the ball just scraped under his body, Australia 2–1.

Tony Vidmar, the old warhorse, stepped up next and smacked the ball into the corner of the net, with Carini sent the wrong way. Australia 3–1!

Estoyanoff slammed the third Uruguayan kick past Schwarzer, Australia 3–2.

Captain Mark Viduka took Australia's fourth shot and was looking confident, but he took a stuttered run up and his shot to Carini's right went wide of the post. The crowd were stunned. Australia were so close and now it seemed to have been snatched away. Surely it would not be one of those World Cup moments of despair.

Zalayeta stepped up to make it all square. Mark Schwarzer was a study of concentration. He was holding his commitment not to move until the very last moment. Zalayeta moved up and hit the ball sweetly and powerfully to Schwarzer's left, but the big keeper had again guessed the right direction. But this shot was hit with power and above the keeper's diving body. As the ball flew above him, Schwarzer's arm reached up and he parried the ball away—it was a truly remarkable save, Australia still 3–2!

It was now up to John Aloisi. He was confident and assured and had no hesitation in putting his hand up to take a penalty. Aloisi hit the ball perfectly, but Carini had also guessed the direction, but this shot was just too good, and it hit the net and unleashed pandemonium. The entire stadium erupted. The country also erupted, and John Aloisi tore down the touch line ripping off his shirt and racing into sporting immortality: Australia, 4–2!

The Socceroos were heading back to the World Cup Finals, and fittingly following the heroics of our 1974 team in Germany. Guus Hiddink was an overnight Australian sporting hero. The Australian preparation for the 2006 World Cup Finals in Germany was unprecedented to even many of the seasoned professionals in the Australian squad. Hiddink took his team to Mierlo in the Netherlands, and the coach subjected his players to a gruelling preparation, both physically and mentally. He had his squad prepared and willing to run through brick walls. Australia also faced two top sides in preparation games. The first in Melbourne was against Greece. The match illustrated just how much Australia had improved. Even with top players like Kewell, Cahill and Aloisi absent, the Socceroos dominated the match and were super impressive in winning 1–0. Mark Viduka was glowing in his estimation of the impact of the coach: 'We keep the ball very well, we don't panic. We play like all the other big teams around the world. It's a tribute to him.' Skoko scored with a long-range shot to give the Socceroos victory.

Australia would play their final match against the Netherlands in Holland. The

Dutch were the third-rated team in the world at the time, with a team of superstars including van Nistelrooy, Robben, van Persie, van Bommel and Sneijder. No firmer test could be imagined before the World Cup. The Dutch should have won this game comfortably but they squandered several great chances, and Schwarzer pulled off four or five outstanding saves to all but stamp his starting berth in the team for the Finals. Hiddink had encouraged a competitive fight for the goalkeeping jersey—Kalac had played against Greece, but Schwarzer had earned his spot in this final hit out. The game ended 1–1 and a draw against such opposition was an impressive result, but the Socceroos were well below their best. Tim Cahill smashed in an equaliser in the 55th minute against the run of play. Luke Wilkshire was shown a red card for a tackle on Bronckhorst late in the game, but Australia showed great defensive resolve to hold out. At the World Cup Finals, Australia was drawn into Group F with Brazil, Croatia, and Japan—a formidable group. The team was now Germany-bound.

2006 World Cup Finals

There was a mad scramble for tickets amid predictions that the World Cup in Germany could be the biggest ever gathering of Australian sports fans for any overseas event. Home country Germany, perennial favourites Brazil and potential challengers in Holland, Argentina, and Italy looked the pick of potential winners. Legendary German player and manager Franz Beckenbauer oversaw the World Cup's organisation as president of FIFA's Organizing Committee. In typical German fashion, the organisation of the event proved an overwhelming success. The Finals were tied to the 1989 tearing down of the Berlin Wall and the collapse of the Soviet Union. It was a celebration of the unification of Germany. The stadiums were excellent, and there were efficient transport systems and good accommodation. Australia would go into their opening World Cup Finals' match against the old enemy, Japan, as a very well-prepared and fit side.

Australia 3, Japan 1
(*Halftime:* 0–1)
Scorers: Cahill (2), Aloisi
12 June 2006
Referee: Essam Abdel-Fatah (Egypt)

Crowd: 46,000
Fritz Walter Stadium, Kaiserslautern, Germany

Australia: Mark Schwarzer, Craig Moore (Joshua Kennedy 61), Lucas Neill, Luke Wilkshire (John Aloisi 75), Marco Bresciano (Tim Cahill 53), Brett Emerton, Scott Chipperfield, Vince Grella, Jason Culina, Harry Kewell, Mark Viduka.
Japan: Yoshikatsu Kawaguchi, Yuichi Komano, Tsuneyasu Miyamoto, Hidetoshi Nakata, Naohiro Takahara, Shunsuke Nakamura, Atsushi Yanagisawa (Shinji Ono 79), Alessandro Santos, Takashi Fukunishi, Keisuke Tsuboi (Teroyuki Moniwa 56 (Masashi Oguro 91)), Yuji Nakazawa.

What a match. What sheer excitement, drama and a nail-biting finish! It was an outstanding Australian team performance, all building to a crescendo with only seven minutes left on the clock. There was a huge Australian contingent in the crowd who went ballistic during those final minutes and through to fulltime. It was a very warm day at 30 degrees with high humidity to test the stamina of the players and the respective coaches, Hiddink and Zico.

The Socceroos began superbly and looked in control. Viduka was proving too much to handle for the Japanese defence of Miyamoto, Tsuboi and Nakazawa. Kawaguchi made two early saves before Bresciano blasted over the bar and shortly after had a weak attempt saved.

The Japanese then had a chance following a foul on Nakata on the edge of the box, but the free kick smacked into the Australian wall. The Australian team's passing and movement between the midfield and attack was fluent and controlled. Viduka skilfully backheeled a ball to Bresciano, whose shot could only be parried away by Kawaguchi before it was cleared. The Australian defence was well-marshalled and looked relaxed and dominant over the Japanese forward line.

The Australian midfield also had complete control of the park and they were dictating the pattern of play superbly. The Japanese had barely made an impact on the game when against the run of play Australia switched off and allowed a goal that should have been an Australian free kick. An inoffensive weak cross from Celtic attacker Nakamura seemed to offer no real threat as Schwarzer moved to gather, but he appeared to be bundled aside by the Hamburg striker Naohiro Takahara and fell to the ground. The ball careered on, evading the defence, and crossed the line for a goal. The goal was a blatant foul, and it incensed the Australian team.

After the game, Hiddink declared: 'OK it happens but you expect a free kick or a yellow or red card but not a goal.' Schwarzer was even more blunt: 'I was smashed off the ball by two of their players as I was about to take a harmless lob inside the box.'

It was a cruel blow and for the first time the Australian team were thrown off their game plan and lost confidence. Australia now had to press forward for an equaliser, and this left some gaps for the Japanese to exploit with sudden and swift counterattacks through Nakata, Takahara, Nakamura and the naturalised Brazilian attacker, Alex Santos. Harry Kewell was sparked into action and he very nearly equalised, but his powerful shot screamed over the bar.

The balance of the game had completely shifted and another goal for Japan could well have sealed the Socceroos' fate. Viduka now seemed well-shackled by Fukunishi at the back for the 'Blue Samurai.' Australia began to look short of ideas on how to break down the Japanese stronghold. Hiddink sensed the moment, and he brought on Josh Kennedy and Tim Cahill. The new assault to unpack the Japanese was an aerial one, with balls pumped into these two spring-heeled, lethal air weapons. With just ten minutes to go, John Aloisi was also introduced. Australia were going for it with nothing to be 'left in the tank'.

The Japanese then suffered a blow with Tsuboi forced off. Lucas Neill went forward to launch a long throw into the nervous Japanese box and the ball bounced off Kennedy falling to Kewell, but he mishit it in the crowded goalmouth. The ball then fortuitously fell to the ever-alert Tim Cahill to smack home the equaliser!

Japan should have scored only minutes later but the unmarked Fukunishi, with Australia storming forward, smacked his shot wide. John Aloisi then held a ball up close to the Japanese penalty area before squaring it to Tim Cahill. He was again ready on the spot to take his time and crack a second shot in, off the post, across the goal, and in!

The Socceroos had hit the front—it was madness. Cahill in his customary fashion set off to the corner flag pursued by players, substitutes and Australian support staff.

Kawaguchi pulled off two great saves from Viduka and Aloisi soon after. Japan nearly forced an equaliser but were denied what looked a legitimate penalty appeal that was waved away. Close to fulltime, John Aloisi ran on before slotting the ball past Kawaguchi. The referee blew fulltime and whether you were an Australian in the stadium, watching on a big screen back home, or in your own lounge room, you simply erupted with joy. Australia had recorded their first ever World Cup Finals' victory!

Even though Tim Cahill had only been on the pitch for 38 minutes, he was justifiably man of the match with his two goals. He was ecstatic: 'It means everything to be here, we dream of this as boys'.

In the other group game, Brazil overcame Croatia 1–0 through a late first-half goal from Kakâ. Ronaldinho was now regarded as the world's best player, and with strikers like Ronaldo and Adriano up front, and Real Madrid wingman Robinho out wide, they looked like such a threatening line-up. Croatia and Japan followed up with a 0–0 result that was a great one for Australia. It left them sitting at the top of the group with Brazil. The next match would be their biggest test—going in against five-time World Cup champions Brazil in Munich.

Australia 0, Brazil 2
(*Halftime:* 0–0)
18 June 2006
Referee: Christian Schraer (Germany)
Crowd: 66,000
World Cup Stadium, Munich, Germany

Australia: Mark Schwarzer, Lucas Neill, Craig Moore (John Aloisi 69), Tim Cahill (Harry Kewell 56), Jason Culina, Tony Popovic (Marco Bresciano 41), Brett Emerton, Mark Viduka, Vince Grella, Scott Chipperfield, Mile Sterjovski
Brazil: Nelson Dida, Marcos Cafu, Ferreira Lucio, Silveira Juan, Fereira da Rosa Emerson (Gilberto Silva 72), Roberto Carlos, Ze Roberto, Leite Adriano (Chaves Fred 88), Ricardo Kakâ, Luiz Ronaldo (De Souza Robinho 72.

The Australian tactics worked a treat through the first half of this game as a packed midfield frustrated and broke up Brazilian forward probes. Australia was not intimidated or overawed by their opponents and demonstrated that they fully deserved to be on the park with the world champions.

The performance of the referees and linesmen for this game was highly questionable with the 25 to 9 foul count at fulltime. Clearly, Brazil was a 'protected species'. The

Brazilians seemed a little off the pace and Ronaldo appeared to be uninterested in the game and carrying a few extra kilos. Australian fans, never short of a quip at the right time, started chanting: One-Ton Ron-al-do, he's a One-Ton Ron-al-do to the tune of the Cuban song 'Guantanamera'.

The Samba Kings had some chances early. Ronaldo flicked a ball back over his head to Kakâ, but his volley was just wide. Viduka then had a crack from 25 yards, but it was well held by Dida. Craig Moore deflected a Ronaldo shot away for a corner soon after. Scott Chipperfield made a break down the left and put it through for Sterjovski to race on to, but he let it run over the by-line thinking he heard the referee's whistle. It had been a whistle in the crowd. Just before halftime, Australia very nearly grabbed the lead when a powerful Bresciano shot was not far away.

The Socceroos were not just there to put up a defensive wall, and in the second half they created some great chances. Harry Kewell had only just come off the bench when Brazilian goalkeeper Dida dropped the ball at his feet, but Kewell unfortunately could not put it away. Tony Popovic had to be replaced by Mark Bresciano with an injury shortly before halftime. Bresciano was nearly through but was brilliantly tackled by Zé Roberto inside the box when about to shoot early in the second half. It was Zé Roberto again who halted Kewell as he burst through not long afterwards.

The goal Brazil had been pushing for came in the 49th minute. Ronaldo, after a few stepovers on the edge of the box, squared the ball to Adriano who was one-on-one with Scott Chipperfield, and he pushed the ball to his lethal left foot and slammed it home past Mark Schwarzer. Ronaldo looked to have been just offside when he received the ball, but the Socceroos were down 1–0.

Harry Kewell was then found in the clear from a long clearance with Dida off his line. Kewell had a crack from 35 yards that was not far away. John Aloisi came on as a substitute and nodded a ball down for Viduka, but his effort ended on top of the net. Bresciano also had a late volley pushed away by Dida.

The world's best player, Ronaldinho, was well-shackled by the Australian defence. The disappointing Ronaldo was replaced by Robinho who, just after coming on, sent a vicious shot just wide of the left post.

The second Brazilian goal came late when Robinho got in the clear and sent a low, swerving shot. Schwarzer got a touch to it, but only managed to push the ball on to the post. It bounced back to the unmarked replacement Chaves Fred to tap home.

Many commentators felt the 2–0 scoreline flattered Brazil and that Australia were unlucky not to have scored, or even drawn the match. The game demonstrated to the world that Australia was a top-class side and that this Brazilian team did not overawe them. Brazil, despite the talent at their disposal, had now gone two games against both Croatia and the Socceroos where they looked flat and far from unbeatable.

It was a jubilant Australian squad after the match. A draw between Croatia and Japan had left Australia in a position of needing only a draw against Croatia to progress to the last sixteen. Harry Kewell was thankfully let off for an outburst against the referee during the Brazil match by the FIFA disciplinary panel.

The upcoming match against Croatia would be the biggest game in Australian soccer history. There was added spice: three members of the Croatian squad, Anthony Serić, Josip Simunić and Joey Didulica had grown up and developed as footballers in Australia. The Socceroos squad also contained five players with Croatian ancestry, including captain Mark Viduka.

The big decision for this game was Hiddink's choice to replace Mark Schwarzer in goal with Zeljko Kalac. There had been the usual unstable Australian soccer media stir-up in the background calling for Schwarzer to be replaced for some time, but it was still a surprise for the penalty shoot-out hero against Uruguay to be replaced.

Australia 2, Croatia 2
(*Halftime:* 1–1)
Scorers: Moore, Kewell
22 June 2006
Referee: Graham Poll (England)
Crowd: 52,000
Gottlieb-Daimler Stadium, Germany

Australia: Zeljko Kalac, Lucas Neill, Craig Moore, Tim Cahill, Jason Culina, Brett Emerton (sent off 87), Mark Viduka, Harry Kewell, Vince Grella (John Aloisi 63), Scott Chipperfield (Joshua Kennedy 75), Mile Sterjovski (Marco Bresciano 71)
Croatia: Stipe Pletikosa, Darijo Srna, Josip Simunic (sent off 90), Igor Tudor, Dario Simic (sent off 85), Marko Babic, Dado Prso, Niko Kovac, Stjepan Tomas (Ivan Klasnic 83), Ivica Olic (Luka Modric 74), Niko Kranjcar (Jerko Leko 65)

The game for qualification to the last 16 was a cracker and contained passion, hysteria, relief, shock, mistakes, and blunders.

The Socceroos were off to a shaky start with Viduka turning the ball over in failing to find Grella. In trying to make amends for his mistake, he chased back and gave away a tame free kick on the edge of the Australian box. Only two minutes in, Croatian dead-ball specialist Darijo Srna stepped up. It was a perfect free kick up over the wall with power, and it went past the diving Kalac.

The Socceroos should have been level only four minutes later when Mark Viduka was rugby-tackled in the Croatian penalty box by Josip Simunić. Graham Poll, who did not have a great game with the whistle, was seemingly the only one who failed to see a clear foul.

Australia was rattled; Croatia were dominating the middle of the park and their back three led by Simunić looked rock solid. The Socceroos were constantly turning over the ball and failing to hold possession. The pattern of the match was set with Australia streaming forward and Croatia happy to sit back and wait for a quick counterattack.

Harry Kewell forced a great save from Pletikosa. Australia had free-kick specialist Mark Bresciano on the bench and Emerton and Chipperfield were not up to his high standard of delivery. Several free kicks and corners were wasted.

However, Hiddink's focus on fitness would be the telling factor. Australia continued to press forward and were able to pin Croatia's fullbacks with our wide options of Emerton, Sterjovski, Chipperfield and Kewell rampaging down the flanks. The pressure finally brought a just result when a threatening Brett Emerton cross saw Dario Simić bundle Cahill away, and then Stjepan Tomas handled the ball. Craig Moore stepped up calmly and slotted the ball home from the spot. 1–1!

Back home in Australia, a picture of then Prime Minister John Howard jumping from his seat in celebration after the penalty illustrated that the Socceroos had arrived and captured the nation's attention like never before.

Croatia nearly scored right on halftime, but Pršo fired into the side netting. The Socceroos looked on top after the break, but they suffered a major blow after 56 minutes when Kovac left Tim Cahill standing and fired a weak shot at Kalac who muffed the shot. It hit his body and bounced up and over him into the net.

Hiddink as a master tactician came to the fore again when he brought on Bresciano after 71 minutes. John Aloisi and Josh Kennedy were also introduced. A brilliant cross from Bresciano should have been rewarded with another penalty as Tomas again handled in the box—more blatantly than the first one but again Poll missed it. The Australians had been turning over the ball and failing to find the killer pass, but with Bresciano on, that all changed. Only 15 minutes remained on the clock when fittingly it was a pinpoint Bresciano cross that found Aloisi's head to flick on to Kewell to volley home with surgical precision! Later reviews questioned whether Kewell was offside, but for once luck went with the Socceroos.

Australia was now at 2–2 and the team that would progress if scores remained level. They were surging forward over the top of Croatia, pressing, chasing, and harassing them at every opportunity. Adding to the excitement and stress, Brett Emerton was red-carded after picking up his second yellow card with only three minutes left on the clock. Poll also issued Dario Simić with a second yellow and he was also marched. Yet Josip Simunić somehow survived dismissal despite having received three yellow cards. He should have been marched for another rugby tackle on Viduka, as well as bringing down Josh Kennedy for good measure. But somehow in all the carnage and chaos, Poll failed to send off the Croatian defender.

Right at the end, Kennedy was again upended in the penalty area and the ball rolled to Aloisi to dispatch, but apparently the whistle had gone to end a remarkable match. The Socceroos were through to face Italy in the last 16—what an achievement!

There was history between our next round opponents Italy and Guus Hiddink. Back in 2002, the Dutchman orchestrated South Korea's 2–1 victory over Italy to reach the quarter-finals of the World Cup. The Italian press called Hiddink *il-mago*, translating as 'wizard' or 'magician'. Italy had to face the Socceroos with the knowledge that their nemesis awaited them. Additionally, there was the stain of Italy's 1–0 defeat at the hands of North Korea back in 1965, Australia's first ever World Cup opponents.

Italy had progressed in 2006 after finishing top of Group E having beaten Ghana 2–0, the Czech Republic 2–0 and drawing 1–1 with the United States. They had a rock-solid defence, and some world-class stars in Totti, Del Piero, Buffon, Cannavaro and Pirlo. Australia would also go into this important match with two important players missing—Harry Kewell was injured, and Brett Emerton suspended. On the plus side, Mark Schwarzer was re-installed as first choice keeper after the Zeljko Kalac experiment against Croatia.

Australia 0, Italy 1
(*Halftime:* 0–0)
26 June 2006
Referee: Luis Medina Cantalejo (Spain)
Crowd: 46,000
Fritz-Walter Stadium, Kaiserslautern, Germany

Australia: Mark Schwarzer, Lucas Neill, Craig Moore, Tim Cahill, Jason Culina, Mark Viduka, Vince Grella, Scott Chipperfield, Luke Wilkshire, Mile Sterjovski (John Aloisi 81), Marco Bresciano
Italy: Gianluigi Buffon, Fabio Grosso, Fabio Cannavaro, Alessandro Del Piero (Francesco Totti 75), Gennaro Gattuso, Luca Toni (Andrea Barzagli 56), Alberto Gilardino (Vicenzo Iaquinta 46), Gianluca Zambrotta, Simone Perrotta, Andrea Pirlo, Marco Materazzi (sent off 50)

The match was full of excitement, pain, jubilation, and controversy. The ground was affected by heavy overnight rain but played in glorious conditions at 23 degrees.

Australia began well and controlled the ball for long periods, stroking it about. They held it for the opening two minutes before a Tim Cahill shot went wide of the mark. Italy packed their midfield and defensive areas to close down Australian penetration. The Azzurri were favouring the quick breakout approach and had their chances in the opening exchanges. Del Piero left Jason Culina and crossed beautifully to Luca Toni who beat Chipperfield to the cross, but his header whizzed past the right post with Schwarzer beaten.

Another Italian through ball found Del Piero whose cross again caused problems with Perrotta laying off to Gilardino, but his shot was deflected clear by Chipperfield's leg. The Australian midfield and defence of Grella, Wilkshire, Culina, Moore, Neill and Chipperfield were performing at the top of their game in closing down players like Pirlo and nullifying Italian advances.

After 20 minutes, Gilardino provided a chance for the tall Luca Toni whose shot was deflected by Craig Moore, forcing Schwarzer to save by tipping the ball over the bar. Only two minutes later, Gilardino and Toni saw Italy's best first-half chance end with Toni's shot saved by Schwarzer's legs.

The Socceroos had their chances as well with Scott Chipperfield pouncing on an

Australian free kick that was poorly cleared. Chipperfield shot low and hard at Buffon who fumbled the first attempt but was quick to regather ahead of the advancing Mark Viduka. Another chance fell to the giant Toni after 34 minutes as Simone Perrotta's cross reached his head, but his effort went up and over the bar.

It was an evenly matched first half; Australia with greater possession but Italy with the bulk of the chances. Three minutes after the break, another Italian counter saw Vincenzo Iaquinta cross from the right wing to Perrotta who teed up Toni, but he again squandered the opportunity by shooting up and over with the goal at his mercy.

The game then saw a dramatic turn in Australia's favour when Marco Materazzi was red-carded for a foul on Marco Bresciano when the Socceroo had been in goal-scoring space. Scott Chipperfield was now getting more space with the man advantage, and pushing forward he brought another great save from Buffon after 58 minutes—sadly, there was no one on the spot to finish off the chance.

The Socceroos dominated the next 30 minutes of the match; the Italians withdrew into a six-man defensive wall. Coach Marcello Lippi even sacrificed forward Luca Toni for another defender in Andrea Barzagli. On the 81-minute mark, John Aloisi was brought on for Mile Sterjovski as the Socceroos went in search of the winner. A corner from Bresciano found the head of the climbing Tim Cahill, but he could only head over. Minutes later, a surging John Aloisi drove a low, hard cross into the box, but Buffon took the ball off the boot of Mark Viduka.

Three minutes of extra time was called; the master Hiddink had two subs up his sleeve for extra time with the Italians having used all of their replacements. They would also be playing with a man down. Australia was full of running and looked the far fitter team.

There was only 40 seconds on the clock when an innocuous Italian break down the left saw Fabio Grosso get away from Marco Bresciano. Grosso was confronted by Lucas Neill coming across to block the threat. Grosso flicked the ball inside and saw Neill go to ground and extend his leg. Heo saw his opportunity and went down over Neill's leg. Neill had made no move towards him, but the Spanish referee awarded a penalty. Totti stepped up and in such a high-pressure moment slammed the ball into the right side of the net past Schwarzer. The referee blew fulltime almost immediately.

It was such a horrible way to go out—an outstretched leg and a feigned fall had seen the Socceroos eliminated. The Australian team and supporters were absolutely gutted. But in looking back, the team known as the 'Golden Generation' could hold their heads high. The performances of the Socceroos against some of the best teams in the world was outstanding.

The 2006 World Cup Finals will not be remembered for an outstanding winning team or the play of a genius individual who dominated the tournament. The quarter-finals saw France and Brazil battle it out, Les Bleus triumphing 1-0. Germany, with home advantage, only progressed 4-2 on penalties at the expense of Argentina. Italy downed Ukraine 3-0 (who would have been Australia's quarter-final opponent) and Portugal outed England 3-1 on penalties. Italy then downed the hosts Germany 2-0 in extra time in the semi-final, and France eliminated Portugal 1-0.

The Final will not be remembered for a classic match but for the referee sending off Zinedine Zidane for head-butting Italian defender Materazzi, who fell to the floor. The referee had no option other than to send off the French superstar. Zidane said it was a response to the Italian player making comments about his family. The match would go down to a penalty shoot-out and Italy held their nerve to win 5-3. Australia could take great heart in the fact that the team that eliminated them from the World Cup had gone on to lift the trophy.

WORLD CUP QUALIFICATION AND FINALS 2010-SOUTH AFRICA

The intervening years— The Australian team, 2006-2010

The decision to hold the World Cup Finals in South Africa was a brave decision on FIFA's part but considering the collapse of apartheid and the election of Nelson Mandela as President of South Africa, a very just one. Mandela had used sport to unify the nation through the 1995 Rugby World Cup that host South Africa won, allowing Mandela to showcase the uniting of the rainbow nation—it was a stroke of genius. But that incredible success and PR work could not disguise the fact that neither Mandela nor the black population followed the wobbly ball code that was historically tied to the brutal apartheid scheme. As I stated in my book the *Aboriginal Soccer Tribe,* under white rule in South Africa, cricket and rugby union dominated. They were sports tied to the apartheid regimes of the past and very much a part of the racial divide there. Soccer became the game of the majority black population, and 'the more popular soccer became with the non-whites the more the whites looked down on it',[2] In that sense, the staging of the World Cup Finals in South Africa meant the world to the black population.

Australia, despite the financial clout of Frank Lowy, could not hold onto their Svengali coach, Guus Hiddink. Like a modern-day footballing 'soldier of fortune' he moved on to greater riches promised by Russia to lead their next World Cup campaign. Hiddink's assistant Graham Arnold was installed as interim coach. Frank Lowy had been instrumental in seeing Australia admitted to the Asian Confederation; there

---

2 Murray, B, The World Game, University of Illinois Press, Urbana and Chicago, 1998, p. 18.

would be no more World Cup qualifiers against South American teams.

Australia had their first outing following the 2006 World Cup Finals in an Asian Cup qualifying match against Kuwait in Sydney. Despite not having any of their major overseas stars lining up, the Socceroos still pulled a very healthy 36,000 fans to the Sydney Football Stadium. The game was significant in the fact that the Australian team contained two Aboriginal players in Jade North and Travis Dodd. It was Dodd, the flying Adelaide wingman, who scored the opening goal in the 2-0 victory. The return match saw Australia beaten 2-0, likely through a combination of heat and lack of preparation.

In October, still capitalising on the wonderful World Cup results in Germany, Australia was able to draw over 47,000 fans to Suncorp Stadium in Brisbane to see a 1-1 result with Paraguay. The Socceroos were then able to field many of their big names against Bahrain in an Asian Cup qualifier at Allianz Stadium in Sydney that they duly won 2-0. In mid-November, the Socceroos were back in action against Ghana in a friendly match in London at Loftus Road that ended in a 1-1 draw.

In early 2007, it was rumoured that another high-profile Dutch coach Dick Advocaat would take over as coach of the Socceroos. Advocaat did go as far as signing a contract, pulling out at the last minute to stay with his Russian club, Zenit St Petersburg. This threw a spanner in the works for Football Federation Australia and Graham Arnold remained in charge for another friendly against Denmark played at Loftus Road in London. The Danes proved too strong winning 3-1.

The Socceroos next went up against China in Guangzhou in a friendly match that the Socceroos won 2-0. It would be nearly three months before Australia went into battle in another friendly, this time against old South American rivals, Uruguay, played at the Olympic Stadium in Sydney. Uruguay gained a sense of revenge for their elimination by Australia for the 2006 World Cup Finals, winning the game 2-1.

The Socceroos then had a warm-up away match against Singapore, winning 3-0 before heading off to their first Asian Cup tournament in Thailand. It was a far from impressive opening as they drew 1-1 with Oman in Bangkok. It was clear that the Asian qualifying route for the next World Cup would not be as easy as some people had predicted. Australia was awful in the second Asian Cup match, going down 3-1 to Iraq. There were rumours of player disputes, a coach under pressure, and both media and public outcry. Then in a complete turnaround, Australia thumped host nation Thailand 4-0 to ensure a rematch with old World Cup foes, Japan. The match against

Japan saw the game locked at 1–1 following extra time. The penalty shoot-out saw the Blue Samurai triumph 4–3 and eliminate the Socceroos from the Asian Cup.

Australia next faced Argentina in a friendly match at the Melbourne Cricket Ground, won by Argentina 1–0 in front of over 70,000 fans. It was again rumoured that Dick Advocaat had relented and agreed to take over as coach of the Socceroos. It was also announced that this would be Graham Arnold's last match in charge.

However, Advocaat again 'did a runner' on Australia and failed to come through as coach. An interim coach in Robert Baan, another Dutchman, would hold the reins against Nigeria at Queens Park Rangers' Loftus Road home ground. Australia won the game 1–0 thanks to a rocket shot from David Carney. It was then announced that Dutchman Pim Verbeek would be Australia's new coach and in charge of their Asian World Cup qualifying campaign. Verbeek had been assistant coach to both Guus Hiddink and Dick Advocaat who were in charge of South Korea at the 2002 and 2006 World Cup Finals respectively. Verbeek did not endear himself to the Australian-based coaching or playing contingent of the A-League, rating it a poor league. He would rely heavily on the overseas contingent and his method was a cautionary approach of two holding midfielders and one lone striker. Australia, as a seeded country due to their FIFA world ranking, were already advanced to round 3 of qualifying for the 2010 World Cup and were drawn against Qatar, Iraq, and China.

Australia 3, Qatar 0
(*Halftime*: 3–0)
Scorers: Kennedy, Cahill, Bresciano
6 February 2008
Referee: Subkhiddin Mohd Salleh (Malaysia)
Crowd: 50,969
Docklands (Telstra Dome) Stadium, Melbourne

Australia: Mark Schwarzer, Lucas Neill, Craig Moore (Brett Holman 77), Tim Cahill (Carl Valeri 67), Jason Culina, Brett Emerton, Luke Wilkshire, Joshua Kennedy (John Aloisi 70), Scott McDonald, David Carney, Mark Bresciano
Qatar: Mohamed Ahmed, Marcone Junior, Ibrahim Al Ghanim, Majidi Siddiq (Wesam Abdulmajid 46), Abdulla Koni, Saad Al Shammari (Mesaad Al Hamad 46), Ali Yahya, Mustafa Abdulla, Khalfan Al Khalfan, Talal Al Bloushi (Waleed Abdulla 78), Fabio Montesin

Only new to the job, Pim Verbeek's tenure as coach was off to a fine start with an impressive 3-0 win at home against Qatar. Verbeek had only 24 hours earlier met the bulk of his squad for the very first time. After the disappointment of the Asian Cup elimination, the win was a relief for the team and their supporters.

Verbeek had promised an attacking approach to the game. Kennedy and strike partner Scott McDonald were up front with Tim Cahill lurking behind them. The fullback pairing of Brett Emerton and Scott Carney were given an open licence to push forward and pump balls into the box for the twin aerial threat of Kennedy and Cahill.

The Socceroos were in control of the game from the opening whistle and stroked the ball about with supreme confidence. It was Kennedy who opened the scoring after ten minutes from a great move that saw the ball moved across the park from right to left and back through the midfield before Brett Emerton was found overlapping on the right. His pinpoint cross found Josh Kennedy to head home.

Eight minutes later, a Luke Wilkshire free kick found the head of Tim Cahill to put Australia 2-0 in front. The Australian midfield were dominating proceedings and Jason Culina was outstanding in dictating and controlling the play, and in particular, feeding a rampaging Brett Emerton on the right. Mark Bresciano was another who was allowed far too much space, and a player like that with latitude would punish anyone.

In the 33rd minute, Scott McDonald found Bresciano on the right to crack home Australia's third goal: 3-0.

Kennedy forced a great save from Ahmed in the Qatari goal just before halftime. Australia could have been five up by the break but for the keeper. Australia's backline of Moore and Neill were in complete charge and were quick to defuse any threat to the Australian goal.

The first half was a truly brilliant display, but Australia did not go on to punish Qatar in the second half. That said, it was a great start for the Socceroos on the road to South Africa qualification. Pim Verbeek confirmed that he was a very good appointment as coach.

Six weeks later, in preparation for its second World Cup qualifier against China, Australia played a warm-up game against Singapore at the National Stadium in stifling conditions. The Australian team was mostly made up of A-league players, but welcomed back Harry Kewell who captained the side in a disappointing 0-0 draw. The game against China would be a tough assignment on this form, but the team would welcome back many of the European contingent for that match. Tactically,

China was leaving no stone unturned as they scheduled the game in the high-altitude city of Kunning.

Australia 0, China 0
(*Halftime*: 0–0)
26 March 2008
Referee: Mohamed Omar Al Saeedi (UAE)
Crowd: 33,000
Tuodong Stadium, Kunning

Australia: Mark Schwarzer, Lucas Neill, Jade North, Jason Culina, Michael Beauchamp, Carl Valeri, Luke Wilkshire, Archie Thompson (Brett Holman 10), David Carney, Vince Grella, Mark Bresciano
China: Zeng Lei, Zhang Shuai, Sun Xiang, Feng Xiaoting, Li Weifeng, Han Peng (Qu Bo 73), Zheng Zhi (Shao Jiayi 68), Zhu Ting, Jiang Ning, Sun Jihai, Zhou Haibin (Xiao Zhanbo 65)

The match confirmed that the Socceroos' move into the Asian Confederation for World Cup qualifying would be very competitive and challenging. The game was played at 1900 metres above sea level. Altitude was not the only hurdle to overcome as the Socceroos would be left without several first-choice players. Only two days were provided for preparation and the coach was also struck down with a stomach bug.

Verbeek went into this match with a clear plan: a very tight backline and congested midfield to deny and blunt Chinese chances upfront, and the tactic worked very well. It was a disciplined Australian performance. Surprisingly China was very cautious, and this approach assisted Australia.

The Socceroos took control of the ball from the first whistle. They knocked the ball around and controlled possession for long periods. Australia was without a genuine striker, but still found opportunities. On a counter, Brett Holman went past Feng Xiaoting and found Bresciano whose shot was brilliantly saved by Zeng Li.

Only ten minutes from halftime, China squandered two great chances to Zheng Zhi and Zhu Ting. China had a reputation as being gun-shy in front of goal and on this performance, they showed just how deficient they were.

After the break, the status quo continued. Australia remained in control of the game and the ball. It was not until the final 15 minutes that China shook itself from lethargy. The speedy Han Peng came off the bench and he injected speed and fear into the Australian defence. In the first instance, he cracked a great volley that Schwarzer saved. Only minutes later, Peng raced through on goal, Schwarzer came out to intercept, clipped him and it was a penalty. Schwarzer, just the man for a penalty, again proved his worth, getting his leg to the shot before gathering it in.

Australia nearly pinched the game in extra time with Jason Culina putting through Bresciano before the ball fell to David Carney, but China's Sun Xiang forced his shot away. The 0–0 result in the end was an outstanding achievement. The Australian defence of Lucas Neill, Michael Beauchamp and Jade North were outstanding at the back.

Frank Lowy could well be perceived as the man with the golden touch. He had established Football Federation Australia, the A-League, and the W-League, then saw Australia end 32 years in the World Cup wilderness to qualify for Germany 2006 before gaining acceptance as a member of the Asian Confederation. These were monumental changes and the perception of both the game and its potential had undergone a massive shift in Australia.

Lowy then looked to pull off the greatest coup of all by putting Australia forward to host the 2018 or 2022 World Cup Finals. It was estimated by researcher and economist John Wilkinson that if successful, the bid to host the world's biggest sporting event could land Australia $5.4 billion dollars in revenue, although other organisations came up with different forecasts, both positive and negative. In any event, as the bid progressed, it became known that it would also have cost as a minimum more than $3.5 billion to fulfill the technical requirements.

The Kevin Rudd Labor government chipped in $47 million dollars in support of the bid, knowing full well the benefits that would flow to the nation if it was successful. But this bid proved to be the first chink in Frank Lowy's armour of success.

It would be two months before the Socceroos were back in action against Ghana, the top-rated African nation and ranked 14th in the world by FIFA. The game was a warm-up match for the crucial games against Asian Cup conquerors, Iraq. Australia downed Ghana 1–0 in front of 29,000 people at the Sydney Football Stadium. Then suddenly it appeared at the last minute that the World Cup qualifier against Iraq would not proceed. The Iraqi government had cancelled both their Olympic Committee and the Iraqi FA. FIFA quickly suspended Iraq from the World Cup competition as a result.

However, Iraq was quick to reply that it was all a mistake and that they never disbanded their Olympic Committee, or the Iraq FA, and the game would proceed.

Australia 1, Iraq 0
(*Halftime*: 0–0)
Scorer: Kewell
1 June 2008
Referee: Ravshan Irmatov (Uzbekistan)
Crowd: 48,678
Suncorp Stadium, Brisbane

Australia: Mark Schwarzer, Michael Beauchamp, Jade North, Jason Culina, Brett Emerton, Luke Wilkshire, Scott McDonald (Brett Holman 65), Harry Kewell (Bruce Djite 76), David Carney, Vince Grella, Mark Bresciano (Carl Valeri 62)
Iraq: Noor Sabri Abbas, Saad Hafidh, Basem Abbas Gatea, Nashat Akram Abid Ali, Emad Mohammed Ridha, Qusay Munir Aboudy, Younis Mahmood Khalaf, Hawar Mulla-Mohammed (Mostafa K Abdulla 84), Haidar Hussain, Ali Hussein Rhema, Mahdi K Ajeel (Salih Sader Salih 68)

The Socceroos came away with the points but could be considered lucky. The Iraqi frontline squandered some top chances and Mark Schwarzer again proved what a top-line goalkeeper he was.

Australia surprisingly was on the backfoot from the first whistle as Iraq swarmed forward, pressing high and creating panic in Australia's inexperienced backline with Lucas Neill missing. Iraq looked particularly dangerous on set pieces. The pacy attackers Hawar, Emad and Mahdi Karim caused no end of problems for the Australian defence. Emad was very unlucky in hitting the crossbar and shortly after with a mix-up between Carney and Beauchamp, he found himself free in the box, but it was Schwarzer again the hero to save. Later in the half, Mahmoud should have scored with a free header but failed to hit the target. It was a relief for the Socceroos to go in level at halftime as Iraq had three outstanding chances missed.

Australia did have some first-half chances. A nice exchange between Kewell and McDonald saw Bresciano presented with an opportunity, but he failed to capitalise.

Harry Kewell looked a new man; fit and rejuvenated and causing the Iraqi team plenty of problems with his slick play.

Only two minutes after the break, a beautiful cross from Brett Emerton was met by Harry Kewell with a beautiful header to score. Australia began to take charge of the middle of the park through Grella, Culina and Wilkshire. They controlled great slabs of possession, but there was not much forward support for McDonald and Kewell.

Iraq had some chances through Emad and Mahmoud that were wasted but the best chance came to Hawar who raced clear of the offside trap, but he shot straight at Schwarzer who saved. Substitutes Bruce Djite and Brett Holman combined well soon after, only for Holman to shoot wide.

The 1-0 win was a great one for the Socceroos and we were in pole position to advance to the final stage.

The return match against Iraq would be played in the neutral venue of Dubai in the United Arab Emirates. Sadly, Iraq was denied the chance to play at home through instability from war and conflict. The games of subterfuge and downright insult for a result surfaced here. Australian supporters were charged $100 a ticket and Iraqi supporters just $10.

Australia 0, Iraq 1
(*Halftime*: 0–1)
7 June 2008
Referee: Kazuhiko Matsumura (Japan)
Crowd: 8,000
Al Ahli Stadium, Dubai, United Arab Emirates

Australia: Mark Schwarzer, Chris Coyne (Joshua Kennedy 64), Michael Beauchamp, Jade North, Jason Culina, Carl Valeri, Brett Emerton, Luke Wilkshire, Harry Kewell (Scott McDonald 70), David Carney, Vince Grella (Brett Holman 46)
Iraq: Noor Sabri Abbas, Saad Hafidh, Basem Abbas Gatea, Nashat Akram Abid Ali (Haitham Tahir 78), Emad Mohammed Ridha, Qusay Munir Aboudy, Younes Mahmood Khalaf, Hawar M Taher (Muhammed Ali Karem 68), Haider A Hussain, Ali Hussein Rhema, Mahdi K Ajeel (Salih Sadwn 68)

The match in Dubai was played in stifling conditions. Australia was still without Lucas Neill at the back and appeared a bit nervy under pressure. The game was decided in the 27th minute of the first half when dangerman Emad Mohammed scored a 'wonder goal'. The skilful and powerful Iraqi player hit a cracking shot from 30 metres that beat the advancing Mark Schwarzer and tore into the top corner of the net, just under the crossbar. It had to be a top shot to beat Schwarzer who had been Australia's saviour on so many occasions through these qualifiers.

A week later, Australia would face Qatar in Doha with the chance to seal a qualifying spot in the last stage of the Asian qualifiers. Mark Bresciano was back in the team. The team would again face extreme heat on the pitch, illustrating the stark and contrasting conditions of these qualifying games.

Australia 3, Qatar 1
(*Halftime*: 0–1)
Scorers: Emerton (2), Kewell
14 June 2008
Referee: Gi Young Lee (South Korea)
Crowd: 12,000
Jassin bin Hammad Stadium, Doha

Australia: Mark Schwarzer, Luke Wilkshire, Michael Beauchamp, Jade North, David Carney, Carl Valeri, Jason Culina, Brett Emerton, Mark Bresciano, Brett Holman, Harry Kewell (Bruce Djite 85)
Qatar: Mohamed Saqr Ahmed, Marcone Amaral C Junior, Abdulla Obaid S Koni (Ibrahim Abdulla Al-Ghanim 33), Yusef Ahmed M Ali (Magid Mohamaed I Hassan 46), Mesaad Ali A M Al Hamad, Fabio Cesar Montesin, Ibrahim Majed A Abdullmajed (Khalfan Ibrahim K H A Al Khafan 65), Talal Ali H Albloushi, Bilal Mohammed B Rajab, Wesam Rizik Abdulmajid, Andres Sebastian S Quintana

Australia opened the game well despite the frenetic noise and support of the home crowd for their team. Qatar on home soil were a different team altogether to the one that gave in meekly to Australia in Melbourne.

Mark Schwarzer again highlighted his importance to the team when he tipped a

Qatari free kick over the bar from Wesam Rizik after only a minute. Australia was soon looking dangerous through Bresciano and Holman. Holman opened the Qatar defence with a pass to Harry Kewell, but his shot was blocked. Holman was again in the picture when his cross nearly beat Ahmed in the Qatar goal.

In the 17th minute, Australia scored to take the lead. Holman again fed a pass through to Bresciano and his low cross was met by Kewell, whose miskick fortunately spilled to Brett Emerton to slot home.

Qatar, far from shocked, roared back and Schwarzer again was forced to make a great save from Soria's well-hit, first-time shot. With their two naturalised South Americans in Sebastian Soria and Fabio Cesar, Qatar were causing the Australian defence all sorts of problems. Cesar, after a terrific run, just failed to find Soria. Soria was nearly through after another good run but was brought down on the edge of the penalty area. Fabio's well-hit free kick was tipped up and over the bar by Schwarzer.

Qatar was a little hard done by, going in at the interval a goal down. Their hopes were then dashed through a quality second goal from the Socceroos. Mark Schwarzer's long kick was flicked on by Harry Kewell to Holman bursting through. He lobbed a ball over the Qatar backline for Brett Emerton to run onto and slot past the Qatar keeper. This second goal deflated the Qatar side and Australia took control of the ball and the match.

Qatar did have a chance for a penalty in the 70th minute when David Carney challenged Soria in the box, but the referee waved it away. Only minutes later, Australia scored again. Harry Kewell had played an outstanding game and was rewarded with a brilliant goal. Holman, who had been a lively presence for Australia from the outset, again got free on the right and sent over a great cross that put the Qatari defence under pressure; they failed to clear, and the ball bounced to Kewell in free space and with time. He controlled the ball with one touch and crashed it past the keeper for goal number three from a very tight angle. The Australian team looked in superb shape and the fitness level of the team was on full display.

Soria had another chance for Qatar from a free kick, but his attempt was gathered by Schwarzer. Then justifiably on their first-half performance, Qatar were rewarded a consolation goal with just a minute left on the clock. Schwarzer again had denied a Qatar shot on goal, but the rebound fell to Khalfan Ibrahim, and he netted from close range. Australia had gone through to the final stage of qualifying with the 3–1 win.

Pim Verbeek subsequently decided to rest too many of his first team members for the return match with China in Sydney. He fielded an experimental side, a move that would draw criticism after the game. China brought a full-strength team to Sydney despite the fact it was a dead rubber for them as they had already been eliminated. The Socceroos would go into the game without the ever-reliable Mark Schwarzer who was suspended following an accumulation of yellow cards.

Australia 0, China 1
(*Halftime*: 0–1)
22 June 2008
Referee: Khalil Ibrahim Al Ghamdi (Saudi Arabia)
Crowd: 70,000
Sydney Olympic Stadium

Australia: Michael Petkovic, Nikolai Topor-Stanley, Matthew Spiranovic, Jade North, Ruben Zadkovich, Carl Valeri, Mile Jedinak (Neil Kilkenny 79), James Holland (David Williams 63), James Troisi (Kristian Sarkies 83), Bruce Djite, Harry Kewell
China: Song Zhen Yu, Sun Xiang, Zhang Yaokun, Li Weifeng, Xiao Zhanbo (Zheng Zhi 73), Xu Yunglong (Wu Hao 69), Wang Dong, Du Zhenyu, Qu Bo, Liu Jian, Gao Lin (Han Peng 87)

In front of a large home crowd, the young Australian team failed to take advantage of the level of support and were beaten 1–0 in a highly entertaining game. The Socceroos fell down in front of goal and squandered some great chances to score.

China took the lead after just eleven minutes when Sun Xiang found himself open and volleyed the ball past stand-in keeper Michael Petkovic. They were then unlucky not to score a second goal from the penalty spot after their initial attempt was ruled out for encroachment.

Australia was now drawn in the final group alongside Uzbekistan, Qatar, Bahrain, and Japan. They would meet Uzbekistan in the first game in September and in preparation undertook two warm-up games against South Africa and the Netherlands. They met Bafana Bafana at Loftus Road in London in mid-August. The game was a tightly fought match and ended 2–2.

In early September, they achieved a wonderful result in Eindhoven, beating the

Netherlands 2–1. The Socceroos were assisted by the Netherlands being reduced to ten men just before halftime, but nevertheless beating a world heavyweight was a huge boost to confidence going into the crucial World Cup qualifiers.

Australia 1, Uzbekistan 0
(*Halftime*: 1–0)
Scorer: Chipperfield
10 September 2008
Referee: Saad K M Al-Faadhli (Kuwait)
Crowd: 34,000
Pakhtakor Markaziy Stadium, Tashkent

Australia: Mark Schwarzer, Lucas Neill, Scott Chipperfield, Jacob Burns, Brett Emerton, Luke Wilkshire, Harry Kewell (Bruce Djite 90), Chris Coyne, Carl Valeri, Brett Holman (Mile Sterjovski 77), Mark Bresciano (David Carney 73)
Uzbekistan: Ignatiy Nesterov, Bahtiyor Ashurmatov, Ilhomjon Suyunov, Asror Alikulov, Islom Innomov, Server Djeparov, Odil Ahmedov, Ulugbek Bakaev (Zayntdin Tadjiyev 69), Vagiz Galiulin (Timur Kapadzea 43), Jasur Hasanov, Maksim Shatskikh

This was a five-star performance that showcased Pim Verbeek as an outstanding tactician. The game also illustrated the fear Asian teams carry going up against the Socceroos. Even though Uzbekistan had not lost a World Cup qualifier in 18 months, they were clearly intimidated by the Socceroos.

The game was not without its problems for Verbeek as Jason Culina and Jade North were both out with a stomach bug. But Verbeek nonchalantly dismissed their loss, remarking: 'That's life, let's get on with the job.'

Australia opened stylishly, controlling the middle of the park through Jacob Burns and Carl Valeri. Lucas Neill and Chris Coyne likewise looked in complete control of any Uzbekistan forward foray. Uzbekistan had its best moments in the opening 25 minutes, but from then on, Australia was in complete control.

The Socceroos scored after 26 minutes with their two fullbacks combining. Luke Wilkshire, a master of the cross, found space to direct over a pinpoint ball for Scott

Chipperfield to meet and head home. Highlighting the level of control the Socceroos exerted after the opening goal, they managed to string together a segment of 37 successive passes. However, despite such dominance and meek resistance, Australia failed to add to their scoreline after the break. Nevertheless, this was a highly professional performance. Pim Verbeek, after an initial hiccup with his statement on the A-League, had now won over the Australia supporters, and also it seemed, Australian soccer's journalistic wolves.

A month later, a very strong Australian line-up was called up by Verbeek to meet Qatar at Suncorp Stadium in Brisbane. Craig Moore, after announcing his retirement earlier in the year, was back in the middle of defence alongside Lucas Neill.

Australia 4, Qatar 0
(*Halftime*: 2–0)
Scorers: Cahill, Emerton (2) Kennedy
15 October 2008
Referee: Khalil Ibrahim Al Ghamdi (Saudi Arabia)
Crowd: 34,230
Suncorp Stadium, Brisbane

Australia: Mark Schwarzer, Lucas Neill, Craig Moore, Tim Cahill, Jason Culina, Brett Emerton (Jacob Burns 87), Luke Wilkshire, Josh Kennedy, David Carney, Scott Chipperfield (Mile Sterjovski 46), Scott McDonald (Brett Holman 69)
Qatar: Abdulaziz Ali Abdullah, Ibrahim Majed Abdullmajed,
Majdi Abdulla Siddiq, Abdullah Obaid Koni, Saad Sattam Al-Shammari (Hamid Ismaeil H Khaleefa 46), Fabio Cesar Montesin (Younes Ali Rahmati 83), Magid Mohamaed Hassan, Mustafa Mohammed Abdulla,
Khalfan Ibrahim Al-Khalfan, Mohammed Gholam Al-Boloushi,
Sebastian Soria Quintana (Yusef Ahmed M Ali 84)

It was a wet night and pitch in this match against Qatar. Tim Cahill was back in the Australian line-up after an eight-month absence, and he played a prominent role in the Socceroos' massacre of Qatar. The Qatari side looked in awe of Australia's playing skills and size. Their Uruguayan import upfront, Soria, was a lone threat against a very well-marshalled Australian backline.

Tim Cahill was on the scoresheet after just eight minutes, and it was all uphill for Qatar from there. Ten minutes later, it was Cahill again tormenting Qatar before he was upended in their box for a penalty that Brett Emerton converted, despite the Qatari keeper Abdulaziz Ali picking the right direction and getting a hand to his shot. Then Soria, in a rare Qatar break, got past three Australian defenders only to lose control at the final moment.

After halftime, Scott McDonald and Josh Kennedy combined to set up Brett Emerton who dispatched his second goal. Josh Kennedy sealed an emphatic victory 12 minutes from the end with a trademark header.

The Socceroos' belief was sky high following this result and a month later they headed to Bahrain full of confidence. However, they were in for a reality check and very nearly embarrassed. The game against Bahrain would highlight the real quality in Asia, and that Australia could never take any game as a given.

Australia 1, Bahrain 0
(*Halftime*: 0–0)
Scorer: Bresciano
19 November 2008
Referee: Masoud Moradi Hasanali (Iran)
Crowd: 10,000
National Stadium, Manamar

Australia: Mark Schwarzer, Lucas Neill, Craig Moore, Tim Cahill, Jason Culina, Brett Emerton (Jacob Burns 87), Luke Wilkshire, Josh Kennedy, David Carney, Scott Chipperfield (Mile Sterjovski 46), Scott McDonald (Brett Holman 69)
Bahrain: Sayed Mohamed Jaafar Sabt Abbas, Mohamed Husain Mohamed Hasan, Salman Isa Ghuloom Ali, Sayed Mohamed Adnan Husain, Abdulla Baba Fatadi, Mohamed Ahmed Mohamed Hubail, Faouzi Mubarak Aaish, Mohamed Noor Abdulrahman (Rashed Abdulrahman Saif Abdulla Aldoseri 79), Aala Ahmed Mohamed Hubail (Abdulla Adnan Saleh Salman Aldakeel 87), Jaycee John Okwunwanne, Husain Ali Ahmed Ahmed Abdulla (Jamal Rashed Abdulrahman Yusufyusuf 75)

A hard-fought win rewarded the Socceroos with top spot in the group following three successive victories. However, it was hardly an impressive performance as Australia were largely outplayed. Any sort of justice would have seen Bahrain win the match. It is possible that a full month since their last outing may have allowed some rust to develop on what had been a largely well-oiled machine up to this point. Bahrain did all of the attacking and Australia were mediocre. Verbeek must have been stunned by this form setback.

Australia's high point was a move of eight successive passes in the opening minute and that was as good as it got. Bahrain then piled on the pressure. Australia's holding midfield of Valeri and Culina were overwhelmed in the middle of the park as Bahrain swarmed forward, and only for a lack of composure in front of goal, they would have been in the lead by halftime. The Nigerian-born Jaycee John was a constant threat but sadly he failed to convert an excellent chance in the first half after pacy left winger Salman Isa opened the Australian defence, but John completely missed his shot.

Another Nigerian convert in Abdulla Fatadi was eye-catching in midfield alongside Mahmood Abdulrahman who seemed to cover every blade of grass. Bahrain penned the Socceroos back with a fluid and pacy attacking formation. Early on it was clear that David Carney and Chris Coyne had their work cut out down the right in containing Fatadi, Mohamed Hubail and Jaycee John.

In the second half, Luke Wilkshire was subjected to a barrage of attacking moves through John, Isa and Faouzi Aaish. There was very little help from the Australian midfield of Kewell, Bresciano and Cahill who all appeared off their game. Josh Kennedy up front was a lone, deserted figure unable to make any impact on the Bahrain twin backline of Mohamed Husain and Sayed Mohammed.

A draw would have been an outstanding and undeserved result for Australia, but a long clearance from Schwarzer threw the Bahrain backline into panic and Bresciano was on the spot to score. On any measure, Bahrain were robbed in losing this game. Goal-scorer Mark Bresciano admitted as much after the game: 'We were very lucky tonight. Bahrain outplayed us. They created a lot more chances. They didn't deserve to lose, and we were lucky to win in the last few seconds... but bloody oath we'll take it.'

The end of the year saw Australia sitting in pole position for their second successive World Cup Finals' appearance. Overall, the performances were noteworthy, with a couple of tepid displays thrown in for good measure. The new year started with an Asian Cup qualifier against Indonesia in Jakarta. Verbeek fielded a largely experimental A-League-based side. In the end, Australia were lucky to come away with a 0–0 result. Verbeek again unleashed on the standard of the A-League players in a performance he rated as 'pathetic'. Australia now had to regroup for the critical match against the old enemy the 'Blue Samurai'—Japan in Yokohama. Verbeek recalled a full strength, largely European-based Socceroos squad.

Australia 0, Japan 0
(*Halftime*: 0–0)
11 February 2009
Referee: Mohsen Basma (Syria)
Crowd: 66,000
International Stadium, Yokohama

Australia: Mark Schwarzer, Lucas Neill, Craig Moore, Tim Cahill (Josh Kennedy 85), Jason Culina, Luke Wilkshire, Scott Chipperfield, Vince Grella, Brett Holman (Richard Garcia 64), Carl Valeri, Mark Bresciano (David Carney 90)
Japan: Ryota Tsuzuki, Yuji Nakazawa, Tulio Tanaka, Atsuto Uchida, Yasuhito Endo, Daisuke Matsui (Yoshito Okubo 58), Tatsuya Tanaka (Shinji Okazaki 83), Shunsuke Nakamura, Keiji Tamada, Yuto Nagatomo, Makoto Hasebe

On any estimate, this was a tradesman-like, methodical performance. Verbeek's set-up again proved outstanding. Japan had a lot of possession, but the Socceroos, marshalled at the back by Neill and Moore, were rarely troubled. Verbeek fielded a five-man midfield of Culina, Grella, Valeri, Bresciano and Holman who closed the middle of the park.

In the first half, Japan did exploit the width on the right through Tetsuya Tanaka who gave Chipperfield a testing period. However, despite possession being in their favour, Japan did not seriously test Schwarzer in the first half.

During the break, Verbeek adjusted his middle and Valeri offered more support to Chipperfield. The tweak worked a treat and Japan did not threaten seriously down the right again. Endo did have one chance, but Mark Schwarzer saved well.

The large Japanese crowd were silenced as the Socceroos saw out the game to gain a valuable point and firm up their position on top of the table.

Another poor performance in an Asian Cup qualifier followed the euphoria of the Japan World Cup result. The Socceroos, albeit a team drawn from the A-League, delivered another below-par performance. Verbeek was not on the sideline for this game having earned a sideline ban, and deputy Graham Arnold was in charge. During the week leading up to the match, the Australian soccer media made much of Verbeek's previous scathing assessment of the quality in the A-League. After this match, there were probably many who shared his opinion. However, Kuwait do deserve some credit for their performance in gaining a 1–0 victory in Canberra. It was not an ideal warm-up for the next World Cup qualifier, but again Australia would be bolstered through the return of their European contingent.

Australia 2, Uzbekistan 0
(*Halftime*: 0–0)
Scorers: Kennedy, Kewell
1 April 2009
Referee: Ali Hamad Madhad Saif Albadwawi (UAE)
Crowd: 57,292
Sydney Olympic Stadium

Australia: Mark Schwarzer, Lucas Neill, Jason Culina, Michael Beauchamp, Luke Wilkshire, Harry Kewell (Brett Holman 74), Scott Chipperfield, Richard Garcia, Carl Valeri (Mile Jedinak 80), Scott McDonald (Joshua Kennedy 59), Mark Bresciano
Uzbekistan: Ignatiy Nesterov, Anvar Gafurov, Hayrulla Karimov (Islom Tuhtahujaev 75), Anzur Ismailov, Sakhob Jurayev, Aziz Ibragimov (Azizbek Haydarov 64), Jasur Hasanov, Server Djeparov, Odil Ahmedov, Farhod Tadjiyev (Anvarjon Soliev 57), Timur Kapadze

Uzbekistan's performance in this match was much improved on their first game against Australia. They played some great football, especially in the first half.

Josh Kennedy came on for Scott McDonald just after halftime and that saw Australia breakthrough in the 66th minute with his header. Only six minutes later, Harry Kewell dispatched a penalty kick to put Australia 2–0 in front. Australia dominated the second stanza with a tiring Uzbekistan crumbling in the face of pressure.

It would be a long two months before Australia stepped onto the field again and sealed their place in the South African World Cup Finals.

Australia 0, Qatar 0
(*Halftime*: 0–0)
6 June 2009
Referee: Abdul Malik Bin Abdul Bashir (Singapore)
Crowd: 7,000
Al Sadd Club, Doha, Qatar

Australia: Mark Schwarzer, Lucas Neill, Jason Culina, Michael Beauchamp, Luke Wilkshire, Harry Kewell (Brett Holman 74), Scott Chipperfield, Richard Garcia, Carl Valeri (Mile Jedinak 80), Scott McDonald (Joshua Kennedy 59), Mark Bresciano
Qatar: Qasem Abdullhamed Burhan, Hamed Shami Zaher, Bilal Mohammed B Rajab, Mesaad Ali A M Alhamad, Ibrahim Majed A Abdullmajed, Mohammed Abdulraab A A Al Yazidi, Talal Ali H Albloushi, Ali Hassan A Yahya (Hasan Khalid H Alhaydos 77), Magid Mohamaed I Hassan (Yusef Ahmed M Ali 83), Ahmed Ali Faris Al-Binali (Majdi Abdulla Siddiq 62), Andres Sebastian S Quintana

The Socceroos were impressive in becoming the third nation alongside hosts South African and Japan to seal their place in the Finals. Despite a goal-less draw, Australia were dominant throughout the game and bombarded the Qatar goal. Goalkeeper Qasem Burhan had an outstanding game for Qatar and denied Australia's attacks on several occasions. The Socceroos had travelled some 10,500 kilometres to earn their spot at the world's greatest football tournament.

Australia returned home to play out their final two games of the qualifying series. The first against Bahrain, who still had a slim chance of making the Finals if they could beat Australia in Sydney. The Socceroos would go into the game with four key players (Lucas Neill, Josh Kennedy, Mark Bresciano and Scott Chipperfield) unavailable for selection. The game showcased the at times dramatic shifts in weather the team had to face throughout this qualifying series—only days before in Doha they played in a scorching 38 degrees and now in a Sydney winter, down to 8 degrees.

Australia 2, Bahrain 0
(*Halftime*: 0–0)
Scorers: Sterjovski, Carney

10 June 2009
Referee: Abdullah Mohamed Masoud Al Hilali (Oman)
Crowd: 39,540
Sydney Olympic Stadium

Australia: Mark Schwarzer, Mark Milligan, Chris Coyne (Jade North 73), Jason Culina, Mile Jedinak (Vince Grella 63), Luke Wilkshire, Mile Sterjovski, David Carney, Harry Kewell, Brett Holman (Nick Carle 84), Scott McDonald
Bahrain: Sayed Mohamed Jaafar Sabt Abbas, Abdulla Abdulrahman Mohamed Marzooq, Salman Isa Ghuloom Ali (Abdulwahab Ali Abdulwahab Husain Alsafi 90), Husain Ali Hasan Ali Mohamed, Abdulla Abdi Omar Yaser (Ahmed Hassan Taleb Mohamed Rashed 87), Mohamed Ahmed Mohamed Hubail, Mohamed Ahmed Yusuf Salmeen, Faouzi Mubarak Aaish (Ismaeel Abdulatif Ismaeel Hasan 76), Mahmood Abdulrahman Mohamed Noor Abdulrahman, Abdulla Ismaeel Omar, Jaycee John Okwunwanne

Bahrain fought bravely for the first half and must have raised the hopes of their supporters for a miracle result, but it was not to be. A missed clearance by midfielder Faouzi Mubarak Aaish ten minutes after the break allowed Mile Sterjovski to race in and take full advantage of the mistake and score the opening goal of the game.

Australia was in coasting mode for the rest of the match, and it wasn't until two minutes from fulltime that they put the icing on the cake and dispatched Bahrain. David Carney curled over a cross to Jason Culina who lurched himself into the air and met it with a bicycle kick of perfection, but the ball crashed into the left post without crossing the line. David Carney following up was on the spot to stab home the second goal.

A week later, Australia would face old foe Japan in their final group game at the MCG and the winner would finish top of their group. The Socceroos had recently been elevated by FIFA to its highest ever ranking of 14th in the world, an incredible achievement and recognition of the teams' performances.

Australia 2, Japan 1
(*Halftime*: 0–1)
Scorer: Cahill (2)

17 June 2009
Referee: Alghamdi Khalil Ibrahim M (Saudi Arabia)
Crowd: 74,100
Melbourne Cricket Ground

Australia: Mark Schwarzer, Lucas Neill, Shane Steffanuto, Jade North, Tim Cahill (Dario Vidosic 84), Jason Culina, Nick Carle (Scott McDonald 77), Vince Grella, Rhys Williams (Jacob Burns 77), Mile Sterjovski, Josh Kennedy
Japan: Seigo Narazaki, Marcus Tulio Lyuji Murzani Tanaka, Atsuto Uchida, Yuto Nagatomo, Yuki Abe, Hashimoto Hideo (Shinzoh Kohrogi 84), Yasoyuki Konno, Daisuke Matsui (Kisho Yano 67), Kengo Nakamura, Shinji Okazaki, Keiji Tamada

The drawing power of the brand Socceroos was on full display. Despite having already qualified for the Finals, they drew a huge crowd of over 74,000 to the MCG.

Against the script, Japan took the lead after 39 minutes when Marcus Tanaka ghosted in unmarked to reach a corner from Shunsuke Nakamura and headed home. But it was left to Japan's perennial tormenter Tim Cahill to take charge of the game in the second half and score twice to deliver a great 2–1 victory. Australia had finished the final qualifying stage on top of their group, scoring 19 goals whilst conceding just four.

Australia would now begin its preparation for the 2010 World Cup Finals. The first game in this process was an outstanding display where they completely dominated Ireland in Limerick. The Socceroos were ruthless in outclassing the Irish 3–0 with goals to Tim Cahill (2) and David Carney. Carney's 30- metre stunner of a final goal summed up the Socceroos' performance.

However, a month later Australia was well below par in going down to South Korea 3–1 in Seoul. This match was a clear reminder that the Socceroos still had much work to do and could not rest on their laurels. Another game against top opposition, the Netherlands, in Sydney saw Australia earn a hard fought 0–0 draw. The Dutch were far superior, but the Socceroos' fighting qualities were on full display. A warning from this game was the lack of penetration upfront for Australia who rarely troubled the Dutch defence. Australia then closed out the year with two hard-fought victories over Oman in Asian Cup qualifiers. The Socceroos' poor early performances meant that they had to win these ties to still be in with a chance. Australia won 1–0 in Sydney and

2–1 in Muscat. The win in the Middle East was meritorious after Rhys Williams had been red-carded after only 16 minutes.

The Socceroos' qualification for South Africa set in motion one of my own greatest wishes and one which was certainly at the top of my 'bucket list': going to a World Cup. The planets were aligning; my new book *The Aboriginal Soccer Tribe* was due for publication in 2010 and interest in the book was building, hence an invitation to attend a Football Writers' Conference in Port Elizabeth at Nelson Mandela University. The Conference was timed perfectly, just before the South African World Cup Finals. I would attend the Conference and then take two weeks' leave from work and join the 'Green and Gold Army World Cup Tour'. I procured ten tickets for matches, including the three group matches for the Socceroos. It was a dream come true and I could not wait. Australia had been drawn into Group D along with Germany, Ghana, and Serbia. It was six months before Australia's opening game, and the preparations began with further Asian Cup qualifiers: first a 2–2 draw with Kuwait followed by a 1–0 win over Indonesia that secured Australia's qualification to the Asian Cup Finals.

2010 World Cup Finals

In May, Australia played a farewell match against New Zealand at the MCG in front of more than 55,000 fans and secured a 2–1 victory. They arrived in South Africa two weeks before the opening games of the Finals to acclimatise to conditions. The Socceroos played two trial games against other World Cup qualifiers, beating Denmark 1–0 in an impressive performance before going down 3–1 to the United States.

I was now in South Africa and undertaking a fantastic event and tour; our base was in Johannesburg and the accommodation was terrific. So many highlights: I visited and stayed in an African game park, went to Soweto, and saw the Apartheid Museum and Nelson Mandela House. I witnessed first-hand the still shocking living conditions of so many black people. The Green and Gold Army arranged a visit to the Zulu community with a large BBQ event that included displays of dancing and singing. The colour, noise (vuvuzelas, the three-foot horns), and excitement of a World Cup was overwhelming and everything I had hoped for. South Africa itself was a country of breathtaking beauty, and as a historian, one of disturbing realities—the past and the brutality of apartheid. The reality of history was very clear, as journalist David Penberthy said: 'In South Africa, soccer has always been the sport of struggle and its teams and players have enjoyed the solidarity of other black nations. In the dark days of apartheid, the South African regime starved soccer of funding and infrastructure, preferring to concentrate on Afrikaner sports such as rugby and cricket.'

Early predictions of Australia's Group D opposition recognised that the Germans were a young side with a long-standing pedigree, Ghana were a side of mercurial brilliance but suspect defence, and Serbia, a young, vibrant team that some predicted could be an outsider to reach the semi-final stage.

We travelled from Johannesburg to Durban for the opening clash with Germany and the trip and arrival at the stadium was electric. Pim Verbeek left no stone unturned in preparation, but in the opener against Germany he was in error. The 4-4-2 system was torn apart by the speed, incisive running, and electrifying pace of this young German team. It was a full-on blitzkrieg. The Socceroos' selection for this game was illogical. Verbeek put midfielder Richard Garcia upfront, and Australia went in without a recognised striker, someone who could hold the ball up. Mark Bresciano and Harry Kewell were left on the bench. Jason Culina was employed in an unfamiliar left midfield role, and he was not comfortable. It was a bizarre move by Verbeek, playing a system he had shunned over the past two years and playing a team that was not a part of his line-ups in the lead-up to the World Cup.

Australia 0, Germany 4
(*Halftime*: 0–2)
13 June 2010
Referee: Marco Rodriguez (Mexico)
Crowd: 62,660
Moses Mabhida Stadium, Durban, South Africa

Australia: Mark Schwarzer, Lucas Neill, Craig Moore, Tim Cahill (sent off 56), Jason Culina, Brett Emerton (Mile Jedinak 74), Luke Wilkshire,
Scott Chipperfield, Vince Grella (Brett Holman 46), Carl Valeri, Richard Garcia (Nikita Rukavytsya 64)
Germany: Manuel Neuer, Arne Friedrich, Sami Khedira,
Bastian Schweinsteiger, Mesut Oezil (Mario Gomez 74), Lukas Podolski (Marko Marin 81), Miroslav Klose (Claudemir Jeronimo Barreto (Cacau) 68), Thomas Müller, Holger Badstuber, Philipp Lahm, Per Mertesacker

The atmosphere in the stadium was amazing. The Socceroos' defence was being severely tested from the kick-off. Australia looked particularly vulnerable down the right side where Thomas Müller was tormenting Vince Grella, Scott Chipperfield and Craig Moore.

The game was only eight minutes old when Mesut Ozil released Müller down the right, and his low, hard cross across the goalmouth was met by Lukas Podolski who crashed a shot past Mark Schwarzer.

Germany then swarmed forward and Australia was forced to withstand a blistering array of attacking chances. A quickly taken free kick released Müller again and his low cross skimmed across the Australian goalmouth with no German attacker able to get a foot to it.

Miroslav Klose then blasted over the bar when clean through. However, Klose made amends after 26 minutes when he rose to meet a cross into the Australian area to head past the advancing Schwarzer for the second German goal.

The Socceroos were barely hanging on in the face of this onslaught, but they managed more through luck to be only 2-0 down at halftime. The young German midfielder Mesut Ozil put on a masterclass and was like a conductor with his orchestra.

Australia's fate was sealed 12 minutes into the second half when Tim Cahill was sent off for a late tackle on German midfielder Bastian Schweinsteiger. Cahill was left in tears and Schweinsteiger later admitted it wasn't a red card.

Reduced to ten men, Australia were 'under the pump' as Germany piled on the pressure. Klose and Sami Khedira both missed golden chances, with Klose shooting wide from just five metres. Müller was on the spot to beat Schwarzer after 68 minutes, and two minutes later, substitute Cacau had an easy tap in following a defence-splitting pass from Ozil to make it 4-0.

Germany played some of the best attacking football that had been seen so far in the tournament. The loss and the number of goals conceded could well have sealed the Socceroos' fate in the group. The Australians were greatly exposed and looked more like an ageing team facing a side full of confidence and youthful enthusiasm.

Pim Verbeek said after the game that he was at fault: 'As coach, you're always responsible. I never blame any of my players. I have no problems saying it's my responsibility.' The post-mortem was blunt: Why did Verbeek make such bizarre changes? Why were Harry Kewell and Mark Bresciano on the bench? Why did a recognised striker in Josh Kennedy not feature? Of even greater concern was the vulnerable Australian defence.

Australia would now have to regroup to face Ghana in Rustenburg in six days in a must-win match. Ghana had beaten a much-fancied Serbia 1–0 in their opening game and Australia would be without arguably their best player in the now suspended Tim Cahill. Much-respected football journalist Mike Cockerill stated after the game that Australia's 2006 'Golden Generation' had passed their use-by date. The knives were out for Verbeek in the Australian press and former Socceroos Charlie Yankos, Mark Bosnich and Robbie Slater were scathing in their assessment, calling it 'un-Australian'. Slater pointed out that Australia: 'played with six midfielders and no recognised striker... You don't mind losing if you give it a shot, but we never did.'

Harry Kewell was expected to be back in the starting line-up to face Ghana as a direct replacement for Tim Cahill. Verbeek surely would revert to his usual 4-2-3-1 formation after the debacle against Germany. Kewell was adamant: 'I'm as fit as I can be. That's what I am here for.' The Socceroos would be facing the entire support of the African continent that was now behind Ghana, the only African nation to win their opening game.

Australia 1, Ghana 1
(*Halftime*: 1–1)
Scorer: Holman
19 June 2010
Referee: Roberto Rosetti (Italy)
Crowd: 34,812
Royal Bafokeng Stadium, Rustenburg, South Africa

Australia: Mark Schwarzer, Lucas Neill, Craig Moore, Jason Culina, Brett Emerton, Luke Wilkshire (Nikita Rukavytsya 84), Harry Kewell (sent off 25), Brett Holman (Joshua Kennedy 68), Carl Valeri, David Carney, Marco Bresciano (Scott Chipperfield 66)
Ghana: Richard Kingston, Hans Sarpei, Asamoah Gyan, John Pantsil, Anthony Annan, Johnathan Mensah, Prince Tagoe (Quincy Owusu-Abeyie 56), Andre Ayew, Lee Addy, Kwadwo Asamoah (Sulley Muntari 77), Kevin Prince Boateng (Matthew Amoah 87)

Both sides displayed the nervous tension surrounding this game. Ghana with a victory would be guaranteed of going through to the next stage, whilst Australia had to win to stay in contention.

Harry Kewell looked dynamic from the start, proving he had finally overcome his nagging groin injury. On eleven minutes, Mark Bresciano, back in the side for Richard Garcia, stepped up to take an Australian free kick from some 30 metres out from goal, and his ferocious shot was dropped by Ghanaian keeper Richard Kingston at the foot of Brett Holman to slot home.

The game erupted after 24 minutes when Jonathan Mensah's shot on goal was said by Italian referee Roberto Rosetti to have been stopped by Harry Kewell's arm. Ghana was awarded a penalty and Kewell was shown the red card—it was a disaster for Australia. Asamoah Gyan stepped up and converted for Ghana whilst Kewell was left fuming and remonstrating wildly with the referee as he was ordered from the field.

It was a cruel blow for Australia, now down a man and with their backs to the wall. However, the Australian defence was marshalled superbly by Lucas Neill and Craig Moore, and they saw Australia to the interval on level terms.

The second half saw Australia drive forward despite being a man short. Both goalkeepers (Mark Schwarzer and Richard Kingston) rose to the occasion with top performances. However, the Socceroos created three outstanding chances in trying to win the game. After 66 minutes, Scott Chipperfield replaced Mark Bresciano and he very nearly rewarded his coach immediately. Luke Wilkshire on the right then delivered a pinpoint dipping cross to the far post and Chipperfield rose highest to meet it, only to send the ball just over the bar. The same two players were involved after 71 minutes when Chipperfield put a beautiful ball through for the overlapping Luke Wilkshire. The fullback took one touch but smacked his shot straight into Ghanaian keeper Kingston. The ball was parried away, but Josh Kennedy pounced. The ball bounced up and Kennedy tried to get over it, but he scuffed his shot, and again it was well saved by Kingston.

The referee called time and the Socceroos could be proud of a fighting performance with ten men. They probably should have still won the game. They would now face Serbia in the final game without a suspended Harry Kewell and Craig Moore, who picked up a second yellow card.

In a surprise result, Serbia beat Germany 1-0. Australia was now in a difficult position: they needed Ghana to beat the Germans and Australia had to upset Serbia.

Alternatively, the Socceroos needed to thrash Serbia whilst Germany did the same to Ghana. The opening result against Germany was like a huge chain around Australia's neck with the negative goal difference. The two red cards to Cahill and Kewell during the two previous games were also very costly.

Australia 2, Serbia 1
(*Halftime*: 1–1)
Scorers: Cahill, Holman
23 June 2010
Referee: Jorge Larrionda (Uruguay)
Crowd: 37,836
Mbombela Stadium, Nelspruit, South Africa

Australia: Mark Schwarzer, Lucas Neill, Tim Cahill, Jason Culina, Michael Beauchamp, Brett Emerton, Luke Wilkshire (Richard Garcia 82), Joshua Kennedy, Carl Valeri (Brett Holman 66), David Carney, Marco Bresciano (Scott Chipperfield 66)
Serbia: Vladimir Stojkovic, Nemanja Vidic, Branislav Ivanovic, Dejan Stankovic, Aleksandar Lukovic, Milan Jovanovic, Nikola Zigic (Marko Pantelic 67), Ivan Obradovic, Milos Krasic (Zoran Tosic 62), Milos Ninkovic, Zdravko Kuzmanovic (Dankko Lazovic 77)

For the first time in the tournament, the Australian team made it to fulltime with an intact team and they achieved an outstanding result in ending Serbia's World Cup hopes. However, Ghana would progress to the next round following another top performance in going down only 1-0 to Germany.

The Socceroos and Serbia were locked up at halftime 0-0. Serbia looked the better side in the first half and controlled possession and the game. But after the break, the Socceroos came out as men on a mission and stunned Serbia. Both Mark Bresciano and Jason Culina nearly scored goals. Goal-sneak Tim Cahill again proved his worth in the air when he out-jumped Manchester United central defender Nemanja Vidić to meet a Luke Wilkshire cross and head home in the 69th minute.

Only four minutes later, Brett Holman burst through the middle of the park and unleashed a long-range shot that skimmed into the Serbian net past Stojković. Just for a moment, there was hope that Australia could go on and completely crush Serbia and advance on goal difference.

However, a substitute for Serbia in Zoran Tosić proved a dramatic change to the game: he hit a powerful volley that Mark Schwarzer could not hold, and Marko Pantelić was on the spot with just six minutes left to pull one back for Serbia. Pantelić then nearly had the equaliser, but he was called offside. Minutes later, Pantelić had the chance to score again and put Serbia through to the last 16, but he blasted the ball over the bar.

Australia held on and achieved a great victory. But their World Cup journey was now over.

On a personal note, being at the World Cup exceeded all my expectations. I saw ten matches including Australia's three games. I saw most of the top teams in action, including Spain, the eventual winners of the tournament, beating Honduras 2–0. The young German side were the most impressive team for me in beating Australia 4–0 in the group stage and demolishing England 4–1 in the last 16 match. They were beaten 1–0 by Spain in the semi-final.

I saw Lionel Messi in action for Argentina in a less than impressive 1–0 win over Nigeria, and I watched Brazil in action on three occasions: beating North Korea 2–1, Côte d'Ivoire 3–1 in the group stage and then a very impressive 3–0 result against Chile in the last 16 stage. They were eventually beaten by the Netherlands 2–1 in the quarter-finals. The Dutch were something of an enigma throughout the series and would go on to their third World Cup Final defeat. Spain were the just winners of the tournament in beating the Dutch 1–0 in extra time with a goal from Iniesta. The Spanish midfield trio of Xabi Alonso, Andrés Iniesta and Xavi were the most creative and brilliant in the world at that time and they were responsible for Spain's victory.

The Socceroos would now regroup and look to 2014 in Brazil. Pim Verbeek was gone to take over as manager of the Moroccan youth national team. Australia would be looking for a new coach and the reality that their star players of the 'Golden Generation' were an ageing team.

I was already in planning mode myself, looking to find a way to get to Brazil for my second World Cup Finals' series. How could I miss out on a Finals' series in Brazil, the land of Jogo Bonito ('the beautiful game') and the home country of Garrincha, Pelé and Ronaldinho? Thankfully, the success of my book *The Aboriginal Soccer Tribe* continued to gain interest across the globe, and I had invitations to speak in England and Canada.

I had also contacted the Federal *University* of *Rio* de Janeiro and the Laboratory of the History of Sport, an area of great interest to me, and they were keen for me to visit at some point in the future.

WORLD CUP QUALIFICATION AND FINALS 2014-BRAZIL

The Intervening Years— The Australian team, 2010-2014

Only two months after their exit from the 2010 World Cup, Australia were back in action with a caretaker manager in charge—national technical director Han Berger was on the sidelines for a game against Slovenia. Australia was beaten 2-0. The very next day, Football Federation Australia announced the appointment of German coach Holger Osieck as the new Socceroos' coach. Osieck had an impressive resume including time as Franz Beckenbauer's assistant coach for the German team that won the 1990 World Cup. He had also coached the Canadian national team that won the 2000 CONCACAF Gold Cup, beating Colombia in the Final. Importantly, he had clocked up time in Asia coaching Japanese club side Urawa Red Diamonds, including winning the 2007 Asian Cup Final.

He had his first game at the helm for Australia with a dull 0-0 draw with Switzerland in St. Gallen. Four days later, the Socceroos had an impressive 2-1 win over Poland in Krakow. Australia continued their winning way under Osieck back in Sydney, downing Paraguay 1-0. In preparation for the Asian Cup in 2011, the Socceroos next ventured to Cairo for a match against Egypt that the Pharaohs won comfortably 3-0. The defeat ended the year for the Australian team.

Australia headed to the Middle East for the Asian Cup and had a friendly match with the United Arab Emirates on the way to acclimatise. The game ended 0-0. The Socceroos opened their Asian Cup campaign with an emphatic 4-0 victory over

India in Doha. Four days later, they faced fellow heavyweight South Korea and fought out a 1-1 draw. Australia squandered some great goal-scoring opportunities in the game. Then in a match they were expected to win easily, the Socceroos were somewhat lucky to beat Bahrain 1-0 in their final group game, with Mark Schwarzer outstanding in goal.

In their Asian Cup quarter-final match, Australia beat Iraq 1-0 in extra time courtesy of a last-minute header by Harry Kewell. The Socceroos then smacked Uzbekistan 6-0 in their semi-final, helped by the fact that the Uzbekistan team had been reduced to ten men. In the other semi-final, Japan downed South Korea 3-0 in a penalty shoot-out. It was no small achievement for Holger Osieck that the Socceroos had reached the Asian Cup Final. The Final itself was largely dominated by Australia but failing to take opportunities up front was costly. Japan won the match in extra time 1-0.

The Socceroos headed to Europe two months later to take on powerhouse Germany. The young German side had only days before played a Euro qualifier and coach Loew made several changes although Schweinsteiger, Müller and Podolski were all in the team. The Socceroos achieved one of their greatest ever victories in beating Germany 2-1. They were down 1-0 at halftime but finished over the top of the Germans in the second half with goals from David Carney and Luke Wilkshire. They achieved revenge for the heavy defeat they had suffered against Germany in South Africa. Coach Holger Osieck after the game stated: 'I'm really proud of the boys, they did a great job.' Osieck was the toast of Australia and football journalist Mick Cockerill declared Osieck was: 'squeezing the very best out of a Socceroos selection which not that long ago looked like it had passed its use by date'. Cockerill was adamant the change from previous coach Pim Verbeek was obvious: 'Osieck exposes his predecessor Pim Verbeek for exactly what he was—arrogant, patronising, and unwilling to acknowledge the crucible of the Australian sporting psyche, having a go.'

Australia next beat old rival New Zealand in preparation for the World Cup qualifiers. The Socceroos were again impressive, beating the Kiwis 3-0 at the Adelaide Oval. The preparations continued with a game against South African World Cup opponents, Serbia, in Melbourne. The game ended 0-0. The final warm-up came with a game against Wales in Cardiff. Australia again produced the goods, downing the Welsh 2-1. The Socceroos would begin their phase 3 World Cup qualifiers against Thailand at Suncorp Stadium in Brisbane.

Australia 2, Thailand 1

(*Halftime*: 0–1)
Scorers: Kennedy, Brosque
2 September 2011
Referee: Abdullah dor Mohammad Balideh (Qatar)
Crowd: 24,540
Suncorp Stadium, Brisbane

Australia: Mark Schwarzer, Lucas Neill, Tim Cahill (Robbie Kruse 71), Brett Emerton (Alex Brosque 79), Luke Wilkshire, Joshua Kennedy, Brett Holman (James Troisi 90), Carl Valeri, Matthew McKay, Neil Kilkenny, Matthew Spiranovic
Thailand: Sinthaweechai Kosin Hathairattanakool, Niweat Siriwong, Chonlatit Jantakam, Datsakorn Thonglao, Teerasil Dangda, Rangsan Viwatchaichok, Adul Lahso, Sompong Sorleb (Suttinun Phukhom 56), Surat Sukha (Arthit Sunthonpit 79), Supachai Komsilp, Jakkraphan Kaewprom

Australia fielded a very strong eleven and the game was expected to be a cakewalk. However, the Socceroos had a real shock awaiting them as the Thai keeper and his defence played heroically in denying Australian chances. The Socceroos' frontline again failed to take advantage of opportunities.

Thailand took the lead against the run of play with a goal from Dangda after 15 minutes, and they went in at halftime still holding their 1–0 advantage.

Josh Kennedy squared the ledger after 58 minutes. Unquestionably, the great worry for Osieck and the Socceroos was the continued failure of the Australian frontline to capitalise on a raft of chances. Alex Brosque scored the winner with only four minutes left on the clock to save Australia a severe embarrassment.

A four-day turn around separated the Socceroos from their second World Cup qualifier. They flew to Saudi Arabia to take on the Saudis in Dammam.

Australia 3, Saudi Arabia 1

(*Halftime*: 1–0)
Scorers: Kennedy (2), Wilkshire
6 September 2011

Referee: Yuichi Nishimura (Japan)
Crowd: 15,000
Prince Mohammed Bin Fahad Stadium, Dammam

Australia: Mark Schwarzer, Lucas Neill, Michael Zullo (Robbie Kruse 79), Sasa Ognenovski, Brett Emerton, Luke Wilkshire, Joshua Kennedy (Mark Milligan 89), Brett Holman (Tim Cahill 87), Mile Jedinak, Carl Valeri, Matthew McKay
Saudi Arabia: Hasan Bader M Alotaibi, Rashed Abdulrahman R Al Rahab, Osama Abdulrzag M Hawsawi, Hamad Mohsen H Almontashari, Abdulla Mohammed A Aldossary, Hassan Muath T Fallatah (Yahia Sulaiman A Alshehri 46), Ahmed Ibrahim Y Ateef (Nasser Al-Shamrani 60), Nawaf Shaker F Alabid (Mohammed Ibrahim M Al Sahlawi 79), Saud Ali M Kariri, Taiseer Jabir A Aljassam, Naif Ahmed T Hazazi

There remained a certain aura of fear in a great majority of Asian nations when facing the Socceroos. It was apparent in this game that Australia won 3-1.

Australia overcame heat and jetlag to ease past Saudi Arabia. The Socceroos' patchy 2-1 victory over Thailand the previous week was unconvincing but at Dammam, two goals by Josh Kennedy and a penalty from Luke Wilkshire lifted the Socceroos to the top of Group D.

Kennedy had opened his account against the Thais and on Tuesday he was at it again, heading a Wilkshire cross into the net just before halftime. The Japan-based striker added a second goal on the 56 minute-mark after cashing in on Brett Holman's defence-splitting pass.

The hosts pulled a goal back through Nasser Al-Shamrani, but Kennedy was then fouled in the box and Wilkshire converted his penalty in the 77th minute.

A month later, the Socceroos were back home and played Malaysia in a World Cup qualifying warm-up in Canberra. They trounced Malaysia 5-0 and Josh Kennedy continued his rich vein of scoring by netting another two goals. Three days later, they faced Oman at the Sydney Olympic Stadium.

Australia 3, Oman 0
(*Halftime*: 1-0)
Scorers: Kennedy, Holman Jedinak

11 October 2011
Referee: Kovalenko Valentin (Uzbekistan)
Crowd: 24,372
Sydney Olympic Stadium

Australia: Adam Federici, Lucas Neill, Michael Zullo (Alex Brosque 86), Rhys Williams (Robbie Kruse 71), Luke Wilkshire, Joshua Kennedy (Neil Kilkenny 90), Brett Holman, Mile Jedinak, Carl Valeri, Matthew McKay, Matthew Spiranovic

Oman: Ali Habsi, Juma Darwish, Mohammed Al-Sheiba, Rachid Al-Farsi, Saad Suhail, Ahmed Mubarak, Abdul Rahman, Ismail Al-Ajmi (Eid Al-Farsi 65), Abdulaziz Al-Miqbali, Amad Al Hosni (Hassan Al-Housni 84), Mohammed Hamed (Hamood Al-Sadi 65)

Australia was without two big names in Tim Cahill and Harry Kewell, but young guns like Rhys Williams, Michael Zullo and Matthew Spiranovic stood up in this match. Brett Holman proved the Socceroos' hero as he scored one and set up another in a convincing 3–0 Australian win in Sydney.

Holman put the Socceroos ahead after just eight minutes when he got on the end of a Matt McKay pass and slammed the ball home after Oman had failed to clear a dangerous Williams cross. It marked the start of Australia's near-total domination of the first half where they cruised in possession, confidently knocking the ball around the park but failing to convert that dominance into goals. At the end of the first 45 minutes, the Socceroos had just three attempts on goal with only one on target. This was scarcely believable given the absolute control they had enjoyed in the game.

In the second half, Oman came out playing with more conviction as they looked for an equaliser. They posed more of a threat for the first 15 minutes.

But the Socceroos dashed Oman's hopes after 65 minutes. Their attack started with key playmaker Holman who intercepted the ball on the edge of the box before setting up Luke Wilkshire. Wilkshire's shot was saved, only to rebound straight to Josh Kennedy who made no mistake and rattled the ball home to double Australia's advantage.

With the score at 2–0, Oman pushed hard to get back into the game and won a free kick on the edge of the Socceroos' box. It forced a great save from keeper

Adam Federici in his only real test of the night.

At the other end, a perfectly flighted free kick from Wilkshire saw Mile Jedinak get just enough of a touch on the ball to defeat Oman's EPL keeper, Ali Al-Habsi, and claim Australia's third goal after 85 minutes. The Socceroos would secure their place in the next round of qualifying with victory—or possibly just a draw—against Oman in Muscat on November 11.

A month later, Australia flew to the Middle East for the return match against Oman in vastly different weather conditions.

Australia 0, Oman 1
(*Halftime*: 0–1)
11 November 2011
Referee: Ali Hasan Ebrahim Abdulnabi (Bahrain)
Crowd: 4,500
Sultan Qaboos Stadium, Muscat

Australia: Mark Schwarzer, Lucas Neill, Rhys Williams (Brett Emerton 72), Luke Wilkshire, Joshua Kennedy, Harry Kewell (Robbie Kruse 53), Brett Holman, Mile Jedinak, Carl Valeri, Matthew McKay, Matthew Spiranovic
Oman: Ali Habsi, Eid Al-Farsi, Hamed Al Bulushi, Hussain Al Hadhri (Ismail Al-Ajim 69), Saad Suhail, Ahmed Mubarak, Abdul Rahman, Abdulaziz Al-Miqbali, Hasasan Al Gheilani, Amad Al Hosni (Qasim Harddan 78), Mohammed Hamed (Fawzi Doorbeen 59)

Australia was an abject disappointment and failed to confirm their place in the next stage of qualifiers in going down to Oman in Muscat. Oman came back with a vengeance following their defeat in Sydney, grinding out a 1–0 win.

Amad Ali scored Oman's only goal in the 18th minute, and the hosts' defence held strong against an increasingly frustrated Australian attack. The failure to convert goal chances was now a major headache for coach Osieck.

Four days later, the Socceroos were given another chance to advance to the next stage, meeting Thailand in Bangkok. The game had to be shifted from its original venue at the National Stadium to the Rajamangala National Stadium following devastating floods. The National Stadium was being used as an Evacuation Centre.

Australia 1, Thailand 0
(*Halftime*: 0–0)
Scorer: Holman
15 November 2011
Referee: Mozaffarizadehyazdi Saeid (Iran)
Crowd: 19,400
Rajamangala Stadium, Bangkok

Australia: Mark Schwarzer, Lucas Neill, Michael Zullo, Luke Wilkshire, Matthew Spiranovic, Brett Emerton, Brett Holman (Robbie Kruse 83), Mile Jedinak (Neil Kilkenny 90), Carl Valeri, Matthew McKay, Joshua Kennedy (Alex Brosque 86)
Thailand: Sinthaweechai Hathairattanakool, Suree Sukha, Niweat Siriwong, Chonlatit Jantakam, Phanrit Nataporn, Thonglao Datsakorn, Vivatchaichok Rangsan (Winothai Teeratep 62), Choeichiu Phichitphong (Pipob On-Mo 80), Supachai Komsilp, Kaewprom Jakkaphan, Kirati Keawsombut (Dangda Teerasil 75)

Brett Holman was the hero as he fired the Socceroos into the final stage of 2014 World Cup qualifying in a hard-fought 1–0 win over a gallant Thailand in Bangkok.

Needing only a point to seal progression to the final round of Asian qualifying starting in June, Australia had to soak up some heavy pressure before Holman's 77th-minute header put the result beyond doubt.

Despite talk of being determined to atone for the shock 1–0 loss to Oman in Muscat four days earlier, the Socceroos were far from convincing on a humid Bangkok evening. But the ever-improving Holman again proved his worth with his second goal in three international matches. The AZ Alkmaar midfielder found Brett Emerton out wide, and the Sydney FC winger sent in a fine cross before Holman steered a header into the back of the net.

Holman admitted that the Socceroos were not convincing but said they had got the result they were after: 'We got the job done, so that's the most important thing and now we can look to the opponents we have in round two and see how we go from there. These sort of games; it all depends on the three points. We did it tonight, not convincingly, but we didn't give away much either so that was the most important thing.'

Osieck admitted it was a tough win but praised his side for its efforts in two tricky away matches: 'I'm pretty pleased for the boys, tough win but a good win. You have to consider... we had two road games, playing in Asia in different countries in the Middle East and South-East Asia, it's always difficult. It's not going to be easy for anybody. Already from three road games we won two, which is definitely a great achievement.'

Emerton was one of two changes to the starting side from the loss in Oman, with Michael Zullo also coming in as the injured Harry Kewell and Rhys Williams made way. Despite beginning with a familiar-looking team, Australia looked disjointed and struggled to control possession for much of the first half.

The visitors were lucky to go into the break level, with the only genuine chance of the half falling to the hosts. Impressive midfielder Datsakorn Thonglao pulled all the strings for Thailand, producing an exquisite through ball in the 35th minute only for Suree Sukha to blast over the bar from close range.

Australia's left side, particularly Zullo, was bombarded by the lively Thais while the Socceroos were restricted to only two shots on goal for the half. Both fell to the head of in-form striker Josh Kennedy, but neither attempt troubled Thailand goalkeeper Sinthaweechai Hathairattanakool. The Thais continued to threaten early in the second half and tension was building until Holman intervened. Thailand's best chance to equalise fell to substitute Poonsak Masuk, but he could not keep a close-range shot down.

Australia moved to 12 points on top of Group D, ensuring it would top the group. Midfielder Matt McKay would be ineligible to face Saudi Arabia in the next match after picking up a second-half yellow card.

The win meant that Holger Osieck's side headed into its final Group D qualifier at home against Saudi Arabia in February knowing the qualifying job was already done, possibly allowing the German coach to experiment with his squad.

The year 2012 promised so much with Australia involved in the final stage of World Cup qualifiers. There were rumblings of discontent in the background—the FFA and head Frank Lowy were left to deal with two rogue billionaire owners of the Gold Coast and Newcastle Jets A-League clubs, Clive Palmer and Nathan Tinkler. Palmer and Tinkler had been courted for their financial clout, overlooking the fact that they were both unpredictable time bombs waiting to go off.

Lowy for the first time was also a target following the World Cup bid debacle, and there were obviously some rebels from the old soccer world coming out from under cover to fire off a few shots at the head of soccer in Australia. Lowy had been a protected species through his run of success, but he now faced growing resentment. Lowy was being questioned and challenged in the media over the rights of the FFA to run the A-League. There had been growing calls for an independent body to run the League, or at best grant greater control for the owners of the clubs. Leading the charge was Clive Palmer, a man with a reputation as a loose cannon at any time. Palmer and Lowy had a heated exchange with Palmer arguing 'that owners need a greater say and better consultation'. Lowy's dictator approach was also being questioned. This malcontent would continue to fester for years to come.

The Socceroos would begin 2012 with their World Cup qualifier against Saudi Arabia. Australia was certain to progress to the final stage of qualifying and finish top of its group, regardless of the result at Melbourne's AAMI Park.

Australia 4, Saudi Arabia 2
(*Halftime*: 1–2)
Scorers: Brosque (2), Kewell, Emerton
29 February 2012
Referee: Dong Jin Kim (South Korea)
Crowd: 24,214
Melbourne Rectangular Stadium (AAMI Park)

Australia: Mark Schwarzer, Lucas Neill, Matthew Spiranovic (David Carney 82), Jade North, Sasha Ognenovski, Brett Emerton, Mark Milligan, Harry Kewell, James Troisi (Archie Thompson 62), Alex Brosque (Nick Carle 87), Marco Bresciano
Saudi Arabia: Waleed Abdullah, Osama Hawsawi, Abdul Al Dossary, Kamel Al Mousa, Mohammad Al Shaloub (Naif Hazazi 79), Nasser Al-Shamrani, Hassan Fallatah, Saud Kariri, Ahmed Al Fraidi (Ahmed Ateef 65), Taisir Al Jassam, Salem Al-Dawsari

Striker Alex Brosque scored a double as a stunning second-half Socceroos' barrage set up a 4–2 win to end Saudi Arabia's World Cup qualifying campaign.

The Socceroos looked in danger of suffering their first loss on home soil in three years when they trailed 2–1 at halftime and that was still the score 72 minutes into the match. But the game then turned dramatically, as the home side piled on three goals in three minutes to ensure it would carry plenty of confidence into the last stage of qualifying for the 2014 World Cup Finals in Brazil.

The Socceroos had made a sluggish start to go a goal down in the 19th minute, courtesy of Saudi Arabia's Salem Al-Dawsari. Brosque later scored Australia's lone goal in the first half when midfielder Mark Bresciano, playing his first game for the Socceroos since the 2010 World Cup, gave the pacy striker a nice through ball to run onto.

After Brosque's 43rd-minute equaliser, the home side paid for some loose defence when Nasser Al-Shamrani received a cross unmarked in the penalty area and fired home in first-half stoppage time.

Brosque was heavily involved in the second-half onslaught. He set up Harry Kewell, who had an excellent match, for Australia's second goal of the night, running past the defence into the left of the penalty area, then cutting the ball back for Kewell's first-touch finish.

Brosque scored himself two minutes later, combining superbly with Brett Emerton, whose perfect chipped cross from the left allowed the striker to speed into the penalty area and head the ball past the Saudi keeper.

Within a minute of the restart, Emerton scored himself, with Bresciano again providing the assist. Emerton had a touch of luck, as a defender's attempted clearance ricocheted off the Australian's boot into the net.

It was fitting that the Socceroos had a dose of luck, as earlier in the second half, captain Lucas Neill was denied what would have been his maiden international goal by an incorrect offside call.

Australia's win was good news for Oman, who overtook Saudi Arabia to progress to the next stage with a 2–0 win over Thailand in Muscat.

Four months later, Australia regrouped for the final stage of World Cup qualification with a warm-up game against Denmark in Copenhagen. The Socceroos were comfortably beaten by the Danes 2–0. Six days later, the Socceroos went into battle with Oman in Muscat in very hot conditions.

Australia 0, Oman 0
(*Halftime*: 0–0)

8 June 2012
Referee: Faghani Alireza (Iran)
Crowd: 11,000
Sultan Qaboos Stadium, Muscat

Australia: Mark Schwarzer, Lucas Neill, Sasa Ognenovski, Luke Wilkshire (Robbie Kruse 82), Harry Kewell (Archie Thompson 58), David Carney, Jade North, Carl Valeri, Matthew McKay, Alex Brosque, Mark Bresciano
Oman: Ali Abdullah Harib Al Habsi, Mohammed Saleh Ali Al-Musalami, Mohamed Albalushi, Raeed Ibrahim Saleh, Mohammed Eid Al Farsi (Ali Hilal Saud Al-Jabri 71), Saad Suhail Juma Al Mukhaini, Obaid Al Mahajiri, Abdul Sallam Amur Juma Al Mukhaini, Ismail Sulaiman Ashoor Al Ajmi, Amad Ali Sulaiman Al Hosni (Waleed Abdallah Al-Saadi 83), Juma Darwish Juma Al-Maashari (Hussain Ali Farah Al Hadhri 66)

The Socceroos kicked off the next stage of their qualifying campaign with a lethargic display against Oman in Muscat. Australia had the better chances during the game, but Oman captain and goalkeeper Ali Al-Habsi had an outstanding game.

Substitute Archie Thompson had three great chances before fulltime but was unable to convert any of them. In a disturbing incident, Australian goalkeeper Mark Schwarzer complained that laser beams were directed at his eyes during the match.

Oman front man Amad Al-Hosni was a problem for the Australian defence throughout the match and forced a sensational save from Schwarzer in the second half.

The Socceroos played with caution throughout the game and were clearly not about to concede against the run of play. This encouraged the Omani part-timers who were inspired by their supporters and the cautious Australian approach to the game.

Harry Kewell and Alex Brosque started up front with tall striker Josh Kennedy and Tim Cahill named on the bench. Jade North started at right-back and Carl Valeri edged out Mile Jedinak for a spot in midfield.

Australia started the match slowly, maintaining possession and hoping to force an error from Oman. Socceroo defender Sasa Ognenovski picked up a yellow card in the sixth minute while Oman's Al Hosni found space in the 10th minute but directed his header straight at goalkeeper Mark Schwarzer.

David Carney and Carl Valeri then called Al-Habsi into action with long-range strikes as Australia started to find their way into the match. Al-Habsi did well to get down low to a Valeri shot from 12 metres out in the 35th minute after good lead-up work from Harry Kewell.

After conditions cooled during the halftime break, Oman upped the pressure on the Socceroos. Al-Hosni thought he had put his team ahead in the 56th minute with a header, only for Schwarzer to dive sharply to his left and push the ball away. Al-Hosni slapped his arms against the ground in frustration and Schwarzer screamed angrily at his team's defence.

Archie Thompson replaced his Melbourne Victory teammate Kewell in the 59th minute and Al-Hosni was at it again nine minutes later with an acrobatic volley that sailed wide.

Brosque had a good chance in the 75th minute after the ball dropped to him in the box, but he failed to score. Archie Thompson couldn't squeeze the ball past Al-Habsi seven minutes later. Robbie Kruse replaced Luke Wilkshire in the final ten minutes and nearly set up a goal, but Thompson's backheel failed to beat Al-Habsi. In injury time, Thompson had another look at goal only to put his glancing header wide.

The Socceroos flew back to Australia to face run-away group leaders Japan in Brisbane in a defining match in the group. The Socceroos needed to improve measurably from the game against Oman in facing the 'Blue Samurai.'

Australia 1, Japan 1
(*Halftime*: 0–0)
Scorer: Wilkshire
12 June 2012
Referee: Khalil Ibrahim Al Ghamdi (Saudi Arabia)
Crowd: 40,189
Suncorp Stadium, Brisbane

Australia: Mark Schwarzer, Lucas Neill, Tim Cahill, Sasa Ognenovski, Luke Wilksire (Robbie Kruse 90), David Carney, Jade North, Carl Valeri, Matthew McKay (Nikita Rukavytsya 64), Alex Brosque, Marco Bresciano (Mark Milligan 13 (sent off 56))
Japan: Eiji Kawashimi, Keisuke Honda, Yuto Nagatomo, Atsuto Uchida (Hiroki Sakai 73), Yasuhito Endo, Shinji Okazaki (Hiroyoshi Kiyotake 87),

Shinji Kagawa (Masahiko Inoha 90), Yasuyuki Konno, Yuzo Kurihara (sent off 89), Makato Hasebe, Ryoichi Maeda

Down a man just after halftime, the Socceroos fought bravely to earn a 1–1 draw in their World Cup qualifier against old rival, Japan. Six years to the day after their epic 3–1 World Cup win over Japan in Germany, Australia again showed their fighting spirit, despite Mark Milligan being red-carded in the 55th minute.

Milligan wasn't the only one seeing red—Socceroos' coach Holger Osieck was seething on the sidelines after watching Milligan receive his marching orders for a diving challenge on Atsuto Uchida.

Only minutes after Milligan's dismissal, Osieck's mood was at explosion point in the 65th minute when Japanese dangerman Keisuke Honda found an unmarked Yuzo Kurihara free in the box and Japan were in front.

A 69th-minute penalty to the Socceroos restored parity and eased Osieck's rage. Referee Khalil Al Ghamdi pointed to the spot after Atsuto Uchida brought striker Alex Brosque down and Luke Wilkshire converted from the spot. The goal lifted the 40,189 Socceroos supporters to urge their team on.

In the 77th minute, Suncorp Stadium nearly erupted when defender Sasa Ognenovski's shot hit the crossbar. There was more drama when Kurihara received a second yellow card in the 89th minute and was dismissed, and Wilkshire's long-range shot was brilliantly saved by Japanese keeper, Kawashima.

Australian coach Osieck praised his charges after the game: 'It was a heroic performance after playing in extremely difficult conditions in Oman and then with the travel back to Australia. What they showed today with one man down is hard to describe. The spirit is unique, what they displayed today. It was very, very unfortunate that we lost (Bresciano) early because he provides that element of creativity that later on, we were missing.'

Osieck protected Milligan from any blame for his red card and was critical of referee Ghamdi for the defensive midfielder's second yellow: 'That was a very, very dubious call from the referee. It was a cross inside, and he clearly went to the ball and didn't even touch (Uchida). How could he give a red card for that? It was beyond my comprehension.'

Tim Cahill, who appeared to be on the outer with coach Osieck after not taking the field in six of their last seven internationals was injected into the starting side for this match and proceeded to terrorise Japan in the first half. Cahill seemed to be everywhere and was present during Australia's best first-half scoring chance in the 19th minute as his header was saved.

Kurihara also defied Alex Brosque and cleared a ball off the line while lying on his back. Frustration caused by Cahill bubbled over when Kurihara received a yellow card for manhandling the ever-moving Australian star moments later.

Japan made a mess of their best scoring chances—Yuto Nagatomo's 33rd-minute cross failed to find a wide-open Ryoichi Maeda and Atsuto Uchida's strike 10 minutes later went well wide. Australia received a major blow when veteran midfielder Mark Bresciano lasted just 13 minutes before being subbed off with what appeared to be a groin strain. He had been a standout in Australia's 0–0 draw with Oman the previous weekend and was again expected to control the game tempo against Japan.

It was a second straight draw for Australia in the final qualifying stage following the 0–0 result with Oman. The draw ended a run of two straight runaway wins by Group B leaders Japan.

A top-two finish in the five-team group would guarantee a berth at Brazil 2014. But clearly Australia wasn't going to get things going all their own way in this group. They followed the Japan match with a couple of friendly games in preparation for what lay ahead. They were well beaten by Scotland in Edinburgh 3–1. They then went to Beirut to face Lebanon, winning 3–0. This was a final warm-up match for the World Cup qualifier against Jordan in Amman on September 11.

Australia 1, Jordan 2
(*Halftime*: 0–0)
Scorer: Thompson
11 September 2012
Referee: Abdullah Baloushi (Qatar)
Crowd: 16,000
King Abdullah International Stadium, Amman

Australia: Mark Schwarzer, Lucas Neill, Tim Cahill, Sasa Ognenovski (Matthew Spiranovic 14), Luke Wilkshire, Robbie Kruse, David Carney, Brett Holman (Archie Thompson 74), Matthew McKay, Alex Brosque, Mark Bresciano (Mile Jedinak 46)

Jordan: Amer Shafi, Mohammed Al Dmeiri (Saeed Murjan 46), Abdulelah Al Hanahneh, Amer Deeb, Mohammad Mustafa Hassan Ali, Odai Al Saify (Anas Hijah 73), Ahmad Hayel, Shadi Abu Hashhash, Basem Fathi, Hassan Abdel-Fattah (Hamza Al Dardour 84), Anas Bani Yaseen

The result of this game threw Australia's qualifying campaign into serious disarray. It was a pitiful performance which coach Holger Osieck described as an 'enormous disappointment'. The loss meant the Socceroos had just two points from three games. They were well off the pace from run-away leaders Japan and in a real fight to get the final second position place.

Australia at least pulled a goal back through substitute Archie Thompson in the last five minutes, but poor finishing and frantic defending allowed Jordan to claim the memorable win. Ranked 87th in the world to Australia's 25th, Jordan was now in second place on four points in Group B.

Coach Osieck was scathing: 'We didn't get into the game, our passing was a disaster, we never could get into our normal rhythm. The disappointment is enormous. We had a very, very poor first half. We played a lot of long balls, and I don't know why that happened.'

Captain Lucas Neill also did not hold back in his assessment: 'We can't afford many slip-ups now. We've got to pick the team that will do the job in each game now. We've got to keep believing and stay positive. There's plenty of points to play for. But if we perform like we did tonight, it's going to be difficult.'

Towering Socceroos' defender Sasa Ognenovski had to leave the field after only 14 minutes with an injury, forcing Osieck into an early reshuffle, and Jordan's high-tempo game unsettled the Australians.

In the 48th minute, Jordan forward Odai Al-Saify skipped down the left and was felled in the penalty area as he cut back inside Mile Jedinak. Qatari Abdullah Baloushi gave the penalty and Abdel-Fattah slotted the spot kick past Mark Schwarzer.

Jordan retreated and allowed Australia to dictate play before the home side produced a stunning counter to grab a second. Al-Saify led a breakout and skipped around Lucas Neill before cutting the ball back for Deeb to fire in at the near post in the 77th minute.

The Australians, who had slumped to a 0–0 draw away to Oman in their opening qualifier, were rattled and Jordan should have had a third, but Deeb clipped his shot just over the bar.

Jedinak then smacked the post with a long-range drive as the Socceroos struggled to find the spark required. They relied on hopeful balls into the area instead. Substitute Archie Thompson then fired his right-foot shot past Shafi. The goal set up a nervy finale with AFC vice-president Prince Ali Bin Al-Hussein amongst those home fans unable to watch. But after Robbie Kruse wasted one last good chance, Jordan held firm, and the world's 87th-ranked side claimed the win.

Japan strengthened its iron grip on top spot in the group with a 1–0 win over Iraq in Saitama. A month later Australia flew to Qatar to face Iraq—a match that could all but have ended the Socceroos hopes of making the finals in Brazil. This was a 'win-at-all-costs' match.

Australia 2, Iraq 1
(*Halftime*: 0–0)
Scorers: Cahill, Thompson
16 October 2012
Referee: Lee Min Hu (South Korea)
Crowd: 2,183
King Abdullah International Stadium, Amman

Australia: Mark Schwarzer, Lucas Neill, Tim Cahill (James Holland 89), Luke Wilkshire, Robbie Kruse (Tommy Oar 79), Brett Holman, Mile Jedinak, Carl Valeri, Matthew McKay, Alex Brosque (Archie Thompson 75), Matthew Spiranovic
Iraq: Sabri Abbas Noor, Ibrahim Ahmed, Khaldoon Ibrahim Mohammed, Akram Nashat (Shafee Osamah 84), Hammadi Ahmed Abdullah (Kareem Mustafa 60), Younis Mahmoud, Ahmed Yaseen Gheni, Shaker Salam, Saeed Samal, Husam Kadhim Jebur Al-Shuwaili, Khalid Muthana Salih (Abdulzehra Ala'a 64)

Australia eased the heat on under-fire coach Holger Osieck and got its World Cup qualification bid back on track after coming from behind to beat Iraq 2–1. However, it looked like another barrage of negative headlines were coming Osieck's way when the Socceroos fell behind to Alaa Abdul-Zahra's goal in the 72nd minute.

But Tim Cahill scored a superb 80th-minute header from a Matt McKay corner, and then substitutes Tommy Oar and Archie Thompson combined to grab an 84th-minute winner and lift the Socceroos to second spot in Group B with five points from four games.

A happy and relieved coach Holger Osieck stated: 'I think we are back in the race ... it is better to operate from the upper position rather than to chase the pack. We were lucky even though it only came in the closing minutes. We managed to score from the chances that we had, unlike the last match against Jordan where we failed to score from the chances that we created, and we lost the match.'

Thompson stated after the game: 'Who keeps telling me I'm old? Who keeps telling us old boys we shouldn't be part of the Socceroos? But hopefully this will shut a few mouths and put us back on track.'

Australia now had its destiny in its own hands with three of its last four games at home, the only exception being a tricky away trip to Japan, who led the group on 10 points. This win against Iraq was a great boost to team morale.

The Socceroos were now in equal second position on the qualifying table with Oman, but only one point ahead of Jordan. Iraq had dropped out of contention. Australia were five points behind unbeaten runaway leaders Japan.

Through to the end of the year, Australia would play several friendlies and Asian Cup qualifiers. They were impressive in downing fellow Asian heavyweights South Korea 2–1 in Hwaseong-si and they followed that with a 1–0 win over Hong Kong in an East Asian Cup qualifier tournament in Hong Kong. The final games saw a 1–1 draw with North Korea and two big wins: 9–0 over Guam and 8–0 against Taiwan. This concluded the 2012 year. The run of results may have given Holger Osieck some breathing room in his survival as coach.

Australia kicked off 2013 with a friendly match against Romania held in Malaga, Spain, going down 3–2. The Socceroos then resumed their World Cup qualifiers with a home game against Oman. In front of a good home crowd the Socceroos were firm favourites. In a major shock, the other group game saw Japan go down to Jordan on the same night. Australia really needed to win to take advantage of that unexpected result.

Australia 2, Oman 2

(*Halftime*: 0–1)

Scorers: Cahill, Holman

26 March 2013

Referee: Ravshan Irmatov (Uzbekistan)
Crowd: 34,603
Stadium Australia, Olympic Park, Sydney

Australia: Mark Schwarzer, Tim Cahill, Luke Wilkshire, Robbie Kruse (Archie Thompson 68), Brett Holman, Mile Jedinak, James Holland (Mark Bresciano 53 (Tommy Oar 77)), Matthew McKay, Robert Cornthwaite, Alex Brosque, Michael Thwaite
Oman: Ali Al Habsi, Mohammed Saleh Ali Al-Musalami, Raed Saleh, Eid Al-Farsi (Jaber Al Owaisi 84), Abdul Aziz, Qasim Said (Ali Hilal 90), Saad Al Mukhaini, Ahmed Mubarak, Abdul Sallam Al Mukhaini, Hassan Al Gheilani, Amad Al Hosni (Ismail Al-Ajmi 68)

Against all expectations, Australia put in a horror performance and were very lucky to end up with a 2–2 draw thanks to a Brett Holman bullet at the death. The shock 2–1 win by Jordan over Japan had dropped the Socceroos back to third place in the Group B Asian qualifiers.

The result left the Socceroos with just one win and six points to show from five games. They were now locked in an intense fight with Jordan and Oman to be the second team through to the World Cup behind clear group leaders, Japan.

In their final three qualifying matches in June, the Socceroos would be looking to snatch at least a point in Japan, then storm home with wins at home against Jordan and Iraq. But judging by the performance against Oman, that looked to be a forlorn hope.

It took only six minutes for Oman to shock Australia. The crowd of 34,603 at Homebush was stunned into silence when speedy forward Abdul Aziz Mubarak left central defender Michael Thwaite stranded for pace and slotted an angled, left-foot drive through the legs of goalkeeper and stand-in skipper Mark Schwarzer.

The dejected Socceroos clearly missed suspended captain Lucas Neill and were lacking confidence and hope. However, Brett Holman was the home-side hero and lifted the team with an impressive performance.

A mistake-riddled first half had Australian coach Holger Osieck howling at his players, as well as exchanging angry words on the sidelines with his Omani counterpart, Paul Le Guen.

The nightmare got worse for Australia soon after the restart when midfielder Mile

Jedinak stuck out his left leg and deflected a low, hard cross past a hapless Schwarzer for an own goal to make it 2–0 to Oman.

However, the Socceroos fought their way back into the game in the second half with grit and determination. Shortly after halftime, Tim Cahill headed home Luke Wilkshire's corner to pull one goal back and was unlucky with a string of other superb headers. Holman then 'saved Australia's bacon' by smashing a drive past Omani goalkeeper Ali Al-Habsi from outside the box.

The Holman goal snatched a point from the depths of despair, but the Socceroos had clearly left themselves an uphill task to reach Brazil. Coach Osieck was again in the firing line with the media and calls were increasing for his dismissal.

Australia flew to Japan for a decisive game in early June. Japan, who had been so impressive throughout qualification except for their recent unexpected loss to Jordan, were favourites and could have put a 'nail in the Australian team's qualifying coffin'.

Australia 1, Japan 1
(*Halftime*: 0–0)
Scorer: Oar
4 June 2013
Referee: Nawaf Shukralla (Bahrain)
Crowd: 62,172
Saitama Stadium, Saitama, Japan

Australia: Mark Schwarzer, Lucas Neill, Sasa Ognenovski, Luke Wilkshire, Tommy Oar, Mark Milligan, Mark Bresciano, Brett Holman (Dario Vidosic 72), Robbie Kruse (Archie Thompson 90), Tim Cahill, Matthew McKay
Japan: Eiji Kawashimi, Yuto Nagatomo, Yashuhito Endō, Shinji Okazaki (Hiroshi Kiyotake 87), Ryoichi Maeda (Yuzo Kurihara 79), Makoto Hasebe, Atsuto Uchida (Mike Havenaar 84), Shinji Kagawa, Yasuyuki Konno, Keisuke Honda, Maya Yoshida

In a complete turnaround, the Socceroos regained their fighting tenacity to earn a draw against the 'Blue Samurai' in Saitama. The performance was a vast improvement on the display against Oman in Sydney.

Only a 90th-minute Keisuke Honda penalty denied the Socceroos a famous victory.

Referee Nawaf Shukralla awarded it after adjudging Socceroos defender Matt McKay to have handballed a Japanese cross.

A cross-turned-shot from Tommy Oar, who was one of Australia's best with his speed on the left, had earlier put Australia 1–0 up in the 82nd minute. Coach Holger Osieck confessed at fulltime: 'Before the game, a draw would have been good but when you are that close ... of course a draw is a little bit disappointing.'

Skipper Lucas Neill and Sasa Ognenovski were outstanding at the back for Australia and on several occasions denied the likes of Honda, Shinji Kagawa and Yasuhito Endō from scoring for Japan. Mark Schwarzer also pulled off a brilliant save from Kagawa early in the game, as Australia struggled to come to terms with the speed and movement of their opponents.

But Australia was having success on the counter, with the precise distribution of Mark Bresciano and Brett Holman, and they could have gone ahead midway through the first half when Holman released Robbie Kruse. But Kruse could not beat the advancing Japanese keeper Eiji Kawashima, and Tim Cahill fired a difficult rebound over the crossbar from distance.

Australia's pressing of Japan began to tire their older legs. The home side began to dictate possession in the second half, with Kagawa going close with a chip that shaved the apex of the goal.

However, Tommy Oar looked to have won the game for the Socceroos when his 82nd-minute cross from the left looped over Japanese goalkeeper Eiji Kawashima, who flapped and failed to save it.

Oar's goal gave the visitors an unlikely lead and while Japan committed numbers forward in search of the equaliser, the Socceroos seemed to be doing well to shut the 'Blue Samurai' out. That was until McKay's indiscretion as the final minute of normal time elapsed. Honda made no mistake with the penalty to deny Australia a victory that would have taken them a long way towards qualification for Brazil. The result left Australia in a precarious position with home matches against Jordan and Iraq that they would both need to win to secure qualification.

The once much-vaunted fear that Asian teams had in facing the Socceroos had evaporated over the course of this campaign and it was clear that the development of the game in Asia was taking massive steps forward. Meanwhile, our own youth development was going backwards. Since its inception in 1981, the Australian Institute of Sport (AIS) had been largely responsible for many of the players that would become known as the 'Golden Generation'. However in 2012, it had been decided that the AIS would no longer be responsible for directly managing elite athlete programs. This was a massive blow and detriment to the successful soccer programs over the previous 30 years—and we have still not recovered.

Australia's two final games would be played at home and there was no room for error. Coach Holger Osieck had become a major target for wrath and blame—his very future hung in the balance.

Australia 4, Jordan 0

(*Halftime*: 1–0)

Scorers: Bresciano, Cahill, Kruse, Neill

11 June 2013

Referee: Abdul Malik Abdul Bashir (Singapore)

Crowd: 43,785

Etihad Stadium, Melbourne

Australia: Mark Schwarzer, Mark Milligan, Lucas Neill, Sasa Ognenovski, Mark Bresciano, Tommy Oar (Archie Thompson 60), Robbie Kruse (Dario Vidosic 86), Tim Cahill, Brett Holman (Tom Rogic 79), Luke Wilkshire, Matthew McKay

Jordan: Amer Shafi Mahmoud Sabbah (Ahmed Abdel-Sattar Nawwas 88), Mohammad Mustafa Hassan Ali, Shadi Nadmi Abu Hash'hash, Basem Fat'hi Omar Othman, Anas Walid Khaled Bani Yaseen, Saeed Hassan Murjan, Amer Deeb Mohammad Khalil (Yaseen Anas Al-Bakhit 67), Khalil Zaid Bani Attiah, Adnan Suleiman Hassan Adous, Odai Yusuf Ismaeel Al-Saify (Hamza Ali Khaled Al-Dardour 67), Ahmad Hayel Ibrahim

This 4–0 win over Jordan at Etihad Stadium meant that the Socceroos were just 90 minutes away from reaching Brazil. Goals to Mark Bresciano, Tim Cahill, Robbie Kruse, and Lucas Neill—the captain's first goal in his 91st international—capped the team's finest effort of the campaign to at last deflect the heavy criticism of both the team and coach. The barbs and hatchet-sharpening had been going on for months and the accusation that the team was past its use-by date were loud and forceful.

Bresciano was dominant in midfield and Kruse a bundle of energy and improvisation down the right. If Neill's goal was historic rather than majestic, the first three were all moments to savour on what proved to be a thoroughly good night for the Socceroos. In the end, the win was as easy as the scoreline suggests. But in the beginning, the nerves and jitters were obvious for both players and supporters; the Socceroos were sluggish to get going.

The mood wasn't helped by an early Jordanian injury that prompted a wave of boos, and only Mark Milligan's long-range shot raised the crowd's pulse.

Holger Osieck made his displeasure clear from the side-line. Australia wasted some chances—Tommy Oar's cross was overhit but retrieved and returned by Robbie Kruse, only for Brett Holman's shot to be blocked by goalkeeper Amer Shafi, and Bresciano then blazed the rebound wide. The agony of this miss was short-lived; seconds later Bresciano made no mistake. The goal was created by Kruse's pass to the right wing and Luke Wilkshire's flicked return ball that sent Kruse striding into the box, his low cross smashed home from six metres by Bresciano.

The Jordanians then switched off and for a period afterwards they were just hanging on. Kruse's break was crudely halted with a challenge that earned Khalil Zaid Bani Attiah a yellow card, then Holman's through ball sent Kruse clear down the right again. This time though his cross was overhit and Cahill, arriving in front of goal at speed, could only deflect it wide.

There was Socceroo confidence everywhere and excellent movement, exemplified by the way Wilkshire kept joining the attack down the right. Only towards the end of the first half did the Australians seem under any threat when Adnan Suleiman missed a great chance for a cross after leaving Matt McKay standing.

Milligan had a great opportunity soon after, but he volleyed Kruse's cross over the top. However, Jordan was coming into the game, dominating possession, and creating chances that Anas Bani Yaseen and Saeed Murjan wasted, heading, and shooting the ball wide.

Archie Thompson was introduced after an hour to the delight of the crowd, and within seconds there was a second goal to celebrate. It began at the back with Ognenovski, then the ball was moved with speed to Thompson, Bresciano and Holman to Kruse on the right—his perfect cross invited Cahill to power home a header.

It was a brilliant move, and the pressure was lifted as the Socceroos stormed forward. They probed the Jordanian defence from left and right. Twice Thompson was almost put clear and Osieck slumped to his knees in frustration, knowing a third goal would 'seal the deal'.

Finally, it came with 76 minutes on the clock. Bresciano moved the ball to the right for Holman, whose pass found Kruse's feet. In a twinkle, the Bayer 04 Leverkusen-bound forward turned his man and drove a low shot that Amer Shafi couldn't keep out.

Thompson then almost 'iced the cake' after being put clear by Wilkshire, but he was denied by a sprawling save from Amer Shafi. From the corner though, Neill leapt highest to turn home a Cahill knock-on and the evening was complete.

The Socceroos had one final hurdle to climb for Brazil: a game against Iraq in Sydney.

The build-up to the final qualifier against Iraq was intense, and like the corresponding Uruguay match eight years before, it was again a sell-out crowd. The Socceroos were holding down second spot on the Asian Group B table and a win would guarantee a berth at the 'Big Dance' in Brazil. But if they lost or drew the game, Oman had the chance to leapfrog the Socceroos, provided they beat Jordan.

Iraq would go into the game without two of their 'big guns' in Younis Mahmoud and Nashat Akram. They were late withdrawals amid speculation of internal divisions in the squad. Added to this, striker Alaa Abdul-Zahra was red-carded in their loss to Japan and suspended.

Still, the Socceroos were not without their detractors—the team continued to be compared in the press to 'Dad's Army'. If they overcame this final hurdle, then at next year's World Cup Lucas Neill would be 36, Mark Schwarzer 41, Sasa Ognenovski and Archie Thompson 35 and Tim Cahill and Mark Bresciano 34; Luke Wilkshire at 32 was one of the young ones.

Iraq, despite player withdrawals, had a very strong record against the Socceroos, having beaten them at the 2007 Asian Cup and also knocking the Olyroos out of the 2004 Olympics. The Iraqi coach, Serbian Vladimir Petrović remained as the only coach to have beaten Australia in a World Cup qualifier at ANZ Stadium when in charge of China, back in 2010. In the final analysis before the game, Iraq would field a severely under-strength side. Except for a few players, they would essentially field their under-20 side. Surely the planets had aligned, and the Socceroos would be bound for Brazil?

Australia 1, Iraq 0
(*Halftime*: 0–0)

Scorer: Kennedy
18 June 2013
Referee: Faghani Alireza (Iran)
Crowd: 80,523
Stadium Australia, Olympic Park, Sydney

Australia: Mark Schwarzer, Lucas Neill, Mark Milligan, Sasa Ognenovski, Luke Wilkshire, Tommy Oar, Brett Holman (Tom Rogic 60), Matthew McKay, Mark Bresciano, Tim Cahill (Joshua Kennedy 77), Robbie Kruse (Archie Thompson 78)

Iraq: Noor Sabri Abbas Hassan Al-Bairawi, Ahmad Ibrahim Khalaf, Ali Bahjat Fadhil, Khaldoun Ibrahim Mohammed, Ali Adnan Kadhim Al-Tameemi, Dhurgham Ismail Dawood Al-Quraishi (Halgurd Mulla Mohammed Taher Zebari 65), Waleed Salem Al-Lami, Saif Salman Hashim Al-Mohammadawi (Osama Ali Mohammed 78), Humam Tariq Faraj Na'oush (Hammadi Ahmad Abdullah 74), Saad Abdul-Amir Al-Zirjawi, Mohannad Abdul-Raheem Karrar

It was an amazing crowd and tense atmosphere for this game. There was a proverbial sea of heaving green and gold. Holger Osieck and his team left it until the last gasp to seal the spot in Brazil. The team and coach had survived poor performances, doubts, and a stuttering final phase of the Asian qualifiers to finally triumph and all was forgotten in the end—the team and fans were left to celebrate a wonderful night amid skyrockets and celebrations.

The young Iraqi side deserved full credit for their wonderful performance that really pushed the Australian team and frayed the nerves of Socceroos' supporters.

Australia dominated from the opening whistle and very nearly scored in the second minute when a passing interchange between Robbie Kruse and Tim Cahill gave Cahill a chance with his left foot, but Noor Sabri saved brilliantly. Even defenders Neill and Ognenovski got in on the action when Neill set up his defensive partner to head over the bar.

Tim Cahill had a few other chances as well; after 28 minutes he headed straight at Iraqi keeper, Noor Sabri. Seven minutes later when the Iraqi keeper fumbled a Matt McKay cross, Cahill, with his back to goal, spun but his shot just went wide.

Despite the pressure and domination of possession, Australia just could not break

Iraq down. The Iraqis remained composed and resolute despite having five teenagers in their line-up. In the middle of the park, Khaldoun Ibrahim and the 19-year-old Saif Salman were standouts. Just after halftime, the Socceroos' supporters' nerves were nearly frayed when Salman crashed a long-distance shot that Mark Schwarzer gathered on the second attempt.

Tommy Oar was beginning to threaten down the left flank. However, the Socceroos when going forward were clearly vulnerable to a counterattack. Rain began to tumble down to dampen supporters' hopes even more. On the hour mark, Osieck brought on Tom Rogic for Brett Holman to set off a loud cheer from the Australian supporters. Rogic made an immediate impact and was giving the Iraqi defence real concerns with his mazy dribbling.

Midway through the half, the Australian supporters went up when Robbie Kruse struck a sweet volley past Noor Sabri, but the joy was short-lived as the referee awarded Iraq a free kick for an earlier foul by Ognenovski.

Emotions were now running high, and Australia pressed forward with a run of corners. In the 77th minute, coach Osieck replaced Tim Cahill with Josh Kennedy. Cahill appeared far from happy with his removal. It was Kennedy's first appearance for 19 months following a terrible run of injuries. Archie Thompson also came on for Robbie Kruse. But it would be left to the lanky Kennedy to claim hero status when he rose into the air to reach a pinpoint Mark Bresciano cross and head home the winner. It set off an incredible roar of celebration. Those of us in the crowd rode our emotions for the final minutes before the referee blew time to set off wild celebrations.

The next day the press hailed Kennedy. Because of his long hair and beard, he was often referred to as 'Jesus' and in this game as 'the Redeemer'. It was, without doubt, a miracle. Personally, I feel Josh Kennedy is one of the most under-rated Australian strikers in the history of the game, brilliant in the air and mobile with good control for a big man. He could hold the ball up well and undoubtedly was hampered during his international career by injuries.

Coach Holger Osieck, a man under severe attack throughout the campaign, was left with the final word: 'It's been a tough campaign, but the boys did a great job. We grew as a team, as a unit and the reward is that we are going to the World Cup. This has given me a beautiful feeling and I am very proud and now is not the time for analysis of the game or to look forward… it is time for joy and celebration.' He added optimistically: 'Hopefully after today's victory I get at least another year.'

A month after this qualifying success, the Socceroos travelled to South Korea to take part in the Asian Football Federation East Asian Cup. Australia went into this tournament with a young experimental side and started with a respectable 0-0 result with the hosts, South Korea. However, two successive defeats, 3-2 to Japan and 4-3 to China, saw the Socceroos finish last on the table. Despite having successfully qualified for the finals in Brazil, coach Osieck was again under fire and the next two warm-up games sealed his fate. I felt for Osieck and his team in the choice of opponents faced for these warm-up games —Brazil in Brazil and France in Paris. Both games resulted in humiliating and embarrassing 6-0 defeats. The FFA reacted immediately and terminated Osieck's contract with both the 2014 World Cup and the 2015 Asian Cup (to be held in Australia uppermost) in their mind.

It was now clear that a drastic overhaul of the Socceroos team was necessary. There was immediate talk of getting a high-profile European or South American coach to take over—this included Guus Hiddink returning, Frenchman Gérard Houllier, or Argentinian Marcelo Bielsa. Nothing materialised. In their first game after sacking Osieck, Australia faced Canada in London, recording a 3-0 win with caretaker coach Aurelio Vidmar in charge.

The FFA finally announced the expected appointment of Ange Postecoglou as the new Socceroos' supremo with a five-year contract. The calls for Postecoglou's appointment had been loud and consistent over the previous 12 months. He had outstanding results with the Brisbane Roar in the A-League and there was much anticipation and excitement over his appointment. The Socceroos would face Costa Rica in Sydney in his first match in charge. Sadly, in the week before the game, Socceroo legend Mark Schwarzer announced his retirement from the Socceroos. The Socceroos downed Costa Rica 1-0 at the Sydney Football Stadium thanks to a goal from Tim Cahill. Sadly again, Lucas Neill was targeted by sections of the home crowd who booed each time he touched the ball and forced him to admonish a section of the hometown supporters.

Ange Postecoglou was given the mammoth task of rebuilding the team. The Australian soccer media had built him up as the Messiah— they all supported his appointment. But Australian soccer media support has always been a fickle and unpredictable beast. The year ended and we rolled into the 2014 World Cup year. Once again I had booked myself onto the Green and Gold Army World Cup Tour and was very much looking forward to it. Australia's group in Brazil was foreboding, with a make-up of Chile, the Netherlands, and current world champions, Spain.

In early March, Australia played a warm-up game against Ecuador in London at Millwall's 'The Den' home ground. The game ended in defeat—the Socceroos were beaten 4–3. The final, customary World Cup warm-up game for the Socceroos at home was played at the Sydney Olympic Stadium in late May. The match against South Africa ended 1-1, but there were glimpses of the possession-style game that Postecoglou was trying to fashion. He was forced to make some strong decisions, none more so than informing long-term captain Lucas Neill that he would not be a part of the 30-man preliminary squad to be announced shortly before the World Cup. Neill had been a champion player and captain, and he was clearly one of Australia's greatest all-time defenders.

Postecoglou also lost a few key players to injury, including likely Neill replacement, Newcastle United's Curtis Good and striker Josh Kennedy. Also missing out was long-time fullback Luke Wilkshire and young gun Tommy Rogic. A final warm-up game was scheduled against Croatia in Brazil the week before the tournament commenced. The Socceroos dominated possession in the first 45 minutes and the backline that Postecoglou settled on — Franjic, Wilkinson, Spiranovic and Davidson — did themselves no harm in a solid performance. There was quick and incisive ball movement from defence into attack. However, the lack of penetration in the final third was a concern. Croatia won the game 1–0.

2014 World Cup Finals

Unlike in South Africa in 2010 where I was able to procure ten match tickets with little trouble, FIFA decreed they would have control over all World Cup ticketing in Brazil. It proved far more complicated and difficult to get any tickets, and I only managed to get three. But importantly, they were all for the Socceroos' games.

There was some concern with growing anti-World Cup demonstrations in Brazil directed at the money spent on hosting it, rather than fixing the shocking inequalities that exist in Brazilian society. It must be said that the nation is far from united around the World Cup, and I sided with the demonstrators and protesters after my arrival. Comments by ordinary Brazilians highlighted the discontent: 'I will cheer for Brazil, as always, but for the first time I don't want them to win. If we win, the government will use it as an opportunity to say what a success it has been and to mask all our problems.'

The nation, just prior to the World Cup opening, was rife with strikes and protests. In Rio, the city was gridlocked by protesting water company workers and a march by striking teachers. Banks were closed because of a security guard strike. It was a country torn in two.

The tournament itself witnessed reigning champions Spain and hosts Brazil amongst the favourites. The other fancied sides drew the usual suspects—a Lionel Messi-led Argentina, the young German team from South Africa had matured into a top side, and the Dutch possessed speed and skill in abundance. The Socceroos were clearly a team in rebuild. How would they fare in this World Cup baptism of fire? First-game opponents, Chile, were a side bristling with skill and confidence coming into this World Cup. Confidence on the streets of Santiago was very high and there was a sense of optimism not witnessed since Chile hosted the World Cup Finals in 1962 and finished third. Coach Ange Postecoglou was adamant: 'If you look at Chile, everyone is so admiring of their style of play and the fact that they're a real chance in the World Cup. They built that. They weren't in that space four years ago. That's got to be our goal, and I see with this group of players there's an appetite for that… We've all got a unique and pretty fantastic opportunity to taste some rarefied atmosphere and we've got to take it in, even myself.'

The first game against Chile was held in the city of Cuiabá. We travelled from Rio to Cuiabá by plane and stayed for two days. Cuiabá was described as a boom town basking in the relentless Mato Grosso sun. It is located close to one of the most famous locations in Brazil, the Pantanal. The Pantanal is the world's largest wetland and 20 times the size of the Florida Everglades. It is an amazing place to see wildlife.

Australia 1, Chile 3
(*Halftime*: 1–2)
Scorer: Cahill
13 June 2014
Referee: Noumandiez Desire Doue (Ivory Coast)
Crowd: 40,275
Arena Pantanal, Cuiabá, Brazil

Australia: Mathew Ryan, Jason Davidson, Ivan Franjic (Ryan McGowan 49), Matthew Spiranovic, Alex Wilkinson, Mathew Leckie, Mark Milligan,

Mile Jedinak, Tommy Oar (Ben Halloran 68), Mark Bresciano (James Troisi 78), Tim Cahill

Chile: Claudio Andres Bravo Munoz, Mauricio Anibal Isla Isla, Gary Alexis Medel Soto, Gonzalo Alejandro Jara Reyes, Eugenio Esteban Mena Reveco, Marcelo Alfonso Diaz Rojas, Jorge Luis Valdivia Toro (Jean Andre Beausejour Coliqueo 68), Arturo Erasmo Vidal Pardo (Felipe Alejandro Gutierrez Leiva 60), Charles Mariano Aranguiz Sandoval, Eduardo Jesus Vargas Rojas (Mauricio Ricardo Pinilla Ferrera 88), Alexis Alejandro Sanchez Sanchez

The stadium in Cuiabá was full of colour and noise including a great contingent of Socceroos' supporters and a very vocal and friendly Chilean fan base. A brave and impressive Socceroos outfit sadly fell agonisingly short against Chile, losing 3-1 in an enthralling World Cup match. There was tremendous excitement. The way Chile opened—with speed, flair, and skill—there were grave fears among us in the stadium that the Socceroos would crumble and collapse to cop another humiliating hiding. But they regrouped, rallied and came into the game.

Nerves unquestionably played a major part in the Australian team's tardy beginning that saw them 2-0 down after just 14 minutes. Goals were scored by Alexis Sanchez and Jorge Valdivia before the Socceroos had a chance to settle. Chile took the lead when Charles Aranguiz managed to get in behind the Socceroos' defence after 11 minutes, and when Eduardo Vargas headed down from the midfielder's cross, Sanchez guided the ball in at the near post. The advantage was doubled when Barcelona forward Sanchez picked out Valdivia and the Palmeiras midfielder hit a dipping shot in off the underside of the bar from 25 yards.

But as the first half progressed, Australia found its feet, led by Mark Bresciano in the middle, Mathew Leckie out wide and Tim Cahill up front. It was Cahill who gave Australia life again, heading home from an excellent Ivan Franjic cross from the right for his record-extending 33rd international goal.

Shortly after, Tommy Oar's cross was met with a firm half-volley from Bresciano, only for keeper Bravo to push the ball around the post. The Socceroos' supporters were up and roaring encouragement, and the team were lifting while Chile looked vulnerable. Tim Cahill was in everything, and he headed over from another Jason Davidson cross as Australia continued to threaten.

Australia upped the pressure in the second half and soon found itself firmly in the ascendancy. Bresciano had a shot brilliantly saved, Cahill had a goal denied for offside, and Leckie continued to terrorise the Chilean defenders.

Chile came close to a third goal when Sanchez threaded through for Eduardo Vargas and the Valencia forward's shot was cleared off the line by Alex Wilkinson. Cahill again demonstrated his renowned aerial ability soon after when he climbed above his marker, Gonzalo Jara, but this time headed over.

Sadly, Australian hopes of securing a point vanished when substitute Jean Beausejour drilled a low strike into the far corner in stoppage time.

Taking out the first quarter of an hour, the Socceroos fully deserved a point at the very least from this game. Tim Cahill gave an honest assessment after the match: 'We really stood up strong and it's just unfortunate. Not a lot went our way tonight, and it showed. They got in twice and punished us, but after that you could see [Chile's] legs were going. We knew we could get something from this game, and when you attack and concede a goal like that it's disappointing.'

The defeat was costly for Australia with Franjic succumbing to a hamstring injury that was likely to end his tournament. Tim Cahill, captain Mile Jedinak and Mark Milligan all picked up yellow cards, meaning they would be treading a disciplinary tight rope in the final two group games.

Coach Ange Postecoglou was understandably disappointed with the result but was proud of the Socceroos' performance: 'It was gut-wrenching, to be honest. I felt especially in the second half we were right on top; we just couldn't get that second goal. I thought if we got the second, we'd go on with it. It's disappointing for the players, after a rusty start ... I thought we were well in the game. Chile has some quality players and at the start they were at their sharpest, we probably gave them too much respect. Once we got the first goal, we got a little bit of belief in ourselves. We kept the ball a little bit better although I thought we lacked a bit of composure at times. We gave away a two-goal start, and in the end that's what killed us.'

The Netherlands displayed awesome power in smashing world champions Spain 5–1 in the other group game. There was no denying that the Socceroos had an almighty hurdle to overcome in their second match against the Dutch. After the game, our supporter group took a charter flight from Cuiabá to Gramado. Founded by German colonists, Gramado reflected German architecture and was so much cooler in the mountains than Cuiabá. It reminded me of Bavaria, a place I visited a lot back in the 1970s. There were pubs and restaurants all reflecting the German influence in the town's history. It was a great place to unwind and await the Socceroos' next match against the Dutch in Porto Alegre. On the morning of 17 June, we were taken by coaches on the short, 110-km journey to Porto Alegre. The city is Brazil's most southern and important port city' and reflects a heavy European settler influence through Portuguese, German, Polish and Italian immigrants. The city is the hometown of Brazilian superstar Ronaldinho. The following match day saw the group transported to the stadium and we were singing up a storm in anticipation of a great Socceroos' performance.

Australia 2, Netherlands 3
(*Halftime*: 1–1)
Scorers: Cahill, Jedinak
18 June 2014
Referee: Djamel Haimoudi (Algeria)
Crowd: 42,877
Estadio Beira-Rio, Porto Alegre, Brazil

Australia: Mathew Ryan, Alex Wilkinson, Ryan McGowan, Matthew Spiranovic, Jason Davidson, Tommy Oar (Adam Taggart 77), Mark Bresciano (Oliver Bozanic 51), Matthew McKay, Mathew Leckie, Mile Jedinak, Tim Cahill (Ben Halloran 69)
Netherlands: Jacobus Cillessen, Ron Peter Vlaar, Stefan de Vrij, Rolando Maximiliano Martins Indi (Memphis Depay 46), Daley Blind, Nigel de Jong, Jonathan Alexander de Guzman (Georginio Wijnaldum 78), Daryl Janmaat, Arjen Robben, Robin van Persie (Jeremain Marciano Lens 87), Wesley Sneijder

We all marched down to the stadium as a large group—it was a glorious day and my seat in the stadium was in a perfect position two sections back, just forward of the 18-yard box for the end that Australia would attack in the first half. Even the most fervent Socceroos' supporter could not have gone into this game with thoughts of victory following the Dutch demolition of world champions Spain in their first game.

Socceroos' coach Ange Postecoglou said before the game that his side intended to attack—and they were true to his words in the opening exchanges. But a flash of quality from Robben saw the Netherlands take the lead against the run of play. The Bayern Munich forward feinted his way past Alex Wilkinson on the halfway line, raced towards the Australian goal and drove in an angled shot for his third goal of the World Cup.

The Socceroos responded immediately with one of the goals of the tournament, Cahill meeting an angled ball from the right with a powerful left-foot volley that crashed in off the underside of the crossbar. The seat I was in was a perfect spot to see this goal. Socceroo supporters in the stadium erupted.

Had midfielder Mark Bresciano and defender Matt Spiranovic shown the same poise as Cahill, Australia could have taken the lead earlier than they did. Bresciano ran onto a low Leckie cross only to shoot over from just inside the area, while Spiranovic got away from his marker at a free kick but side-footed an eight-yard shot straight at keeper, Jasper Cillessen.

Mat Leckie also had a goal disallowed after he was adjudged to have fouled Daley Blind. But Australia continued to press and went in front when an Oliver Bozanic cross struck the hand of Daryl Janmaat and the referee pointed to the spot. Jedinak struck it firmly past Cillessen!

However, the lead did not last long, as Van Persie netted his 11th goal in 10 internationals soon afterwards, controlling the ball before turning and firing into the roof of the net.

Australia then again opened up the Dutch defence and Tommy Oar crossed for Leckie, who chested rather than headed the ball straight at Cillessen. But it was Depay who decided the outcome of the game, the 20-year-old PSV Eindhoven winger curled a shot just beyond the reach of Mat Ryan. Ryan should have saved this attempt; it was a soft goal.

The win ensured that the Netherlands secured a last-16 place in the 2014 World Cup, whilst Australia were now out of the tournament. Progress to the last 16 for the Dutch was secured after holders Spain were eliminated by Chile 2–0. Both Cahill and Van Persie were both ruled out of their teams' final group games after being shown their second yellow cards of the tournament in this match.

Press reports of the Socceroos' performance were glowing: 'Australia is the lowest-ranked team here, but it was a heroic effort, an incredible goal by Tim Cahill and they should have won the game. That minute cost them with Mathew Leckie missing the chance at one end and the goalkeeper's mistake at the other. What a game, what a World Cup.'

Ange Postecoglou offered praise of his team's showing: 'I just wanted the players to get the reward for the way they went about things today. I have put a lot of pressure on the players and the staff that we are going to be a certain type of team and take it to world-class opposition, but it is one thing saying it and another thing doing it. They did that today but didn't get their reward. It's heartbreaking and massively disappointing.'

As a spectacle, to have been there for this match was a privilege. It was such a great game to watch, a swash-buckling approach by an Australian team against a top-class side.

The Green and Gold Army hosted a post-game party and dinner with an open bar. It was the perfect way to reflect on the match. Two days later, we flew on to Curitiba for the Socceroos' final game against Spain.

Australia 0, Spain 3
(*Halftime*: 0–1)
Scorers: Cahill, Jedinak
23 June 2014
Referee: Nawaf Abdullah Ghayyath Shukralla (Bahrain)
Crowd: 39,375
Arena da Baixada, Curitiba, Brazil

Australia: Mathew Ryan, Alex Wilkinson, Ryan McGowan, Matthew Spiranovic, Jason Davidson, Matthew McKay, Mile Jedinak, Tommy Oar (James Troisi 61), Oliver Bozanic (Mark Bresciano 72), Mathew Leckie, Adam Taggart (Ben Halloran 46)
Spain: Jose Manuel Reina Paez, Juan Francisco Torres Belen, Raul Albiol Tortajada, Sergio Ramos Garcia, Jordi Alba Ramos, Andres Iniesta Lujan, Jorge Resurreccion Merodio, Xabier Alonso Olano (David Josue Jimenez Silva 83), Santiago Cazorla Gonzalez (Francesc Fabregas Soler 68), Fernando Jose Torres Sanz, David Villa Sanchez (Juan Manuel Mata Garcia 56)

Spain overcame the Socceroos 3–0 in the final group game. Australia certainly did not lack support in the crowd of 40,000, but looked jaded and tired in this match after their heroics against Chile and the Netherlands. They also missed their gun,

Tim Cahill, through suspension. Both sides were already out of the tournament, and it showed. In the final analysis, the Socceroos performed above expectations at the 2014 World Cup Finals, whereas Spain, as defending champions and one of the favourites, were an abject disappointment. Clearly time had caught up with their side and they were but a shadow of the 2010 team.

In the opening 30 minutes, Spain's play against the Socceroos was characterised by misplaced passes, uncertainty in defence and a lack of bite in the final third. Australia started positively in the first half, looking to set a quick tempo early on with snappy passes and pressure on the Spanish midfield. But Spain eventually got into the tussle, keeping the ball for lengthy spells, with Villa a regular attacking outlet down the left.

The first warning shot came as Santi Cazorla saw a shot blocked in a crowded area, before a low Villa cross beat everyone as the ball skimmed across the face of goal. Cazorla's cross then got past the onrushing Mat Ryan, but the Australian defence cleared the danger.

However, the ever-reliable David Villa, whose inclusion was one of seven Spanish changes for this match, then scored a familiar, classy goal. His flicked, backheeled finish from Juanfran's cross nine minutes before the break capped a move that was typical of Spain in their glory years. Andrés Iniesta had threaded a pass down the right to overlapping fullback Juanfran. The Atletico Madrid player squared to Villa, whose clever finish outfoxed keeper Mat Ryan.

Australia almost hit back immediately, but Spanish goalkeeper 'Pepe' Reina hacked the ball clear in a goalmouth scramble.

Spain improved greatly after the break. Australia had an early chance, but James Troisi couldn't control the ball on the sideline. After increasing pressure, Del Bosque's men eventually doubled their lead in the 69th minute when Iniesta's ball split the defence and found Torres, who side-footed in. That was the Chelsea forward's first World Cup goal since 2006. It was a fine mark for Iniesta who was playing his 100th game for Spain.

Mathew Leckie proved to be Australia's main dangerman, cutting inside to constantly trouble Spain down the right flank with his pace. The Socceroos had opportunities to test Spain's backline with two Tommy Oar free kicks, but none of them resulted in clear-cut chances. Spain was always the dominant side in the second half, despite the introduction of Mark Bresciano.

The final goal of Spain's campaign came eight minutes from the end. This time it was Fàbregas; the Chelsea midfielder, who had a falling out with Del Bosque during the build-up to the match, played a lovely, lofted ball to Mata at the far post. The Manchester United player barely looked up before poking the ball under the body of Ryan.

Defeat meant the Socceroos that went to Brazil became, statistically, the worst-performed of the four Australian teams to contest the World Cup Finals to that point. Even the part-timers of 1974 managed to scramble a point in their final match against Chile on a waterlogged pitch in Berlin. Coach Ange Postecoglou suggested that it seemed the physical and mental exertion of an arduous campaign had finally taken a toll. He observed that this World Cup had given his team an accurate measure of the gap that separates his team from the best. Against Chile and the Netherlands, it was a costly mistake here or there that meant goals were conceded or opportunities squandered. Against Spain, the inability to maintain pressure and composure let the Spanish off the leash. Clearly the absence of Tim Cahill was a huge loss against Spain and neither Adam Taggert in the first half nor Ben Halloran in the second came close to replacing the 34-year-old. One journalist noted that taking Cahill's place at this World Cup was like being handed Mick Jagger's microphone.

With the Asian Cup around the corner in 2015, this tournament was always going to play a major role in that preparation, and there were several positive features of the Socceroos' play that could be carried forward.

It was back to Rio for the final leg of my wonderful stay in Brazil. The excitement and colour of a World Cup in Brazil was something special to savour. I loved the vibrant city life. The World Cup Finals themselves threw up several surprises, including the Spanish early exit. England were again an abject failure, losing to both Italy and Uruguay, and earning just a point to finish bottom of Group D. Brazil, playing at home, were greatly favoured in this tournament but were not overly impressive in the group stage and only managed to defeat Chile on penalties in the second round before going past Colombia in the quarter-finals.

The young German side from South Africa in 2010 had matured into a top-class side and they cruised into the semi-finals after defeating France 1–0. The semi-final match between Brazil and Germany delivered a result of seismic proportions as the Germans demolished, humiliated, and destroyed the aura of Brazilian football, winning 7–1. The Netherlands, a great side, were defeated by Argentina on penalties in the other semi-final, and Lionel Messi was through to a World Cup Final. The Dutch inflicted further pain upon Brazil in winning the third-place match 3–0.

Germany were favourites against Argentina, and they controlled possession and had the greater chances, but had to wait until extra time to seal their win with a great goal from Götze. He skilfully controlled a cross from Schurrle, then twisted to volley home the winner. The Germans were worthy winners.

The Socceroos headed home to prepare for the 2015 Asian Cup and the qualifiers for the 2018 World Cup in Russia. After yet another wonderful World Cup experience, I was already hoping and planning for Russia.

Head coach Guus Hiddink (left) with assistants Graham Arnold (centre) and Johan Neeskens (right) watching over training in Stuttgart, June 2006.

Mark Viduka, Craig Moore, Tim Cahill, and Harry Kewell celebrate Australia making the round of 16 at the 2006 World Cup in Germany. Moore and Kewell both scored in the 2-2 draw with Croatia which was enough to progress.

Lucas Neill with head coach Pim Verbeek in Brisbane prior to a World Cup qualifying match vs Qatar. Australia won 4-0, October 2008.

With Craig Johnston in South Africa, June 2010.

The Socceroos line-up against Ghana ahead of their 2010 World Cup match in Rustenburg, South Africa. The game was a 1-1 draw.

Soaking up the atmosphere at the *Estadio Beira-Rio* in Porto Alegre, Brazil, at the World Cup match between Australia and the Netherlands. The Netherlands won 2-3, June 2014.

Tim Cahill celebrates his 'wonder goal' vs the Netherlands at the 2014 World Cup. It should have won the goal of the tournament but was ranked second.

With 'Kossie' (John Kosmina) in Brazil, June 2014.

Captain Mile Jedinak holds aloft the Asian Cup – won on home soil, January 2015.

Aaron Mooy in the World Cup qualifier vs Jordan, March 2016.

Matthew Jurman on the ball in the first of the play-offs to make the 2018 World Cup vs Honduras, San Pedro Sula, November 2017. Australia drew 0-0 and won the return leg at home, 3-1.

With Ned Zelic in Russia, June 2018.

With Jacob Burns in Russia, June 2018.

Denmark's Martin Braithwaite and Australia's Aziz Behich in their group stage match at the 2018 World Cup, Samara, Russia. The match was a 1-1 draw.

Awer Mabil controls the ball during the match vs Saudi Arabia, November 2021.

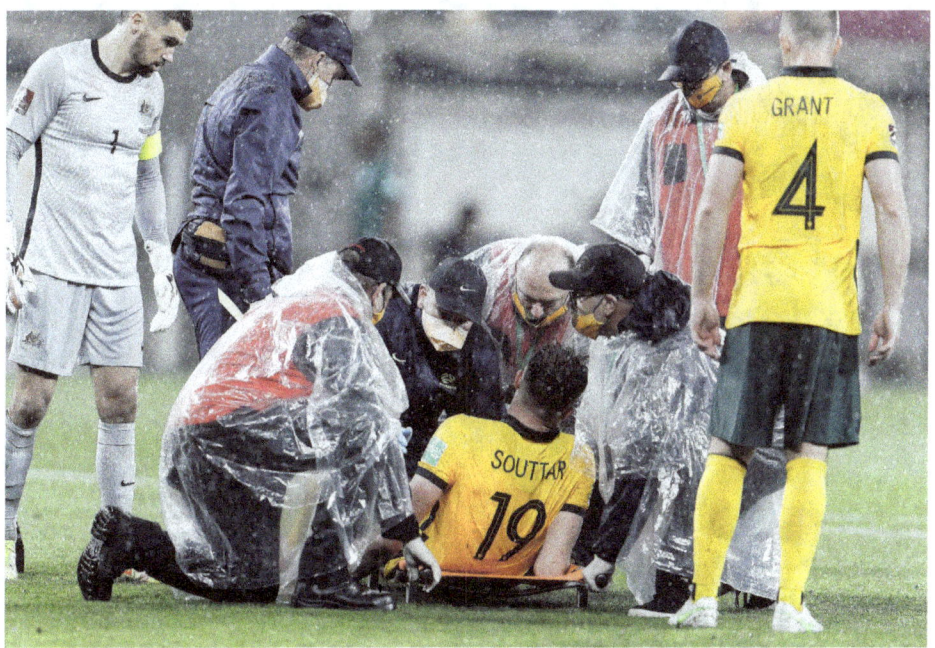

Harry Souttar is taken away on a stretcher during the World Cup qualifier vs Saudi Arabia in November 2021, watched by goalkeeper Mathew Ryan and defender Rhyan Grant. Australia suffered a form slump during Souttar's absence in subsequent qualifiers but both Souttar and the team recovered to qualify for the 2022 World Cup in Qatar.

With Australia's Head of Delegation and Qatar 2022 Ambassador, Tim Cahill AO, for the farewell match ahead of the 2022 World Cup, vs New Zealand, September 2022.

Australia vs Denmark at the 2022 World Cup.

One of the standouts in the successful 2022 World Cup squad, Jackson Irvine at home in Melbourne soon after the tournament holding a copy of the Encyclopedia of Socceroos Centenary Edition (Fair Play Publishing), December 2022.

WORLD CUP QUALIFICATION AND FINALS 2018-RUSSIA

The Intervening Years— The Australian team 2014-2018

As a historian, Russia, like Brazil, held a massive attraction for me: the revolution—Lenin, Stalin and the overthrow of the Czar and the rise of communism; the history connected with Napoleon and Hitler's failed invasions of Russia; the literary giants including Leo Tolstoy, Alexander Pushkin, Fyodor Dostoevsky, and Ivan Turgenev, to name but a few. The Bolshoi Ballet and the culture of Russian life all were major magnets for me, and all I needed was the Socceroos to qualify again for another World Cup Finals to make a visit.

Australia's build-up for the Asian Cup, and further down the line, World Cup qualification began immediately on the team's return home from Brazil. They first undertook a match against quality opposition—Belgium in Liege, losing 2-0. They followed up with a hard fought 3-2 victory over Saudi Arabia in another friendly, played at Craven Cottage in London. Two more friendly games were held against Middle Eastern opposition, Australia drawing with the Arab Emirates in Abu Dhabi and then going down to Qatar 1-0 in Doha. The Socceroos ended their year with a loss against the reigning Asian champions, Japan, losing 2-1 in Osaka. On the evidence of those five games, Ange Postecoglou would have his work cut out to transform his team into a real chance of success in the Asian Cup, only six weeks away.

Hosting the 2015 Asian Cup was a landmark moment for the game in Australia. Great crowds, excitement, tension, and elation were all parts of the journey. The

Socceroos opened with two impressive wins—4–1 over Kuwait, and then 4–0 over Oman. A reality check was in store at Suncorp Stadium in Brisbane, as the team went down to South Korea, 1–0. Australia then rebounded to beat China 2–0 in the quarter-final before dispatching the United Arab Emirates, 2–0 in Newcastle.

The final against South Korea was a thrilling classic with a huge crowd of over 76,000 urging the Socceroos on. Australia took the lead just before halftime through Massimo Luongo and looked to be on top. The second half saw the team controlling the game and seemingly assured of victory until South Korean star Son Heung-Min equalised on the 90-minute mark. Australia must have felt like they had been hit by a bus—to be so close and have the silverware seemingly snatched away was heartbreaking. However, Postecoglou lifted his team and in extra time they scored through James Troisi to claim the title as champions of Asia.

Australia followed with two impressive World Cup qualifier warm-up games in Europe. First, facing world champions' Germany in Kaiserslautern, there was a very impressive 2–2 draw, followed by a 0–0 result against Macedonia in Skopje. The Socceroos' first World Cup qualifying hurdle was an away trip to face Kyrgyzstan.

Australia 2, Kyrgyzstan 1
(*Halftime*: 1–0)
Scorers: Jedinak, Oar
16 June 2015
Referee: Khamis Mohammed Al-Marri (Qatar)
Crowd: 18,000
Dolen Omurzakov Stadium, Bishkek, Kyrgyzstan

Australia: Mat Ryan, Ivan Franjic, Tim Cahill (Tomi Juric 87), Mark Milligan, Matthew Spiranovic, Mathew Leckie, Aziz Behich, James Troisi (Matthew McKay 71), Mile Jedinak, Nathan Burns (Tommy Oar 56), Alex Wilkinson
Kyrgyzstan: Valery Katsuba, Valerii Kichin, Daniel Tagoe, Azamat Baimatov, Viktor Maier, Farhat Musabekov (Ildar Amirov 66), Bakhtiyar Duyshobekov, Edgar Bernhardt, Anton Zemlianukhin, Mirlan Murzayev (Vadim Kharchenko 72), Vitalij Lux (Almazbek Mirzaliev 80)

Australia kicked off their qualification campaign for the 2018 World Cup with a less than impressive 2–1 win over Kyrgyzstan. Nevertheless, a winning start was a good way to begin. The home side were treated like heroes at the end. Ranked 177th in the world, they looked every bit as capable as the Socceroos, ranked 114 places above them. This was arguably the most significant match Kyrgyzstan had ever played at home. Even Prime Minister Temir Sariyev was on hand to welcome the players. Fuelled by that patriotism, and with the stadium's new lights beaming for the very first time, their players sensed the weight of history.

The Socceroos were off to a flying start and needed only 30 seconds after kick-off to take the lead. Following a lightning move, Australia gained a free kick and Mile Jedinak stood over the ball 20 yards out from goal. His low shot took an outrageous bounce off the bumpy pitch and gave Kyrgyzstan goalkeeper Valery Katsuba no chance. However, while the sold-out 18,000-strong crowd at the Dolen Omurzakov Stadium let out a collective groan after Jedinak's strike, their players wasted no time lamenting their misfortune.

Unfortunately, it was the only decent Australian move of the entire first half. Kyrgyzstan, initially stunned after going behind, quickly recovered to take charge of the game and lay siege to the Australian goal. They played with a verve and determination the Socceroos lacked. Australia, playing with as close to a full-strength line-up as injuries would allow, were industrious enough, especially the captain Mile Jedinak and Mathew Leckie. But overall, they looked nervous, unimaginative, and lacked composure. Perhaps they had just expected the home side to sit back and take a battering. Maybe the crowd, who were outstanding throughout, got to them.

Two of Kyrgyzstan's most dangerous players, Viktor Maier and Edgar Bernhardt were playing in the German Regional League and the Polish Second Division respectively at the time. The Turkey-based Mirlan Murzayev caused big problems for the Australian defence, and the left-back Valerii Kichin looked as if he would be a good addition to the Russian Premier League the next season. Kyrgyzstan created several chances, the best of them a wonderfully crafted move that ended with German-based striker Vitalij Lux thrashing his shot into the side-netting, temporarily sending the stadium wild.

Australia did stem the flow on occasions. Matt Spiranovic had a chance to double Australia's advantage on the half-hour mark, but his header from a corner drifted wide.

The onslaught continued after the interval, as did the floodlights in their first outing.

Kyrgyzstan made all the play, but that started to change around the hour mark after winger Tommy Oar came on for Nathan Burns. Then after 67 minutes, Oar got on the end of a Mark Milligan pass and struck the ball past goalkeeper Valery Katsuba to increase Australia's lead.

The goal was against the run of play and Kyrgyzstan deserved more for their domination throughout. They certainly kept Mat Ryan busy right until the end and got some reward two minutes into injury time when substitute Almazbek Mirzaliev headed in from a corner.

After the game, Ange Postecoglou said the only surprise for him was Kyrgyzstan's level of fitness: 'I thought they would die away a little towards the end, but maybe that was the crowd factor. They gave them the energy they needed. In terms of ability, we knew they could play because we had watched them a fair bit. If anything, we looked a bit underdone with a few players who hadn't played for a while and that showed in the end. We tried to force things a bit too much in the first half. It was hard for us to keep passing through the lines and we lost possession a bit too easily, which allowed them to counterattack. We got a bit better in the second half, particularly when Tommy Oar came on and we looked a bit more threatening.'

The final score flattered Australia, but they at least returned home with the points. Postecoglou would surely remind his players that nothing on the road to Russia could be taken for granted. Captain Mile Jedinak admitted as much, recognising the game as a tough assignment and far more difficult than many had imagined: 'Let's not kid anyone. You look at results across Asia and in the context of things, it was a very positive result. It puts us in good stead from here. We know we can perform better and we're under no illusions but, considering the circumstances, I'm very happy with taking three points.'

The Kyrgyzstan fans were left celebrating, giving their team a heroes' reception after the match, and then mobbing them as they got on to the team bus.

It would be nearly three months before Australia had their second qualification game against Bangladesh in Perth.

Australia 5, Bangladesh 0
(*Halftime*: 4–0)
Scorers: Leckie (2), Rogic, Burns, Mooy
3 September 2015

Referee: Vo Minh Tri (Vietnam)
Crowd: 19,495
HBF Park, Perth

Australia: Adam Federici, Jason Davidson, Matthew Spiranovic, Bailey Wright, Tarek Elrich, Mark Milligan (Jackson Irvine 76), Aaron Mooy, Massimo Luongo, Mathew Leckie (Tim Cahill 62), Nathan Burns, Tom Rogic (Christopher Ikonomidis 62)

Bangladesh: Mohammad Sahidul Alam, Topu Barman, Mohammed Yeasin Khan, Mohamed Nasirul Islam Nazir (Yeamin Ahmed Chowdhury Munna 46), Ashraf Mohamed Linkon, Jamal Harris Bhuyan, Mohamed Mamunul Islam Mamun, Hemanta Vincent Biswas (Mohamed Monaem Khan Raju 37), Mohammed Enamul Hoque (Abdul Baten Mojumdar Komal 87), Mohamed Jahid Hasan Ameli, Mohammed Jewel Rana

The Socceroos destroyed Bangladesh in their World Cup qualifier with a ruthless 5–0 victory in Perth. The reigning Asian Cup champions were never troubled against the world's 173rd-ranked team, who were well off the pace in every department.

It took just six minutes for Australia to open the scoring and the way they did so was a pointer to the utter dominance they would enjoy. A simple cutback from Massimo Luongo found Mathew Leckie in the box and he routinely placed the ball underneath the outstretched glove of Bangladeshi goalkeeper, Sahidul Alam, who was under siege all night long.

Desperate to make the most of his recent call up to the national squad, 28-year-old Tarek Elrich controlled the right side of the pitch and played a large part in both early goals. QPR's Massimo Luongo, the player of the Asian Cup, was also involved in plenty of Australia's key moves. Making his first international appearance in more than a year, midfielder Tom Rogic added the next two goals in the 8th and 20th minutes, the latter aided by a wicked deflection that went down as an own goal. Rogic was running the show in his long-awaited return to the midfield.

Nathan Burns provided the next just before the half-hour mark as he swooped on a loose ball for his debut international goal. The scoring slowed up considerably from that point on, thanks in part to some tardiness from the home side and some good saves by keeper Sahidul Alam.

Aaron Mooy made it 5-0 in the 61st minute with a long-range screamer from outside the box. Mooy trapped the ball outside the area, then turned and curled the ball past Sahidul. In truth, the margin could and should have been far greater, but Australia clearly coasted through the second half and missed some easy chances from close range. It all made for a party atmosphere for the crowd of 19,495 at HBF Park in Perth, the biggest crowd at that venue for a football match. The turnout was a strong statement from the Perth public in the first Socceroos game held there in a decade.

Coach Postecoglou had attempted to play down the chances of a massacre and tried a new diamond midfield formation and some fresh combinations, but he would have taken next to nothing from the match. Some of his selections were intriguing, not the least the decision to bench Tim Cahill, who had been unveiled as stand-in skipper the day before the match. Mark Milligan took the captain's armband and led with aplomb, providing brilliant service from midfield, but the result was effectively never in doubt.

Postecoglou rejected suggestions he was preparing his side for life without Cahill: 'We're not looking at a post-anyone era. At the moment what we are looking at is a team that is continually evolving and will continue to evolve until we get to the place where we feel that we can challenge for the World Cup.'

Five days later, the Australian team were back on a plane to Tajikistan for another World Cup qualifier. This was an uneasy assignment to undertake. Tensions had been rising in the former Soviet Union territory for some time and over the previous 48 hours before the Socceroos arrival, 17 people were killed in a shoot-out between militants and the police in the capital. It was reported that eight of the dead were police. Officials announced after liaising with authorities in Dushanbe that the situation remained calm—businesses, government services and the airport remained open.

The long and ongoing dispute between the FFA and the players' union over a collective bargaining agreement was another distraction that Postecoglou could have done without. He rightly raised objections, stating it was affecting the preparation of his team. He was later admonished by the FFA and forced to apologise. That wasn't exactly the right lead-up to the final stages of the World Cup qualifiers for Russia.

Australia 3, Tajikistan 0
(*Halftime*: 0–0)
Scorers: Milligan, Cahill (2)
8 September 2015

Referee: Jameel Juma Abdulhusain Mohamed (Bahrain) Republican Central Stadium, Dushanbe

Australia: Adam Federici, Jason Davidson, Tim Cahill, Mark Milligan, Matthew Spiranovic, Mathew Leckie (Tommy Oar 78), Bailey Wright, Aaron Mooy (Tom Rogic 68), Matthew McKay (Nathan Burns 68), Ryan McGowan, Massimo Luongo

Tajikistan: Alisher Dodov, Farkhod Vasiev, Eraj Rajabov, Davronjon Ergashev, Khurshed Makhmudov (Parvizdzhon Umarbaev 63), Jakhongir Dzhaillov, Nuriddin Davronov, Dilshod Vasiev, Fatkhullo Fatkhuloev, Akhtam Nazarov (Akhtam Khamrakulov 74), Manuchekhr Dzhaillov

It was far from pretty, but the Socceroos were poised to book their place in the next round of World Cup qualification after battling to a 3–0 win against a gallant Tajikistan. Coach Ange Postecoglou played down his side's first-half struggles against the Central Asian minnows, who were under siege all night long yet frustrated the visitors by holding them out for nearly an hour.

But once Mark Milligan broke the deadlock in the 57th minute, the gulf in class between the Asian Cup holders and the world's 153rd-ranked side became quickly apparent. Mark Milligan's opener came after a goalmouth scramble from an Aaron Mooy corner. Tajikistan was unable to clear the ball and Milligan was on the spot at the back post to toe the ball home.

Stand-in skipper Tim Cahill made it 2–0 in the 74th minute, expertly tucking home a cutback from Ryan McGowan. Many of the raucous, 19,000-strong crowd then started filing for the exits.

Cahill grabbed his second in second-half stoppage time, heading in a Tommy Oar cross.

Postecoglou was adamant after the match that the Socceroos never felt concerned by their inability to score. Australia appeared out of ideas in attack until the first goal came and Tajikistan's will gave in, but that was mostly because unfamiliarity with the artificial pitch led to overblown crosses and mis-hit balls in the final third.

Australia would step into the cauldron of Amman International Stadium in Jordan for their next match. This was a match for the two top sides in the group and it would not be a welcoming atmosphere. Australian football fans were ripped off and faced the threat of crowd violence. There were clear messages of unnerving intimidation for the Socceroo players, officials, and supporters before the game. Tickets designated for Australian fans cost 50 Jordanian dinars (around $101), despite tickets being locally available for 3 JD (around $6). The Department of Foreign Affairs and Trade's (DFAT) advice for supporters travelling to Jordan was updated: 'You should be aware that there is a possibility of crowd violence when attending soccer matches in Jordan. The environment is generally not family friendly and sexual harassment of female fans is not uncommon.'

It was expected that a handful of die-hard fans would travel from Australia for the match, with a few hundred expats from the region also expected to attend the game. Jordan would be looking to give the Socceroos a hostile welcome. Several Socceroos spoke of the hostile atmosphere on the country's last, and only, match in Amman, which ended in a 2-1 win for Jordan in 2012. Home captain and veteran goalkeeper, Amer Shafi said they would draw on that memory when they took the field: 'The match was very tough ... but we play very tough in our country.'

Australia 0, Jordan 2
(*Halftime*: 0–0)
8 October 2015
Referee: Maasaki Toma (Japan)
Crowd: 11,462
Amman International Stadium

Australia: Adam Federici, Jason Davidson, Mark Milligan, Matthew Spiranovic, Mathew Leckie, Bailey Wright (Tomi Juric 77), Tom Rogic (Tim Cahill 67), Tommy Oar (Nathan Burns 46), Aaron Mooy, Massimo Luongo, Tarek Elrich
Jordan: Amer Shafi Mahmoud Sabbah, Baha Abdel-Rahman, Mohammad Al-Basha, Oday Zahran, Yaseen Anas Al-Bakhit (Mahmoud Zatara 87), Abdallah Deeb, Rajaei Ayed Fadel Hasan (Sharif Adnan Nassar 88), Ibrahim Zawahreh, Hassan Abdel Fattah, Hamza Al-Daradreh (Monther Abu Amara 90), Mohammad Aldmeiri

Ange Postecoglou's dream run in the qualifiers came to a thudding halt in Amman. The Socceroos went down to Jordan 2-0, leaving the Middle Eastern nation to claim top spot in Group B. A penalty in the 47th minute gave Jordan the advantage, before a second goal five minutes before fulltime handed them a decisive victory over Australia.

Postecoglou said that while the result was disappointing, there was still hope for the team: 'It's one loss, I mean, right now it doesn't feel good, but I still think we are making progress and certainly from our perspective we will still push on with what we have started here, and I've got no doubt we will get to a good place. Once they got a goal up, the game became a little bit chaotic, a lot of disruptions, we couldn't get into any flow. We had a couple of chances but overall, we just lost control of the game.'

The Socceroos dominated the first half but failed to breach the Jordan defence. Hassan Abdel-Fattah struck from the penalty spot immediately after the resumption following a foul on Hamza Al-Daradreh by Matt Spiranovic.

Australia pushed hard to restore parity, but it was Jordan who found the net again, Al-Daradreh scoring with five minutes remaining to put his team on 10 points from four matches.

Both of Jordan's goals were contentious. The first one came after Nathan Burns was dispossessed in midfield and a long ball was sent through that saw Matt Spiranovic concede a penalty. The second goal came after yet another 50/50 hustle, this time involving Jason Davidson after 84 minutes. He and his opponent both fell in the clash, and it saw the ball then passed into space for Al-Daradreh to pounce and score. If anything, Davidson might have been called for obstruction after he seemed to trip himself first and then angled his body in front of his opponent, which may have contributed to the push he received.

Tim Cahill was lucky not to be spotted for knocking over a player off the ball late in the game. Cahill might have already been aggrieved at again being a late substitution onto the field. It seemed that coach Ange Postecoglou might have been fading him from first-team selection just in case he didn't last until the 2018 World Cup.

After three relatively easy games in this first group phase of World Cup qualifying, Australia had failed its big test away to Jordan. The Socceroos tried to control the game via possession, but they wasted both possession and chances. Jordan ambushed Australia and deserved to be winners. To be out-smarted once is bad enough; for it to happen twice in successive World Cup qualifying campaigns shows an inability to learn. Whether it was arrogance, in that Australia still had the mindset about Asia that 'we should just beat these teams,' there still seemed some residual notion of that.

Right now, Australia was the third best of the second-placed teams. They also had the luxury of three of their final four matches at home, so had a great chance to reverse the result against Jordan and accrue enough points so that finishing second in their group would most likely be enough to qualify. The only away match was to be against Bangladesh, while Kyrgyzstan, Tajikistan and Jordan were the home matches.

The big takeaway from this game against Jordan was that Australia needed to change its approach when playing overseas against Middle Eastern teams. Arguably Jordan controlled the game much better despite conceding possession. Once Jordan took the lead just after halftime, Australia allowed their frustration to affect their game.

A month later Australia was back in action on home soil against Kyrgyzstan. After licking their wounds from the defeat against Jordan, this was the chance for redemption and to 'right the ship' for World Cup qualification.

Australia 3, Kyrgyzstan 0
(*Halftime*: 1–0)
Scorers: Jedinak, Cahill, own goal
12 November 2015
Referee: Kim Sang Woo (South Korea)
Crowd: 19,412
Bruce Stadium, Canberra

Australia: Adam Federici, James Meredith, Bailey Wright, Ryan McGowan, Trent Sainsbury, Mark Milligan, Aaron Mooy, Mile Jedinak (Tom Rogic 61), Massimo Luongo, Tim Cahill, Tomi Juric (Nathan Burns 28 (James Troisi 73)
Kyrgyzstan: Pavel Matiash, Valerii Kichin, Talant Samsaliev, Viktor Maier, Azamat Baimatov (Kozubaev Tamirlan 77), Islam Shamshiyev (Vitalij Lux 58), Ildar Amirov, Ivan Filatov (Uulu Kairat Zhyrgalbek 46), Duishebekov Bahtiyar, Musabekov Farkhat, Edgar Bernhardt

The Socceroos scored a 3–0 victory over Kyrgyzstan in Canberra, securing three vital points to consolidate second spot in Group B. Captain Mile Jedinak and Australia's all-time leading goal scorer, Tim Cahill, scored either side of halftime, before an own goal from Kyrgyzstan forward Ildar Amirov put the result beyond doubt.

Jedinak, back as national skipper after a three-game absence, was a composed influence in a high-intensity match in which an athletic Cahill could have been mistaken for a version of himself 10 years earlier. The experienced duo directed Australia's youthful outfit but enjoyed the spoils themselves in front of nearly 20,000 fans at Bruce Stadium.

The Socceroos applied all the pressure in slippery conditions, duly delivering on coach Ange Postecoglou's unapologetic pre-match vow to attack 'relentlessly'. They started frantically and their full- throttle approach played through Kyrgyzstan's defence, very nearly resulting in a goal to Cahill after just one minute of play. He produced a stunning aerial manoeuvre to send Jedinak's deflected cross goalward, but goalkeeper Pavel Matiash was on hand to stop it with an impressive leaping effort.

Fifteen minutes later, Cahill hit the woodwork after Aaron Mooy's driving run towards goal was blocked by Matiash and the ball fell to Cahill. The gulf in class was painfully clear against the visitors, who were without threatening forwards Anton Zemlyanukhin and Mirlan Murzayev, and they lacked the counterattacking drive that gave Australia a horrid scare in Bishkek back in June. Australia was by far the better team, but like so many of these matches against lower-ranked opponents, their quality does not ensure anything until they get in front.

Kyrgyzstan was stubborn; Australia 'huffed and puffed' and bluffed and threatened, but for 40 minutes they could not quite 'blow the Kyrgyzstan house down'. Despite dominating in both possession and territory, Australia was often dispossessed by Kyrgyzstan, who turned up to defend in the desperate hope a shock upset might keep their World Cup dream going. Australia did not so much devour its South Asian counterparts, but rather they 'ate them up slowly', maintaining the intensity until the visitors buckled.

The Socceroos had a scare when Viktor Maier went down after a Meredith challenge, but play was waved on. Australia almost took the lead in the 37th minute when another fine pass from Mooy found Burns. His shot was saved, and Milligan could not get on to the rebound at close range as the ball was scrambled to safety. Amid chances aplenty, proceedings looked to have gone awry when striker Tomi Juric exited late in the first half with an apparent groin injury. But his replacement Nathan Burns went straight 'in for the kill', peppering Kyrgyzstan's goal.

Burns' first of a flurry of opportunities gifted Mark Milligan an enviable chance to open the scoring, but the midfielder somehow managed to fire wide in front of a beckoning goal. In the end, it didn't matter. Moments later, Islam Shamshiyev took down Burns just inside the box in the 39th minute and South Korean referee, Kim

Sang-woo, pointed to the spot. Mile Jedinak stepped up to power a shot right of Pavel Matiash and into the Kyrgyzstan goal. Massimo Luongo also hit the back of the net just before halftime, but he was ruled offside.

Five minutes after the break, Cahill extended the lead when he latched on to a slick, no-look pass from Aaron Mooy and slotted home in the bottom-left corner for his 42nd Socceroos goal.

With just over 20 minutes remaining, Mooy put his corner into the box, and in trying to head the ball clear, Kyrgyzstan's Ildar Amirov put it over his own goalkeeper, guaranteeing the Socceroos' victory. Cahill could have finished with a hat-trick on the night if not for two excellent saves by Matiash in stoppage time.

The result left the Socceroos at second in Group B qualifying, one point behind Jordan, with their next game a clash with Bangladesh in Dhaka. The victory set up Ange Postecoglou's team for the psychologically and logistically difficult trip to Bangladesh, where they could take another step on the road to Russia 2018 qualification. Postecoglou had said that even before the withdrawals through injury of players like Matt Spiranovic and Mathew Leckie in the lead-up to the game, he was inclined to make changes. He had been unimpressed with the way his players had performed in the Middle East last time out. However, no-one quite expected the side he did put out. Australia went into this game loaded with central midfielders (Jedinak, Mark Milligan, Aaron Mooy and Massimo Luongo all started) and two strikers in a sort of 4–2–2–2 formation, with Mooy and Luongo pulling into wider areas, and the fullbacks, particularly debutant James Meredith on the left, getting forward.

Five days later, Australia made the long journey to Bangladesh and were given a great favour by Kyrgyzstan who downed Jordan 1-0 in Bishkek, giving the Socceroos the chance to take back top spot in the group with a win.

Australia 4, Bangladesh 0
(*Halftime*: 4–0)
Scorers: Cahill (3), Jedinak
17 November 2015
Referee: Wang Di (China)
Crowd: 19,730
Bangabandhu National Stadium, Dhaka

Australia: Adam Federici, James Meredith (Jason Davidson 57), Bailey Wright, Joshua Risdon, Alex Wilkinson, Aaron Mooy (Thomas Oar 46), Mile Jedinak, Matthew McKay, Massimo Luongo (James Troisi 46), Tim Cahill, Nathan Burns
Bangladesh: Mohammad Sahidul Alam, Rayhan Hasan, Topu Barman, Mohammed Yeasin Khan, Jamal Bhuyan, Mohammed Mamunul Islam, Mohammad Ziban (Aminur Rahman Sojib 87), Hemonta Vinsent Biswas, Mohammed Nasirul Islam, Mohammed Monaem Khan Raju, Abdul Batem Komal

The 'Tim Cahill show' travelled to Bangladesh, with the Socceroos' talisman netting a first-half hat-trick in Australia's 4–0 win in Dhaka. Australia had only arrived in Bangladesh the day before the game due to security concerns. Only a month before, Australia's world champion cricket team postponed their tour of Bangladesh after the Australian government advised them to stay at home because of potential militant attacks.

Cahill scored three times inside 37 minutes, while skipper Mile Jedinak also struck to send Australia to the top of their qualifying group ahead of main rivals, Jordan. It was all one-way traffic in favour of the Australians, who easily controlled possession despite struggling to move the ball around freely on the long-grassed surface. At times, Ange Postecoglou's team were sloppy against their lower-ranked opponents, an off touch here, a wayward ball there.

Aaron Mooy shone bright as usual with a hand in every goal, and whenever he found space, and there were acres of it, the aerial threat of Cahill was waiting. There was not a Bangladeshi defender in sight for the former Everton man's first when he nodded in a deep free kick from Mooy on six minutes.

It was nearly half an hour later before the Melbourne City star also set up the second with a through ball to debutant Josh Risdon, and the in-form Perth Glory defender crossed for Cahill to volley home.

Five minutes later, the Socceroos' all-time leading goal scorer added another to his total by adding the finishing touch to a cross from Mooy, who had latched onto a sublime through ball from the recalled Matt McKay.

Crystal Palace midfielder Jedinak got in on the action just before the interval with a textbook header from close range after Bailey Wright headed across the box. At the break, James Meredith came on for Jason Davidson, and Tommy Oar and James

Troisi for Mooy and Massimo Luongo.

If the first half was a raging goal-fest, the break gave way to a mediocre second half. The crowd perked up briefly as the home side made a couple of swoops forward, while Jedinak went close again 10 minutes from time. But his tremendous overhead kick was parried to safety by Bangladeshi keeper Sahidul Alam.

After the game, Postecoglou said: 'We came here to win the game. It was difficult conditions for us tonight. In the first half it was good but the second half we were a little scrappy. In the end I was happy with the performance with the players, three points for us and with it we go home. Knowing what the boys have been through the last few days, both physically and mentally, we lost our focus and concentration in the second half. But with everything that's going on, the players, the staff have handled themselves impeccably and (I'm) pleased we can get through unscathed.'

Australia would have a long break before World Cup action resumed in the New Year. In fact, it was not until March 24, 2016, that the Socceroos would be back on the pitch. Australia was now in top spot and well-primed to win their final games and be ready for the final qualifying World Cup round to begin at the end of the year.

Australia 7, Tajikistan 0
(*Halftime*: 2–0)
Scorers: Luongo, Jedinak, Milligan, Burns (2), Rogic (2)
24 March 2016
Referee: Fahad Jaber Al-Marri (Qatar)
Crowd: 35,439
Adelaide Oval

Australia: Mathew Ryan, Mathew Leckie (Robbie Kruse 76), Bailey Wright, Apostolos Giannou, Aaron Mooy, Brad Smith, Mile Jedinak (Mark Milligan 46), Nathan Burns, Ryan McGowan, Trent Sainsbury, Massimo Luongo (Tom Rogic 67)
Tajikistan: Alisher Tuychiev, Tukhtasunov Dalerdjon, Rajabov Eraj, Dzhalilov Dzhakhongir, Ergashev Davronjon, Davronov Nuriddin, Aliev Jahongir, Makhmudov Khurshed (Akhmedov Manuchehr 60), Sharipov Faridun, Nazarov Akhtam (Vasiev Dilshod 35), Dzhalilov Manuchehr (Saidov Kamil 73)

The Socceroos thrashed Tajikistan in this match. Apo Giannou made his Socceroos debut and had a hand in three goals. His deft touch laid on a ball for Massimo Luongo's 2nd-minute opener.

Australia earned two penalties either side of halftime for their second and third goals. Captain Mile Jedinak converted the first opportunity and Mark Milligan the second.

The Socceroos' fourth goal came from Nathan Burns after he received a nice cross from Aaron Mooy. Mooy also played a major role in the fifth goal of the night when his 25-metre free kick allowed substitute Tom Rogic to thunder a shot that hit the crossbar before crossing the line in the 70th minute.

Two minutes later, Rogic scored a second goal from a Giannou assist to make it 6–0. A brilliant header from Burns after receiving a Ryan McGowan pass three minutes before fulltime gave the Socceroos their seventh and final goal in a comprehensive win.

Australia now looked forward to facing second-placed Jordan in Sydney and a likely qualifying phase formality. Earlier in this World Cup qualifying campaign it appeared that coach Ange Postecoglou had begun preparing for Socceroo life—post-Tim Cahill—by leaving 'Timmy the gun' on the bench. Cahill was now 36 years of age and come the 2018 Russian World Cup would be 38 and this must have been weighing upon the coach's mind. But Cahill, through sheer grit and performances, demonstrated that he was not ready for the football retirement home—his aerial ability, poacher's instinct and the fear he instilled in the opposition was enough to demonstrate his importance to Postecoglou, and that Cahill was well and truly primed for Russia as his long-term goal.

Australia 5, Jordan 1
(*Halftime*: 3–0)
Scorers: Cahill (2), Mooy, Rogic, Luongo
29 March 2016
Referee: Kim Jong Hyeok (South Korea)
Crowd: 24,975
Sydney Football Stadium

Australia: Mathew Ryan, Tim Cahill, Mark Milligan, Joshua Risdon, Mathew Leckie (Christopher Ikonomidis 64), Bailey Wright, Robbie Kruse

(Nathan Burns 72), Aaron Mooy (Massimo Luongo 64), Brad Smith, Trent Sainsbury, Tom Rogic

Jordan: Amer Shafi, Mohammed Al Basha, Baha Abdelrahman, Ehsan Manel Haddad, Monther Abu Amara (Abdallah Deeb 46), Amad Saleh (Yousef Al-Rawashdeh 46), Oday Zahran, Yaseen Bakheet, Rajaei Ayed Fadel Hasan, Ibrahim Zawareh, Hamza Aldaradreh (Baha Faisal Mohammad 75)

The Socceroos sought and gained revenge for their loss in the Middle East earlier in the campaign. The passage at times had been a bit bumpy but in the end the Socceroos finished on top of the group and would now progress to the final qualifying stage for the 2018 World Cup in Russia.

Tim Cahill again provided evidence of his importance by scoring a double and Robbie Kruse had three assists as Australia beat Jordan 5–1. The 36-year-old Cahill scored twice in the first half as the Socceroos broke down Harry Redknapp's side to win convincingly. The win in Group B meant that Australia entered the third and final phase of Asian qualifying for the 2018 World Cup in Russia.

Hangzhou-based Cahill had now scored 47 goals in 89 internationals for Australia, and 22 goals in 27 World Cup matches. While Cahill again topped Australia's goal scorers against Jordan, it was German-based Kruse who got a rousing ovation when he was subbed late in the second half after providing the final ball for three of the Socceroos' goals.

Australia's other goal scorers were home-based midfielder Aaron Mooy, Celtic's Tom Rogic and QPR midfielder Massimo Luongo.

After the match, coach Postecoglou enthused over the team's performance: 'It's been two strong performances (including Tajikistan) and I think people are starting to appreciate the way the boys are playing now and the belief they have in what we're doing. Jordan was a dangerous opponent, they had everything to play for, yet there was never going to be anyone but us winning on the night.'

Former West Ham, Tottenham and QPR manager Redknapp, who was hired by Jordan's Prince Ali to help his country's World Cup qualifying bid, confessed: 'They were a different class to us, they were a much better and stronger team than we were. So, it was difficult, they had a bit too much quality and they looked a lot fitter than us, they were sharper... There was a big gulf in class tonight. The players did their best. We all did our best but what can you do?'

Australia needed patience to prise open their combative opponents, but once the home side scored the opener in the 24th minute, the visitors broke wide open. Bayer Leverkusen's Kruse delivered a pinpoint cross for stand-in skipper Cahill to tap into an empty net in the 24th minute.

Kruse was again the provider 15 minutes later when he released midfielder Mooy on the left and he slotted the leather past goalkeeper Amer Shafi for 2-0. He made his third assist in the opening half with another lovely cross and Cahill met it with his head for his second of the night. Australia led 3-0 at halftime.

Tom Rogic ensured there was no way back for Jordan with his third goal in the last two World Cup qualifiers and Australia's fourth in this match in the 53rd minute. Luongo scored the Socceroos' fifth goal just five minutes after coming on as a substitute. Yousef Al-Rawashdeh was fortunate not to see a red card when he scythed down Kruse in a vicious tackle which left him clasping his left knee on the ground. But Kruse resumed before being subbed by Nathan Burns with 20 minutes left. Abdallah Deeb scored a consolation goal for Jordan in the final minute of time.

It would now not be until September that the Socceroos would do battle in the final Asian Group qualifying stage. Australia was to be grouped with Japan, Saudi Arabia, the UAE, Iraq and Thailand. In the interim, they prepared well with three games against quality opposition, losing to England 2-1 at the Stadium of Light in Sunderland and undertaking a two-game series against Greece in Sydney and Melbourne. The matches against the Greeks were played before large crowds. The Socceroos beat Greece 1-0 in the opener and then lost 2-1 in Melbourne.

Australia 2, Iraq 0
(*Halftime*: 0–0)
Scorers: Luongo, Juric
1 September 2016
Referee: Alireza Faghani (Iran)
Crowd: 18,923
HBF Park, Perth

Australia: Mathew Ryan, Mark Milligan, Bread Smith, Milos Degenek, Trent Sainsbury, Tom Rogic, Aaron Mooy, Massimo Luongo (Jackson Irvine 78), Mile Jedinak, Mathew Leckie (Apostolos Giannou 85), Tomi Juric (Robbie Kruse 65)

Iraq: Mohammed Hameed, Ahmed Ibrahim, Ali Adnan Kadhim (Yaser Safa Kasim 60), Alaa Ali Mhawi, Dhurgham Ismail, Suad Natiq Naji (Alaa Abdul Zehra 80), Saad Abdulameer, Ali Hisny Faisal (Amjed Waleed Hussein 64), Ahmed Yaseen Gheni, Ali Abbas, Justin Hikmat Azeez

The Socceroos were off and running on the road to Russia, overcoming a dogged Iraq with a 2–0 World Cup qualifying win in Perth. Second-half goals to Massimo Luongo and Tom Juric delivered Australia victory.

A first half of frustration gave way just before the hour mark when Luongo arrived on the spot to thrash home Juric's squared ball. The striker made sure of the result on 65 minutes when Mark Milligan successfully drew attention from Aaron Mooy's corner, allowing Juric to tap home from a metre.

The result, if not the performance, pleased Postecoglou, who spoke of the importance of winning home games during this decisive qualifying group stage. Sterner tests awaited, including the United Arab Emirates in scorching Abu Dhabi heat. But with a shot count of 20-6 and 72 per cent of possession in this match, the Socceroos could be content.

Australia was denied twice by the woodwork before cutting through, and they allowed simple errors to creep into their play. On 26 minutes, Mathew Leckie's majestic long-range header reduced goalkeeper Mohammed Hameed to a bystander, only to bounce off the inside of the post and away. Mile Jedinak, who was uncharacteristically astray in his passing, then headed Mooy's cross just over the bar soon afterwards.

At halftime, it felt like the Socceroos had control of the play, but not the contest. Improved intensity after the break soon had the Iraqis swamped. A fine move between Jedinak and Mathew Leckie ended with Mooy crashing an attempt onto the bar. Australia had their swagger back, and a breakthrough seemed inevitable.

When it did come, on 58 minutes, Juric was the most grateful man in Perth. The tall striker contrived to botch the simplest of tap-ins, but a minute later, he had his redemption. Juric picked himself up after the abominable miss, crossing for Luongo, who didn't make the same mistake. Australia didn't let up, and it was Juric who made the game safe from Mooy's set piece shortly after. On his competitive debut, Miloš Degenek impressed at right-back, while substitute Robbie Kruse fizzed with energy.

Five days later, Australia was in Abu Dhabi to tackle the United Arab Emirates. The

UAE had a large and fervent home game crowd to spur them on, particularly after they had beaten the 'Blue Samurai' (Japan) only days before.

Australia 1, UAE 0
(*Halftime*: 0–0)
Scorer: Cahill
6 September 2016
Referee: Mohd Amirul (Malaysia)
Crowd: 40,983
Mohammed Bin Zayed Stadium, Abu Dhabi

Australia: Mathew Ryan, Brad Smith, Matthew Spiranovic, Trent Sainsbury, Ryan McGowan, Tom Rogic (Massimo Luongo 64), Mark Milligan, Aaron Mooy, Mathew Leckie, Tomi Juric (Tim Cahill 71), Robbie Kruse (Nathan Burns 90)

UAE: Khalid Eisa, Ismail Ahmed, Mohamed Ahmed Gharib (Abdulaziz Hussain Haikal 24), Mohanad Salem Ghazy, Walid Abbas, Ismail Al Hammadi, Omar Abdulrahman, Khamis Esmaeel, Amer Abdulrahman (Salem Saleh Al Rejaibi 77), Ahmed Khalil (Mohammed Alraqui 62), Ali Ahmed Mabkhout

Australia was off to a flyer with two wins in their opening two games and were now on top of the group. Tim Cahill came off the bench to deliver Australia a stunning smash-and-grab success over the UAE in their World Cup qualifier. The striker's second-half volley, his 48th goal for the Socceroos, produced a 1–0 win and maintained Australia's winning record on their path to the 2018 tournament in Russia.

For more than an hour at Mohammed Bin Zayed Stadium, the Socceroos toiled but threatened to come up short in oppressive conditions. Cahill changed that within four minutes of his arrival, timing his run into the box to volley home Brad Smith's inch-perfect cross. Coach Ange Postecoglou and the travelling coaching staff embraced, despite the sticky weather, delighted at their well-executed plan. Postecoglou said: 'We only needed him for 20 minutes over these two games and he delivered. Smithy's put in a great ball. Timmy must have them all on a retainer because it was the best ball of the night. We kept going until the end and got the goal we deserved and justifiably go away with three points.'

Cahill paid tribute to his team-mates who endured 90 minutes of pain in draining conditions: 'I scored but it was because of the collective performance ... If you ask me if I think I'm going to score when I go on the pitch, of course I do. Everything the boss asked of us, we did. We hung in there.'

Anything short of victory would have been an injustice for an Australian team which produced one of the performances of Postecoglou's tenure. In front of an energetic crowd of more than 40,000 (including injured captain Mile Jedinak), the Socceroos dominated from the kick-off. Robbie Kruse and Tom Rogic saw fierce first-half strikes saved, while Aaron Mooy menaced with both corner kicks and a direct free-kick that was headed over. But without a knockout punch, UAE remained in the contest.

Talented midfielder Omar Abdulrahman showed his ability to conjure something from nothing. Socceroo defenders were twice forced to make last-gasp clearances from Abdulrahman's chipped balls, with Trent Sainsbury and Smith stopping one-on-one chances.

After the break, Australia's torment of the UAE goal continued. Mooy unleashed a half-volley onto the bar during a spell of utter dominance, while at the other end, Ali Mabkhout spurned a mighty chance by volleying over from close range. It would be a costly miss, with Cahill leaving his mark and Australia withstanding late pressure to claim a famous victory. The win put Australia on top of the qualifying group after two matches, ahead of the next month's clashes with Saudi Arabia and Japan.

A month later Australia would face their sternest test with the two games against Saudi Arabia and Japan. These games would deliver a great bearing on the top positions of the group.

Australia 2, Saudi Arabia 2
(*Halftime*: 1–1)
Scorers: Sainsbury, Juric
6 October 2016
Referee: Ravshan Irmatov (Uzbekistan)
Crowd: 51,616
King Abdullah Stadium, Jeddah

Australia: Mathew Ryan, Trent Sainsbury, Matthew Spiranovic, Mark Milligan, Aaron Mooy, Brad Smith, Mile Jedinak, Tom Rogic (Jackson Irvine 85),

Robbie Kruse, Mathew Leckie (Massimo Luongo 61), Tomi Juric (Tim Cahill 85)
Saudi Arabia: Yasser Al Mosailem, Hassan Muath Fallatah, Omar Ibrahim Othman (Motaz Hawsawi 70), Osama Hawsawi, Mansour Al Harbi, Salman Alfaraj, Yahya Al-Shehri (Fhad Almuwallad 67), Nawaf Alabid, Abdulmalek Al Khaibri, Taiseer Al Jassam, Naif Hazazi (Nassir Alshamrani 79)

The Socceroos hung on for a 2–2 draw with Saudi Arabia as striker Nasser Al-Shamrani again proved the troublemaker. A draw may have disappointed some but the Socceroos' improving mentality boded well for their World Cup campaign. Amid the hot and humid conditions of Jeddah's King Abdullah Stadium, Socceroos' boss Ange Postecoglou captured the team's post-game mood accurately and succinctly: 'It's a good point, but you feel we could have got more out of it.'

Saudi Arabia started the brighter of the two sides, hurrying and hassling the Australian defence with a high press, and striking with a clarity of purpose and quality of execution. Their fifth-minute goal followed excellent lead-up work from Nawaf Alabid, who used close control and an attacking mindset to put a sharp ball through for Yahya Al-Shehri. His inch-perfect cutback was well dispatched by the late-arriving Taiseer Al Jassam. It was a passage of play that cut straight through the Australian defence and sent an early warning shot across the bows of those that denigrate the ever-improving quality of Asian football.

And yet, with Australia seemingly there for the taking, there were two serious limitations: a creeping psychological fragility and Dutch coach Bert van Marwijk's conservative inclination, always presented as a potential limitation for the home side. With the crowd behind them and confidence streaming through their players, this game was Saudi Arabia's to lose.

The usually excellent Aaron Mooy missed passes. Robbie Kruse and Mathew Leckie lacked spark in attack, and even skipper Mile Jedinak looked off his game. But if Saudi Arabia invited their opponents upon them, then conversely Australia deserved praise for the manner in which they accepted the invitation. As the half developed, the Socceroos began to raise their intensity. Mooy's industry began to sway the balance in the heart of the field, and Rogic increasingly looked the pre-eminent playmaker on the pitch. Brad Smith, nervous in his opening exchanges, then decided to take on his man, working inside and producing a driving run and shot that clattered the post. Australia were then well and truly in the ascendancy.

It was Trent Sainsbury who executed the goal, but it was an equaliser that hailed from the self-belief that Ange Postecoglou had spent years trying to instil within the Socceroos. The 51,616-strong crowd had a vocal lead supporter spurring the 'Green Falcons' on, but they were silenced. Postecoglou bellowed for his team to keep focused, stay sharp and to rise above.

Dutch coach van Marwijk looked uneasy, his eyes twitching as he paced the technical area. The otherwise excellent Omar Hawsawi then succumbed to injury, but the Socceroos refused to allow what initially looked a dubious call for the stretcher to break their rhythm. And less than a minute later, they took a deserved lead. Kruse, so often Australia's Theo Walcott, executed a perfect cross and Tomi Juric was on hand to finish ruthlessly.

However, Alshamrani coming on in the 79th minute displayed supreme confidence to equalise for Saudi Arabia, only a minute after his introduction. His goal lifted his team-mates—and the crowd. The Socceroos might feel aggrieved to have dropped crucial points, but the improved mentality they showed throughout this performance placed them in good stead for the campaign ahead.

The result in Jeddah was a top-draw effort and solidified Australia at the top of the group; now would come the important match against the old foe Japan, back home. The 'Blue Samurai' had not had the best of starts and needed to turn things around.

Australia 1, Japan 1
(*Halftime*: 0–1)
Scorer: Jedinak
11 October 2016
Referee: Nawaf Shukralla (Bahrain)
Crowd: 48,460
Docklands Stadium, Melbourne

Australia: Mathew Ryan, Trent Sainsbury, Matthew Spiranovic, Ryan McGowan, Aaron Mooy (Mathew Leckie 82), Brad Smith, Mile Jedinak, Apostolos Giannou (Robbie Kruse 57), Tomi Juric (Tim Cahill 70), Massimo Luongo, Tom Rogic
Japan: Shusaku Nishikawa, Masato Morishige, Tomoaki Makino, Gotoku Sakai, Maya Yoshida, Makato Hasebe, Hotaru Yamaguchi, Yu Kobayashi

(Hiroshi Kiyotake 81), Shinji Kagawa, Genki Haraguchi (Yuichi Maruyama 90), Keisuke Honda (Takuma Asano 84)

Australia and Japan played out another exciting chapter in their rivalry, drawing 1–1 in their World Cup qualifier at Docklands Stadium in Melbourne. Any thoughts that Japan would be tentative against an in-form Socceroos outfit were blown out of the water after just five minutes when Genki Haraguchi darted into space in the box and slid the ball past Mat Ryan for the opening goal.

Australia looked out of sorts as Japan's pressing completely stopped the Socceroos from playing their favoured passing game, and the Aussies were perhaps lucky not to be further behind at the break.

A somewhat revitalised Socceroos outfit showed signs of improvement after halftime, and the more vibrant outlook paid dividends when Tomi Juric ran onto a cross from Brad Smith before being bundled over by goal-scorer Haraguchi in the box to win a penalty. Captain Mile Jedinak converted with venom from the spot to make it 1–1, and from that point the Socceroos piled on the pressure in search of the go-ahead goal.

Australia controlled possession and brought on attacking weapons Tim Cahill and Mat Leckie to 'go for the kill', but all the while Japan continued to create great chances of their own on the break. Mat Ryan made the game's best save from Yu Kobayashi's header 15 minutes from time, and substitute Takuma Asano may well have found a decisive goal had his feet been a size bigger.

The Socceroos' next best chance came from a looping Matt Spiranovic header that sailed relatively harmlessly over the bar. In the end, neither side could break the deadlock, and the Japanese would most likely leave Docklands the happier after securing a valuable away point against their main group rivals.

Australia's last qualifying game for 2016 would be against Thailand, away in Bangkok. Thailand was currently on the bottom of the group table and were hardly expected to trouble the Socceroos. Normally this would be a match that the Australian team would be confident of getting a result, but this game was greatly affected in the aftermath of the death of the former Thai King some weeks prior. Initially it was expected that the match would be postponed due to undertaking a year of mourning to mark the monarch's passing. But the Thailand Football Association confirmed the game would go ahead. Initially it was announced that supporters attending the game would need to dress in an appropriate manner, with no football supporters' colours or logos. There were to be no drums, flags, megaphones, whistles, or banners. There would also be no chanting of team songs. Then, two weeks out from the game there was an amendment: banners, songs, symbols, and people dressing as they saw fit were all to be allowed.

Australia 2, Thailand 2
(*Halftime*: 1–1)
Scorer: Jedinak (2 penalties)
15 November 2016
Referee: Fahad Jaber Al Marri (Qatar)
Crowd: 36,534
Rajamangala Stadium, Bangkok

Australia: Mathew Ryan, Milos Degenek, Jamie Maclaren (Nathan Burns 58), Matthew Spiranovic (Jackson Irvine 78), Mathew Leckie (Mark Milligan 58), Robbie Kruse, Aaron Mooy, Brad Smith, Mile Jedinak, Trent Sainsbury, Tom Rogic
Thailand: Kawin Thamsatchanan, Theerathon Bunmathan, Adison Promrak (Nattapon Malapun 82), Sarach Yooyen, Siroch Chatthong (Rungrat Phumichantu 90), Teerasil Dangda, Prathum Chutong, Tanaboon Kesarat, Chanathip Songkrasin, Tristan Do, Pokklaw A-Nan

Before the game, the only question was: by how many goals would Australia beat Thailand? And that faith seemed justified after Mile Jedinak's early penalty reflected the Socceroos' obvious ascendancy.

But after the pesky Dangda equalised midway through the half, the game turned on its axis. Thailand gained in confidence, capitalising on Australian errors, and it was no surprise when they took a second-half lead. Thereafter it was desperate stuff from the visitors, and it took some eye-catching cameos from Nathan Burns and Mark Milligan to help snatch a late point. It was as sluggish and off-key a performance as Ange Postecoglou had overseen in his time in control of Australia. Aaron Mooy endured his poorest game in a gold shirt and players all around him looked lost.

Japan's win over Saudi Arabia meant that after five matches, Australia would drop to third in Group B, and if the UAE defeated Iraq there would be four teams separated by just one point at the halfway mark of this group phase.

It was not where Australia expected to find themselves after winning their opening two matches. Despite skipper Mile Jedinak's two penalty goals, Ange Postecoglou's disjointed national team handed last-placed Thailand their first point in the final phase of qualifying at Bangkok's Rajamangala National Stadium.

The way coach Postecoglou stormed off at the break signalled a halftime lashing was coming, yet it made little difference. Australia continued in a lacklustre fashion. Postecoglou switched to a diamond formation, substituting Maclaren and Leckie for veteran Mark Milligan and forward Nathan Burns.

The changes had an almost immediate effect as Siroch Chatthong fouled Jedinak and allowed him to restore parity with a penalty. But even after the in-form Jackson Irvine was brought on for an injured Matt Spiranovic, there would be no winner.

A frustrated Postecoglou said after the match that his side was unable to dictate terms: 'We got a little bit careless with our ball possession and we couldn't really control the game like we wanted to. As soon as it became a game of end-to-end, they obviously got into it, and it's kind of their game and from my perspective it's not the way we want to play the game.'

However, he remained optimistic about Australia's chances of qualification and said it was too early to panic: 'I still think we're well placed. I mean we've had three tough away trips, we haven't lost, and we're pretty strong at home. I think from a qualification point of view I certainly don't think there's extra pressure but that's external sort of buzz.'

This was a new sensation for coach Ange Postecoglou, long the pin-up boy of the Australian football media and tagged as the Messiah of Australian football coaching expertise. He had achieved unprecedented success with the Brisbane Roar playing a brand of football unseen in this country. It was exhilarating and exciting to watch and led to two successive A-League Championships with a style that earned them the tag of 'Roarcelona'. He gained the job of Socceroos' coach in the wake of Holger Osieck's sacking in late 2013 and led a young Australian side to Brazil for the 2014 World Cup and the following year in arguably the Australian national team's greatest moment, winning the Asian Cup in 2015. Clearly recent results highlighted that the long honeymoon period with Ange and the Australian soccer media was over. He was now under scrutiny and copping criticism.

Australia 1, Iraq 1
(*Halftime*: 1–0)
Scorer: Leckie
23 March 2017
Referee: Kim Jong Hyeok (Korea Republic)
Crowd: 3,270
PAS Stadium, Tehran, Iran

Australia: Mitchell Langerak, Milos Degenek, Mark Milligan, Mathew Leckie, Bailey Wright, Tomislav Juric (Tim Cahill 72), Robbie Kruse (Brad Smith 62), Aaron Mooy, Mile Jedinak, Massimo Luongo, Jackson Irvine (James Troisi 82)
Iraq: Mohammed Hameed, Ahmed Ibrahim, Ali Bahjat Fadhil (Ahmed Yaseen Gheni 56), Ali Adnan Kadhim, Mohannad Abdul-Raheem Karrar, Amjad Kalaf Al-Muntafik (Amjed Attwan Kadhim 46), Dhurgham Ismael, Alaa Ali Mhawi, Mahdi Kamil Shiltagh (Hammadi Ahmed Abdullah 74), Saad Abdulameer Al-Dobjahawe, Rebin Ghareeb Solak

Australia lost further ground in Group B of the World Cup qualifiers as they were held to a 1-1 draw by Iraq in Tehran. The game was played in shocking conditions. It was a fourth consecutive qualifying stalemate for Ange Postecoglou's side. It came after Postecoglou unveiled a 3-2-4-1 formation at the PAS Stadium, but his team clearly battled to adjust.

Pre-match predictions of a battle turned out to be accurate. Steady rain throughout the day exacerbated what was already one of the worst pitches Australia had played on in recent years, and at times the new-look back three of Mark Milligan, Miloš Degenek and Bailey Wright looked unable to cope.

Despite an earlier defeat in the reverse fixture, Iraq was the better side this time around and were unfortunate to fall behind to a Mathew Leckie header after 39 minutes. It looked as though the Socceroos would see out the second half and claim a crucial win, but substitute Ahmed Yasin deservedly levelled for the hosts 14 minutes from the end to earn a share of the spoils.

Iraq made the brighter start in the match, with Ali Adnan cutting in from the left to fire over early and Mohannad Abdul-Raheem then forcing a smart stop from Mitchell Langerak. It was only through some wasteful Iraqi finishing and some desperate defending (such as Milligan's last-second intervention to deny Amjad Kalaf a certain goal in the 22nd minute) that Australia remained level. Kalaf then lifted a finish over the crossbar soon after and the Iraqis' general poor finishing proved costly for them.

Australia took the lead through Leckie after Jackson Irvine and Aaron Mooy had fired warning shots. With six minutes of the half to play, Leckie met Mooy's corner superbly and powered his header inside the left-hand post. Iraq was subsequently grateful to Mohammed Hamed as he denied Robbie Kruse, Tomi Juric and Mooy either side of the break, while Langerak was alert to parry Ahmed Ibrahim's effort away.

As the game wore on, Iraq found another gear and secured a point after 76 minutes as Ahmed Yasin slid in to convert Ali Adnan's low cross from the left. The Iraqis needed a piece of expert defending in stoppage time, as the Socceroos almost stole victory in the closing moments—Tim Cahill's header from Mooy's corner needed to be cleared off the line.

Both teams had chances to win in a frantic finale, but it was undoubtedly the Socceroos who would have been happier with the point in the circumstances. However, while Australia temporarily moved level with second-placed Japan in Group B, having played a game more, this was a missed opportunity to keep up the pressure at the top as group leaders. Saudi Arabia won 3–0 in Thailand. Victory against the UAE back in Sydney the following Tuesday would now be crucial if the Socceroos were to secure a top-two spot and qualify automatically for the World Cup Finals in Russia.

The criticism of Postecoglou's decision to change his customary 4–3–3 system to a 3–2–4–1 line-up was rising and roundly condemned by the critics. A major bone of contention with the media was that the players were unaccustomed to the roles they were to play. Critics howled protest that the opposition often played into the spaces left on the flanks that exposed the Australian defence to quick counterattacks through transition. Australia would go into their next match against the UAE in Sydney as a team that were still unbeaten, but having had four successive draws, they were now losing touch with the top-two teams, Saudi Arabia and Japan.

Australia 2, United Arab Emirates 0

(*Halftime*: 1–0)
Scorers: Leckie, Irvine
28 March 2017

Referee: Ahmed Abu Bakar Al Kaf (Oman)
Crowd: 27,328
Sydney Football Stadium

Australia: Mathew Ryan, Milos Degenek, Brad Smith, Mark Milligan, Mathew Leckie, Bailey Wright, Tomislav Juric (Tim Cahill 71), James Troisi, Mile Jedinak (Mustafa Amini 89), Trent Sainsbury, Jackson Irvine (Robbie Kruse 81)
UAE: Ali Khaseif, Walid Abbas (Ismaeil Matar 79), Tariq Ahmed (Mohamed Abdulrahman 37), Mohanad Salem, Ali Ahmed Mabkhout, Ahmed Barman, Ahmed Khalil (Khamis Esmaeel 55), Abdelaziz Sanqour, Ismail Al Hammadi, Ismail Ahmed, Omar Abdulrahman

It was nervy and it was tetchy, but the Socceroos just got the job done to keep its stuttering World Cup qualifying campaign alive at the Sydney Football Stadium. With ground to make up on Japan and Saudi Arabia and needing to win *all* its remaining home games, Australia kept its campaign chugging along with a 2–0 win.

Set-piece expertise came to the fore as a first goal in international football for Jackson Irvine and a headed finish from Mathew Leckie, both coming from corners, saw the hosts home in a stop-start encounter. The UAE were never out of contention until very late in the match.

There were early warning signs for the hosts when Ali Mabkhout nearly broke through before Mat Ryan was forced to mop up an uncertain back pass. But those early nerves were soon settled when Jackson Irvine glanced in his goal via a corner in the eighth minute.

That goal fired up Australia for a time, with Leckie spurning a chance from a sharp angle on the right just two minutes later. Star UAE midfielder Omar Abdulrahman then curled a good-looking free kick towards goal, forcing Ryan into a diving parry.

A surging run from James Troisi saw him arrow in towards the UAE area soon after, only to blaze his shot from outside the box over the bar. Mark Milligan then shot straight at the keeper from distance after a break down the left flank.

Australia probed throughout the second stanza without much reward, with Leckie nutmegging two players on the wing only to see his cross towards Brad Smith cut out at the last second. Abdulrahman had a chance himself at the other end but shot straight at Ryan, before UAE's frustrations were compounded when Leckie fouled the big-haired midfielder on the edge of the box, only for the referee to wave play on.

Leckie was involved in all of Australia's best movements, robbing his man on the right flank, bursting forward and feeding Troisi, who could only blaze over from inside the area. But the game was made safe on the 77th minute, via another corner, as Leckie rose highest to hit an unstoppable header home from Troisi's delivery.

The win saw the Socceroos temporarily go level on points with Group B joint leaders, Japan and Saudi Arabia—though both those teams had a game in hand.

It would be another three months before Australia would battle with Saudi Arabia in Adelaide in the most crucial tie of the qualifying stage. The Socceroos had to win to stay in the hunt for a top-two spot for automatic qualification and third place would see another round of sudden death play-offs.

Australia 3, Saudi Arabia 2
(*Halftime*: 2–2)
Scorers: Juric (2), Rogic
8 June 2017
Referee: Ravshan Irmatov (Uzbekistan)
Crowd: 29,875
Adelaide Oval

Australia: Mat Ryan, Milos Degenek, Brad Smith (Aziz Behich 46), Mathew Leckie, Tomi Juric (Massimo Luongo 85), Aaron Mooy, Mile Jedinak, Ryan McGowan, Trent Sainsbury, Jackson Irvine (Robbie Kruse 63), Tom Rogic
Saudi Arabia: Yasser Al-Mosailem, Osama Hawsawi, Abdullah Al Dossary, Omar Ibrahim Othman, Mohammed Al-Burayk, Salman Al Faraj, Yahia Al Shehri (Abdulafttah Asiri 82), Mohammed Al Sahlawi, Abdulmalek Al-Khaibri (Abdullah Ateef 69), Taiseer Al Jassam, Salem Al-Dawsari (Salman Muwashar 82)

Before the game, the Australian players linked arms and gathered around the centre circle for a minute of silence honouring the victims of the Manchester and London terror attacks just a couple of weeks prior. Controversy arose when the Saudi Arabian team didn't follow suit. The Saudis were booed by Australian supporters.

A very open first half saw four goals with the Saudis coming back twice to go in at the break 2–2 after Tomi Juric bagged a brace for the hosts.

After just six minutes, Saudi keeper Yasser Al Mosailem made a crazy mistake with the ball in hand, slipping when kicking it out of his box. The clearance went straight to Juric and from about 25 metres out the Luzern striker dispatched it into the back of the net.

After 22 minutes, superb inter-play between Al-Sahlawi and Al-Dawsari through the middle opened up Australia's defence and the Saudi star raced through and coolly slipped it low and past Mat Ryan.

Australia's lead was restored after 35 minutes when Mat Leckie's pace down the right got him to the by-line. His measured cross found Juric's head, and with no marking, the big striker guided the ball home, his second goal of the night.

With just seconds left in the half, on the transition, a pinpoint ball over the top opened up Australia and Al-Sahlawi lurking on the opposite post met a low cross to volley home a superb equaliser.

After an uncertain first half, the Socceroos looked far more assured in the second half with half-time substitute Aziz Behich adding plenty of class and energy to the home side's second stanza.

After 64 minutes, Aaron Mooy laid the ball off for Tom Rogic and the Celtic star let fly with a long-range strike. His left-foot rocket burst into the net and gave the Aussies a lead for the third time on the night. Only the month before, the classy midfielder had delivered match-winner exploits for Celtic in the Scottish Cup Final.

Rogic's goal proved to be the winner in this crucial game as well. Coach Postecoglou enthused in the aftermath: 'He's a hell of a player. And the best is ahead of him, no doubt about that.'

The win elevated Australia to the top of the Asia Group B table with Japan and Saudi Arabia. However, Australia was still in third place on goal difference, so the battle was not over.

Rogic said after the game: 'We made it a little difficult for ourselves in the first half, but we showed our quality and limited their chances in the second half and went on for the win. I thought the goal was coming. We started to get on top in the second half and I just wanted to get the boys on the right way and to get the win, which was the most important thing.'

Australia undertook a couple of preparation games before their final group games.

They were well beaten by an all-star Brazil at the Melbourne Cricket Ground, 4-0.

In mid-June, as Asian Champions they played Germany in the Confederations Cup in Sochi, Russia. In a fighting performance the Socceroos went down 3-2. They then fought out a 1-1 draw against Cameroon in St Petersburg. The final match saw Australia needing to beat Chile by two goals to advance to the semi-final stage, but they were held 1-1 in Moscow. The game saw Tim Cahill reach a milestone of 100 games for the Socceroos.

Australia now prepared to face Japan in the crucial World Cup qualifier in Saitama. The Socceroos were hanging on a precipice and needed to win or at least gain a draw to keep their hopes of finishing in the top-two places of the group alive to gain automatic qualification for Russia.

Australia 0, Japan 2
(*Halftime*: 1–0)
31 August 2017
Referee: Alireza Faghani (Iran)
Crowd: 59,492
Saitama Stadium

Australia: Mathew Ryan, Brad Smith, Mark Milligan, Matthew Spiranovic, Mathew Leckie, Robbie Kruse, James Troisi (Tomi Juric 61), Trent Sainsbury, Massimo Luongo, Jackson Irvine (Mustafa Amini 86), Tom Rogic (Tim Cahill 70)
Japan: Eiji Kawashima, Ideguchi Yosuke, Shoji Gen, Yuto Nagatomo, Takashi Inui (Genki Haraguchi 76), Yuya Osako (Shinji Okazaki 86), Hotaru Yamaguchi, Makoto Hasebe, Takuma Asano (Yuya Kubo 89), Hiroki Sakai, Maya Yoshida

Japan booked their place in the 2018 World Cup with an emphatic 2–0 win over Australia in Saitama. Takuma Asano scored late in the first half before 21-year-old midfielder Yosuke Ideguchi covered himself in glory with a sumptuous finish in the 82nd minute as the 'Blue Samurai' sealed a sixth straight appearance in the global showpiece.

Ange Postecoglou's side enjoyed long periods of possession throughout the match against Japan but were unable to make it count. The Socceroos were without star midfielder Aaron Mooy through illness, while Tomi Juric could only start on the bench due to an injury that kept him from training all week.

After an even start, Mathew Leckie came within inches of the opening goal, controlling Massimo Luongo's lay-off before sending a deflected effort off the base of the left-hand post from the edge of the area. Five minutes before the break, Asano broke the deadlock after Nagatomo clipped a fine delivery in from the left, and the Japanese winger side-footed a simple volley past Mat Ryan.

Postecoglou introduced Juric in the second half as the Socceroos began to push for a way back into the contest, and fellow substitute Tim Cahill came within inches of meeting a Robbie Kruse cut-back at the far post. Trent Sainsbury made a brilliant goal-line block to deny Ideguchi a second, but it proved in vain for Australia, as the 21-year-old cut inside from the left before rifling an unstoppable shot past Ryan and into the top corner from 20 yards out in the closing minutes.

Australia was now left with a final game at home against Thailand—a game they needed to win by a large margin to improve their goal difference—and then hope that Japan could beat or at least draw with Saudi Arabia away. It was now a game of chance; the Socceroos were in a round of Russian roulette to get to Russia in 2018. If they couldn't get the results they needed, they would face a sudden-death game against the third-placed team in the other Asian qualifying group, which at this point was looking like Syria.

Australia 2, Thailand 1
(*Halftime*: 0–0)
Scorers: Juric, Leckie
5 September 2017
Referee: Liu Kwok Man (Hong Kong)
Crowd: 26,393
Melbourne Rectangular Stadium (AAMI Park)

Australia: Mathew Ryan, Milos Degenek, Tim Cahill (Robbie Kruse 57), Mark Milligan, Mathew Leckie, Bailey Wright (Jamie Maclaren 71), Tomi Juric, Aaron Mooy, Alex Gersbach (James Troisi 67), Trent Sainsbury, Tom Rogic
Thailand: Sinthaweechai Hathairattanakool, Perapat Notechaiya, Theerathon

Bunmathan, Adison Promrak, Tristan Do (Mongkol Thosakrai 90), Sanrawat Dechmitr (Sirod Chatthong 73), Chanathip Songkrasin (Nurul Sriyankem 79), Pokklaw Anan, Chalermpong Kerdkaew, Teerasil Dangda, Pansa Hemviboon

The Socceroos were unimpressive in gaining a 2-1 win over Thailand. They would now have to wait and hope that Japan at least gained a draw against Saudi Arabia to achieve automatic qualification for the World Cup.

The result was well short of the large win and goal difference boost that Australia needed. The first half was one of immense frustration for the Socceroos. They had chance after chance, only to be denied by desperate blocks on the line, or by the goal posts. Mooy fired one in from outside the box, only to meet the base of the upright with the keeper beaten. Cahill then tried his luck from the edge of the area, only to see his attempt hit both posts as the ball squirted loose from the onrushing attack. There was a hairy moment for the Thailand stopper soon after as he appeared to carry the ball outside the box, but Juric's free kick was blazed over the bar.

Even keeper Ryan saw nerves get the better of his judgement as he raced out to take down a Thai forward outside the box, earning him a yellow card.

Having been frustrated in the first half, Australia needed to burst out of the gates in the second, but despite a litany of chances—40 shots in the match, 13 on target—the match remained goal-less until the 69th minute. Juric got on the end of an all-too-inviting Aaron Mooy cross from the left, beating his marker to nod home wide of the keeper.

The second half had started in panic mode, with Trent Sainsbury putting in a last-ditch tackle in the box, springing an Australian counterattack which saw a Tom Rogic thunderbolt denied by the Thai keeper. Increasingly desperate, Alex Gersbach fired in a left-footed volley from a corner, but again it was blocked by desperate Thai defenders. More chances came flooding in for Australia, but none would find the net. Rogic again found space in the box to set up a rasping left-footer, only to find the upright instead. Rogic had yet another pop from distance, forcing a good one-handed save from Thai keeper Hathairattanakool, before a succession of crosses into the box and mad scrambles saw Thailand survive another wave of Australian attacks.

At the other end, Australia's defence was doing its best to gift Thailand a goal, with both Mat Ryan and Sainsbury giving possession away in their own area, but the visitors spurning their chances to equalise.

Again, Rogic was set up to curl one in from outside the area, sitting the ball up nicely before attempting a shot on the bounce, but he only landed it on the roof of the net. Bedlam would follow as the ball pinged around in Thailand's box, begging to be poked over the goal line, but no such finish would materialise. Juric would try his luck from distance but could only sting the palms of Hathairattanakool. Troisi broke clear and nearly produced an astute finish, but he watched his left-footed drive fly agonisingly wide. Mooy flashed a shot from distance, before Troisi chested it down and lashed a volley straight at the keeper.

The expected floodgates never opened, and Australia's collective 'goose' looked to be cooked when Pokklaw levelled the scores with less than 10 minutes remaining. But Leckie, who had underperformed for much of the match, finally enjoyed a fruitful—and perhaps crucial—moment, when he side-footed home a calm finish with four minutes left to restore the lead and deliver victory.

The fallout after this result was huge; there was a massive backlash against coach Ange Postecoglou from the ever-ready Australia soccer media who had been sharpening their knives and hatchets for some time over both the Socceroos' results and Postecoglou's formation. Fox Sports pundits and former Socceroos Mark Bosnich and Robbie Slater led the charge, demanding he be sacked. Bosnich went so far as to declare that the coach was using the Socceroos as 'an experimental laboratory'. It was confirmed that Australia would face Syria in do-or-die, two-leg play-offs. The winner would then go on to the final play-off against the fourth placed team in CONCACAF—either Panama, the United States or Honduras. The first game against Syria would be played in Malaysia as Syria was in a war-torn state. This neutral venue clearly enhanced Australia's chances.

Australia 1, Syria 1
(*Halftime*: 1–0)
Scorer: Kruse
5 October 2017
Referee: Alireza Faghani (Iran)
Crowd: 2,150
Hang Jebat Stadium, Malacca, Malaysia

Australia: Mathew Ryan, Milos Degenek, Mark Milligan, Matthew Jurman, Mathew Leckie, Tomi Juric (Tomas Rogic 83), Robbie Kruse

(Massimo Luongo 70), Aaron Mooy, Aziz Behich, Josh Risdon
(Nikita Rukavytsya 63), Trent Sainsbury

Syria: Ibrahim Almeh, Hadi Al Masri, Mouaiad Al Ajjan, Omar Kharbin
(Mardik Mardikian 80), Mahmoud Al Maowas (Firas Al Khatib 76),
Omar Al Somah, Yousef Kalfa (Oday Al Jafal 46), Tamer Haj Mohamad,
Zahir Al Medani, Khaled Al Mbayed, Fahd Youssef

A precious away goal put the Socceroos in the driving seat to reach the final stage of World Cup qualifying after their 1–1 draw with Syria in Malaysia. With five minutes to play, Australia was on the cusp of a best-case scenario away win in the first leg of their cut-throat, play-off tie. But a controversial late penalty goal to Omar Al Somah gave the war-ravaged nation the equaliser they craved to cancel Robbie Kruse's 40th-minute opener at Malacca's Hang Jebat Stadium.

With the second leg in Sydney in mind, coach Ange Postecoglou left Tom Rogic, Massimo Luongo and Jackson Irvine on the bench and gambled with the greenest members of his squad for this match. It paid off handsomely. Uncapped Matt Jurman, thrust into a three-man defence alongside Trent Sainsbury and Miloš Degenek, looked like an old hand. Trimmed-down right-back Josh Risdon, capped just three times, was a hive of industry at right wing-back and relieved a high-playing Mat Leckie of his defensive responsibilities. That re-jig bore fruit five minutes before the break when Leckie blazed to the right by-line and cut inside to turn a defender and let rip. Kruse timed his run perfectly to divert the shot home.

Under the weight of the previous month's failure to qualify directly for a fourth straight World Cup, the Socceroos had their work cut out on an uneven pitch with 'a sea of red' to break down. Their steady display yielded chances—Tomi Juric twice hitting the post in consecutive shots and Leckie somehow skying a sitter with ample time. Captain Mark Milligan, who endured extra attention all night, pulled the midfield strings alongside Aaron Mooy and unwound from 25 metres to force a full-stretch save from Syrian goalkeeper Ibrahim Alma.

Syria brought pace, and none were more searing than Al Somah. As Australia searched for a killer second goal, the dangerman and his cohort amped up the pressure, slicing through the Socceroos' defence with increasing regularity and forcing a succession of corners and free kicks. Mat Ryan, hardly called upon in the first stanza, was suddenly in the firing line and made a string of saves including one superb injury-time effort to deny Syria a goal. But there was nothing the Brighton and Hove Albion gloveman could do when Syria was awarded a penalty after contact from Leckie on Al Somah, who duly converted from the spot.

The second half of this qualifying campaign had been wobbly from the outset and that the Socceroos had under-performed is an understatement. The media blowtorch upon coach Postecoglou had continued on his resistance to pull back on his three men at the back, in the face of criticism, was either a reflection of an incredible self-belief or just plain stubbornness. The critical game in Sydney was the last chance saloon for the Socceroos.

Australia 2, Syria 1
(*Halftime*: 1-1)
Scorer: Cahill (2)
10 October 2017
Referees: Ravshan Irmatov (Uzbekistan) Ilgiz Tantashev (Uzbekistan)
Crowd: 42,136
Sydney Olympic Stadium

Australia: Mathew Ryan, Milos Degenek, Matthew Jurman, Trent Sainsbury, Brad Smith (Aaron Mooy 11), Mark Milligan, Mathew Leckie, Robbie Kruse, James Troisi (Nikita Rukavytsya 73), Tim Cahill, Tom Rogic (Tomi Juric 96)
Syria: Ibrahim Alma, Mouaiad Al Ajjan, Jehad Al Baour, Mahmoud Al-Mawas (sent off 94), Omar Al Soma, Ouday Abduljaffal (Firas Mohamad Al Khatib 61), Tamer Hag Mohamad, Hamid Mido (Esraa Al Hamwiah 75), Mohamad Zaher Almedani, Mardek Mardkian (Osama Omari 91), Fahad Youssef

The Socceroos edged a 10-man Syria 2–1 in extra time to progress to the intercontinental World Cup qualifying play-off after a tense stand-off in Sydney. The build-up to the match was dominated by news that Aaron Mooy had been demoted to the bench, and things could not have started worse for Australia when Al Soma broke with ease through the middle to slot past Ryan, putting Syria ahead in the sixth minute and sending the visiting fans into raptures.

An injury to Brad Smith soon after saw Mooy brought on, allaying whatever fuss was caused by Ange Postecoglou's selection. Nerves were settled almost immediately as Mathew Leckie burst brilliantly down the right before hitting an inviting cross for Cahill, who thumped in a headed equaliser for his 49th strike in Australian colours.

Mooy proceeded to link up brilliantly with Tom Rogic and Kruse down the left in an attacking triumvirate that proceeded to toy with the Syrian defence, thanks to some excellent passing combinations. Those combinations helped put James Troisi into the box to feed Cahill, but his right-footed finish was blocked by a defender's thigh with the goal beckoning.

The teams were locked at 1-1 (and 2-2 on aggregate) at halftime.

Both sides struggled to create chances of genuine quality in the second half, as the tense contest petered out to a draw in regulation minutes, sending the decider to extra time. Substitute forward Nikita Rukavytsya then had two golden-edged opportunities to end the tie. Put through early in the first added period, his low, left-footed drive stung the palms of Syrian keeper Hamid Mido, before a pinpoint cross found him in acres of space, only for him to volley straight at the keeper from point-blank range.

Syria was reduced to 10 men after Mahmoud Al-Mawas picked up a second yellow after fouling Kruse on the flank, leaving the visitors to shut up shop in the hope of frustrating Australia. The Socceroos had been constantly frustrated throughout regular time, and through much of extra time, before Tim Cahill rolled back the years with his headed winner to put Australia through to a November play-off against North and Central America's fourth-best team. Robbie Kruse was put through into the area, and with his back to Cahill, twisted around to cross for the 37-year-old to head home in signature fashion for a remarkable half-century of goals in Australian colours.

But the drama wasn't over, as Syria won a late free kick just outside Australia's area with the seconds counting down. Up stepped Omar Al Soma, who hit a rasping shot against the post with Mat Ryan beaten. Syria, a fairy tale team in Asia's World Cup qualifying story, were literally inches away from progressing—at Australia's expense— even though they were down to 10 men. A goal for Al Soma would have levelled the aggregate at 2-2 and put Syria through on the away goals rule.

After the game, Cahill confessed: 'I knew I was going to score, I didn't touch the ball much but in the end I delivered. That's what I've done my whole life and I'll continue to do it.' In another interview, Cahill expressed his fears leading into the game: 'I have a great relationship with the boss, and regardless of the decisions he makes—playing me, not playing me, giving me 10 minutes or 90 minutes—I always respect his decisions. (But) there were a few times I was a bit nervous seeing the subs getting ready to come on. Thankfully, I think he thought this was my time and I felt it was too... I went into it thinking this was possibly my last game (for Australia) if things did not go well... There was never a shadow of doubt in my mind. I was ready.'

Ange Postecoglou delivered a bombshell announcement in the wake of the win that he would resign as Socceroo coach before the World Cup in Russia. Of course, there was still a two-game play-off to be won against Honduras. Clearly Football Federation Australia was caught on the hop, and they were reportedly very unhappy over his announcement. There were widespread calls to sack him immediately. Respected soccer journalist Ray Gatt stated: 'The only option, as I see it, is that an interim coach is installed for the two home-and-away qualifiers against Honduras next month while FFA search for a permanent replacement to take Australia to the World Cup Finals in Russia next year—if we make it.'

Postecoglou had been a target for the media across the previous six months particularly his refusal to back away from his change to the formation which, on results, did not bear up. Ray Gatt expressed that 'the coach over that time was cranky, moody... The body language has been telling and some of his press conferences—where even the most innocuous of questions has raised his hackles—have been eye opening.' This was not something new to Ange Postecoglou. A coach of undoubted high quality, he seemingly possessed an Achilles heel in dealing with media attacks. Back in 2006 during an SBS television interview whilst Australia's Under-20s' coach, he entered a heated 12-minute exchange with television reporter, Craig Foster. Postecoglou erupted over the questions surrounding his second failed attempt to qualify Australia for the World Youth Cup. He subsequently vacated the position as youth coach, and it appeared he again now was pressing the 'ejector seat button' following media attacks.

It was clear Postecoglou was departing even if the Socceroos overcame Honduras. The FFA must have been tested on what to do but eventually agreed to let him stay at the helm until after the play-off with Honduras. It was not ideal and must have been a difficult situation for the players. Honduras would be a difficult hurdle, and if they got through to Russia, the Socceroos would prepare and go in with a new coach.

During their qualification rounds, Honduras preferred playing their home games in San Pedro Sula rather than the capital. San Pedro Sula had until recently held one of the world's highest murder rates. The atmosphere at Honduran home games was famously tense and hostile.

Australia 0, Honduras 0

(*Halftime*: 0–0)

9 November 2017

Referee: Daniele Orsato (Italy)

Crowd: 38,000

Estadio Olimpico Metropolitano, San Pedro Sula, Honduras

Australia: Mathew Ryan, Matthew Jurman, Josh Risdon (Milos Degenek 84), Bailey Wright, Tomi Juric (Nikita Rukavytsya 89), Aaron Mooy, Mile Jedinak, Aziz Behich, Trent Sainsbury, Massimo Luongo, Jackson Irvine (Tom Rogic 74)

Honduras: Donis Salatiel Escober Izaguirre, Henry Adalberto Figueroa Alonzo, Emilio Arturo Izaguirre Giron, Alfredo Antonio Mejia Escobar, Anthony Ruben Lozano Colon (Carlo Yair Costly Molina 73), Carlos Ovidio Lanza Martinez (Michaell Anthony Chirinos Cortez 60), Romell Samir Quioto Robinson, Alexander Augustin Lopez (Mario Roberto Martinez Hernandez 66), Jorge Aaron Claros Juarez, Brayan Antonio Beckeles, Johnny Eulogio Palacios Suazo

The game was played in very hot and humid conditions on a pitch that was best described as 'green sand'. Before kick-off, the crowd went to work to intimidate the Australian team by stamping their feet madly so that the concrete stand vibrated. Horns, drums, whistles, chants, and taunts also greeted the Australian team. It was revealed after the game that the Australian team had been preparing for the game and noise by using sign language and hand signals to combat the din. The conditions were clearly set up to favour Honduras, but it resulted in one of Australia's best performances in twelve months.

It was a game of few chances and the best of them fell to the Socceroos. With an ounce of luck, they could have won the game and gained an away goal that would have counted double. But Honduras and Australia played out a goal-less draw in the first leg of their intercontinental World Cup play-off at the stadium described as a tomb for visiting teams.

The Socceroos were initially awarded a penalty early on for a foul on Bailey Wright, but the referee then changed his mind and awarded a free kick to Honduras. The Socceroos' defender had beaten Escober to the ball and was fouled. Italian referee

Daniele Orsato immediately pointed to the spot, silencing the raucous Honduran crowd. The Honduran players then surrounded the linesman, arguing against the decision. Australian captain Mile Jedinak stood over the ball on the penalty spot. The referee consulted with the linesman and then reversed his decision, deeming Wright to be offside, Replays showed that he was onside by at least a metre.

Luzern striker Tomi Juric had the best opportunities. In the first half, an excellent touch took him past the defence before he fired just wide from 16 yards. Mile Jedinak, returning from a long injury break, was immense playing in front of the back three.

After the break, Massimo Luongo (who had one of his best games for some time) tested Escober with a 25-metre drive before setting up Juric, but his header was tipped over the bar by Donis Escober. Australia also had a great chance late, when breaking from defence Josh Risdon had two players standing in front of an open goal, but his cross was placed behind Aziz Behich and Jackson Irvine.

Carlo Costly had a late chance for Honduras, but Mat Ryan denied the 35-year-old. Cahill remained on the bench during the match with an ankle injury. Postecoglou said he would only risk him if it was necessary. Australia would be hoping that he would recover for the second leg.

The Honduran football media community reflected on the uphill battle their team faced following Australia's performance in San Pedro Sula. The sports paper *Diez* stated: 'Honduras was pardoned in the Olympic Stadium. The Australians missed two clear chances that could have given them an unbeatable advantage in the close contest against a diminished Bicolour squad. The main weapons of Honduras disappeared—neither Alex Lopez nor less Romell Quioto could prevail.'

Honduras would cling to the knowledge that a score draw in the return leg would be enough to get them through the tie. Honduran players Maynor Figueroa and Alberth Elis were both suspended for the first leg and might prove the difference for the return match.

The Honduran press were glowing of the Australian performance: 'You have amazing players, amazing touch. But the match is open, and we have a chance in Australia. But I'm really impressed with the level of skill of some of your players.'

Coach Diario Mas lamented his team's failure to take advantage of playing at home and acknowledged Australia were the better side: 'The team (Honduras) had everything in their favour, good weather, full stadium ... but they lacked offensive power.'

Socceroos' coach Ange Postecoglou felt his team had been underestimated and disrespected by the Honduran media ahead of the game.

Australia was again fortunate that they had chartered a direct Qantas flight back to Sydney. It was déjà vu of the 2005 game against Uruguay. Australia would be back in Sydney some 24 hours before Honduras who would endure a gruelling flight via Los Angeles. Whilst confidence was high, some recalled the confidence following the Socceroos 1-1 draw with Iran in Tehran and their subsequent home draw in the return leg of the doomed qualifying campaign for the France World Cup in 1998.

Australia could call upon Mat Leckie and Mark Milligan for the return leg with Honduras. Both had been suspended for the first leg. They would also have Tim Cahill and Robbie Kruse returning from injury.

Australia 3, Honduras 1
(*Halftime*: 0–0)
Scorer: Jedinak (3)
15 November 2017
Referee: Nestor Pitana (Argentina)
Crowd: 77,060
Sydney Olympic Stadium

Australia: Mathew Ryan, Tim Cahill (Tomi Juric 66), Mark Milligan (James Troisi 89), Matthew Jurman, Mathew Leckie, Bailey Wright, Aaron Mooy, Mile Jedinak, Aziz Behich, Trent Sainsbury, Tom Rogic (Robbie Kruse 77)
Honduras: Donis Salatiel Escober Izaguirre, Maynor Alexis Figueroa Rochez, Ever Gonzalo Alvarado Sandoval, Bryan Josue Acosta Ramos, Emilio Arturo Izaguirre Giron (Henry Adalberto Figueroa Alonzo 42 (Mario Roberto Martinez Hernandez 73)), Anthony Ruben Lozano Colon, Romell Samir Quioto Robinson (Eddie Gabriel Hernandez Padilla 75), Alberth Josue Elis Martinez, Jorge Aaron Claros Juarez, Brayan Antonio Beckeles, Johnny Eulogio Palacios Suazo

After their longest and most drawn-out World Cup qualification, Australia were finally through to their fourth successive World Cup Finals after this win. They made their supporters' nerves jangle until the second half, but the Socceroos got the job done, earning a 3-1 victory over a determined Honduras outfit to book their place in Russia.

Socceroos' warrior Mile Jedinak, known for his lustrous beard and bone-crushing tackles, opened the scoring with a deflected free kick in the second half before two strikes from the penalty spot sealed a superb hat-trick for the midfielder.

The Honduran goal from Figueroa came with the last kick of the game when it meant nothing. The visitors' spirit waned visibly from the 82nd minute when Bryan Acosta's free kick from a dangerous position sailed well over the crossbar. That was the moment the crowd let out a victorious roar, knowing there was no chance of another Iran '97-style' stuff up.

The Socceroos opened the scoring after the best move of the match. Tom Rogic took the game by the scruff of the neck. The Celtic midfielder broke forward, slaloming past defenders before he was eventually chopped down on the edge of the area. Instead of going high over the wall, Jedinak blasted the free kick low, and it deflected off the hip of Figueroa and into the net to unleash a mighty roar from the Olympic Stadium crowd.

The next 18 minutes were the most hectic of the match, with Honduras now forced to attack and the Australians sensing a second goal in the offing. It was always going to be the Socceroos who scored again, and when a dangerous attacking move resulted in a clear handball from Acosta, Jedinak stepped up and calmly slotted into the corner past a diving Escober.

The third goal came when newly introduced Robbie Kruse blitzed the Honduran defence with his fresh legs and was hacked down by Jerry Palacios. The defender was booked, but probably should have been sent off, and the Australian captain once again scored from the spot before chugging down the sideline in a slightly more restrained version of John Aloisi's 2005 victory sprint.

The Hondurans played the perfect game from their point of view in the first half. With only 28 per cent of possession, they managed to limit Australia's opportunities to a couple of half-chances. The away side started wasting time early as well, with a keen eye on the distant prospect of extra time and penalties. Whenever there was a chance to add an extra roll after a strong Australian tackle, they did. Whenever they could 'mistakenly' place the ball on the wrong spot for a free kick, they did. These were the tactics of a street-smart side, and they worked well.

Australia could not find their main man Cahill who was isolated up front, and their most creative players (Mooy and Rogic) were unable to get regular combinations going. The Socceroos' best chance came in the 37th minute when Cahill, frustrated at being isolated up front, picked the ball up on the left wing and left two players 'for dead' before feeding Behich, who teed up Rogic in a great position in the box. However, the midfielder didn't hit the ball sweetly and it was an easy save for keeper Donis Escober.

Honduras looked most dangerous when the rapid, strong, and skilful Alberth Elis attacked down the right, but he was often a lone figure getting forward. The Australians lifted in the second half, and whether it was due to exhaustion from Honduras or an upbeat tempo from the hosts, the game began to stretch and Rogic took control.

The Socceroos were heading to their fourth straight World Cup, even if it took an energy-sapping 29 months of qualifying games to get there.

I was immediately looking to book my way to Russia for my third successive World Cup venture. Russia was another bucket-list destination for me with its rich history. The Socceroos had been thrown into chaos over the departure of their coach Ange Postecoglou. Only days after securing the Socceroos' place in Russia, he commented that the previous nine months had been very difficult and 'that he had been deliberately undermined'. He said in an interview with Fox Sports that the attacks upon him had impacted on his family and left him emotionally drained. He had accepted a position as coach of Japanese club Yokohama F. Marinos, but he saw it as a gateway to Europe: 'The ambition is to coach in Europe.'

It was not until into the New Year that Dutch coach Bert van Marwijk was unveiled as the Socceroos' coach for the 2018 World Cup. His appointment was just short term—for the World Cup and not beyond. Van Marwijk had coached at the highest levels, including winning the UEFA cup with Feyenoord in 2002 and having taken his own country, the Netherlands, to the 2010 World Cup Final where they were beaten 1-0 by Spain. He carried a background knowledge of the Australian team having coached Saudi Arabia against the Socceroos during the qualifying stage. Nevertheless, he would have his work cut out for him on such short notice.

Van Marwijk was a sound choice but was known as a coach that did not take risks, preferring a safety-first approach. He was quick to dispel any model left by former coach Postecoglou: 'I'll do it my way. I'm respectful of the former coach. (But) we will do it my way. I'm a realistic coach and I like creative football—I like to have the ball. But I also like to win, that's the most important thing.' He was adamant that the first game against France was the key game: 'For me, at this moment there is only one thing that counts and it's the first game.' Van Marwijk acknowledged the

Australian qualities: 'They can play football and they try to play. They are strong, physically strong.' It was announced that Graham Arnold would take over as the Socceroos' coach after the World Cup in Russia for the full four-year cycle up to 2022 and the Finals in Qatar.

Australia opened their World Cup preparations in Europe under van Marwijk with a 4-1 loss to Norway in Oslo. They followed up with a 0-0 draw with Colombia at Fulham's Craven Cottage. This time the Socceroos decided against a farewell World Cup match at home and had two games against solid opposition in the Czech Republic and Hungary. The first game against the Czech Republic was impressive as the Socceroos crushed the Czechs 4-0. The game was notable for the debut of young gun Daniel Arzani who had burst onto the recent A-League season like a thunderbolt with his great control and incisive running. Arzani was an X-factor player for the future. The final warm-up game was against Hungary in Budapest and the Socceroos again won, this time 2-1. Arzani again came off the bench and scored his first goal for the Socceroos. These two wins would see Australia head to Russia with a degree of confidence and optimism.

2018 World Cup Finals

This was a huge chance for Russia and its President, Vladimir Putin, to show off the country to the world by hosting the biggest global sporting event on the planet. Billions of dollars had been spent and the planning was meticulous. There were some concerns leading into the tournament in relation to the size of the country and the distances between venues. I was again faced with a ticket dilemma with FIFA in charge and restricted to just three tickets—fortunately for all of Australia's games.

The Socceroos were drawn in Group C alongside France, Denmark, and Peru. Our games would be played in Kazan, Samara, and Sochi. It remains the greatest show on Earth, and Russia and Moscow were truly amazing places to experience. I was booked into the Green and Gold Army Moscow-based trip, staying at the Salut Hotel. Large numbers of Mexicans were also staying at the hotel so every time you went down to the lobby, it was like a full-blown fiesta. There were guitars, drums, trumpets and singing with a good amount of drinking thrown in. That is another attraction of the World Cup—meeting the supporters from so many nations. I ran into a group of French supporters at Gorky Park before their clash with the Socceroos and it was fantastic. Likewise, the large contingent of supporters from Peru en route to Sochi and at the stadium were in full-on party mode.

Australia 1, France 2
(*Halftime*: 0–0)
Scorer: Jedinak
16 June 2018
Referee: Andres Cunha (Uruguay)
Crowd: 41,279
Kazan Stadium, Kazan, Russia

Australia: Mat Ryan, Josh Risdon, Aziz Behich, Trent Sainsbury, Mark Milligan, Mile Jedinak, Mathew Leckie, Aaron Mooy, Robbie Kruse (Daniel Arzani 84), Andrew Nabbout (Tomi Juric 64), Tom Rogic (Jackson Irvine 72)
France: Hugo Lloris, Benjamin Pavard, Lucas Hernandez, Raphael Varane, Samuel Umtiti, N'Golo Kante, Corentin Tolisso (Blaise Matuidi 78), Paul Pogba, Antoine Griezmann (Olivier Giroud 70), Kylian Mbappe, Ousmane Dembele (Nabil Fekir 70)

Australia performed well against the highly rated French side and gave its supporters, numbering over 10,000 at the match, a real buzz. The game overall was not a spectacle, but Australia was so close to pulling off a draw. History was made with the World Cup's first video assistant referee (VAR) decision to award a goal in the 81st minute. The Socceroos were unlucky when a Paul Pogba shot took a wicked deflection off Aziz Behich and spun up over the top of Mat Ryan, came off the crossbar and crept in.

The opening goal had seen Australia's Josh Risdon penalised for a sliding challenge on Antoine Griezmann, allowing the Atletico Madrid forward to dispatch a penalty. Parity was restored minutes later when French defender Samuel Umtiti handled Aaron Mooy's free kick, and Australia equalised through Mile Jedinak's penalty.

Kylian Mbappe sparkled early on, racing beyond the Australia backline to test goalkeeper Mat Ryan after 93 seconds. That sparked a concerted offensive by Didier Deschamps' team, but Australia stemmed the tide as the half progressed. The Socceroos did well to curb the early onslaught. Kylian Mbappe, Griezmann and Pogba all had shots on target inside the first five minutes, meaning Ryan was the busiest man in the Kazan Arena. It was looking ominous for Australia, but fortunately Ryan was up to the task, pulling off four solid saves with the match just eight minutes old.

The longer the game went on, the more Australia dared to believe. Trent Sainsbury was instrumental in keeping the flamboyant French forwards scoreless in the opening 45 minutes. But it was the Socceroos who had the first and only real chance of the half when Aaron Mooy's wicked free kick was flicked on by Mathew Leckie, before the ball took a deflection off the boot of Corentin Tolisso and forced goalkeeper Hugo Lloris into a low save to his left. The French seemed rattled, while the Socceroos began to settle.

Sainsbury was immense at the heart of the defence. Not only did he make crucial interventions when needed, but his organisation of the backline and his reading of the play was outstanding. His partner at the back, Mark Milligan, also hardly put a foot wrong. The Socceroos looked compact and composed—exactly how Bert van Marwijk had been urging them to play. Mile Jedinak and Mooy in the middle of the park provided cover in defence and maintained the Socceroos' solid structure.

Technology provided the talking points in an otherwise flat encounter that failed to inspire. In a frenetic four minutes during the opening of the second half, VAR was used twice to influence goals. Risdon was the first player to be adversely affected with a penalty awarded a minute after the Australian fullback appeared to touch the ball onto Griezmann before the striker went down. Bert van Marwijk's side then received a penalty of their own, with Umtiti's handball confirmed by Uruguayan referee Andrés Cunha after it had been checked on VAR.

While all the pre-match talk was of France's much vaunted front three—Dembele, Griezmann and Kylian Mbappe—they were largely ineffective. Mbappe, the youngest Frenchman to play in a major tournament at 19 years and six months, offered the most danger but was contained by a well-drilled Australian defence, coupled with a plodding French midfield. Griezmann did score from the penalty spot, but he looked a shadow of the player who had scored seven times and provided two assists in his past two major tournaments. Both he and Dembele were withdrawn after 70 minutes.

Olivier Giroud, Griezmann's replacement, struggled to get involved but he crucially provided the ball to Pogba, advancing from midfield, for the winning goal.

With limited time to prepare, Van Marwijk gave his Socceroos' side the appearance of being well worthy of earning a creditable draw. Australia was aiming to emulate their 2006 World cup achievements, the only time they had previously qualified from the group stages in four appearances at the Finals. There was enough promise in this showing to suggest they could approach the next game against Denmark with optimism.

French coach Didier Deschamps stated: 'The opening match is always a dangerous one and we are very happy to have won today, we are in a good position. It was a highly difficult match; the Australian team was very good and as far as France is concerned, we were not quick enough going forward.'

Bert van Marwijk commented: 'We showed guts, and we could be ourselves, but the next game is another game and this gives us confidence. The French did not know what to do for large parts of the game, but France is not my problem, and I will not talk about them. I wish them luck.'

On reflection, it was an impressive opening by the Socceroos. However, the 2-1 defeat was a tough result to stomach. France was favoured to win the World Cup but needed the VAR and a lucky deflection to steal the win after being drawn into a tough battle with the Socceroos. There was much to like about the Australian performance and plenty to look forward to when they took the field against Denmark and Peru, yet van Marwijk couldn't hide the bitter taste of defeat: 'To lose with such a lucky goal, it was disappointing. I think we can be proud of the way we played against one of the best teams in the world. We also had chances. Yeah, I'm (confident going into the rest of the games) but I'm disappointed about the result. I think we at least deserved a point.'

Australia now prepared for their second game against Denmark. While the result against a top side like France was uplifting, being amongst the 10,000 Australian fans in the stadium, the majority were screaming for Tim Cahill to be brought onto the field. He was 38 years of age but had been the Socceroos' most potent weapon during the qualifiers. He also brought an element of unease into the thinking of any opposition, particularly with balls in the air into the box. One only need think back to the exploits of veteran Roger Milla with Cameroon at the 1990 and 1994 World Cup Finals to imagine Cahill's potential impact.

Australia 1, Denmark 1

(*Halftime*: 1–1)

Scorer: Jedinak

21 June 2018

Referee: Antonio Mateu (Spain)
Crowd: 40,727
Samara Arena, Samara, Russia

Australia: Mat Ryan, Josh Risdon, Aziz Behich, Trent Sainsbury, Mark Milligan, Aaron Mooy, Mathew Leckie, Mile Jedinak, Robbie Kruse (Daniel Arzani 68), Andrew Nabbout (Tomi Juric 75), Tom Rogic (Jackson Irvine 82)
Denmark: Kasper Schmeichel, Henrik Dalsgaard, Jens Stryger Larsen, Simon Kjaer, Andreas Christensen, Thomas Delaney, Yussuf Poulsen (Martin Braithwaite 59), Lasse Schoene, Christian Eriksen, Pione Sisto, Nicolai Jorgensen (Andreas Cornelius 68)

Denmark was a quality side, make no mistake, but this was a game Australia needed to win and should have gone after. But inexcusably, they were tentative and took ages to click into gear.

Again, Tim Cahill warmed the bench and was given no minutes to inspire and lift his team-mates. Just him being on the pitch could have been the spark that ignited the Australian players. I truly believe that 15 to 20 minutes of Cahill in both opening games could have ignited something from the Socceroos. Instead, it was a cautious, no-frills approach. Young Daniel Arzani again came off the bench and that was a positive move, but Cahill was left watching on.

The Socceroos' World Cup pulse was still beating after this draw—but only just. Mile Jedinak, with help from the VAR, cancelled out Christian Eriksen's early stunner as the Socceroos drew 1-1 with Denmark at Samara Arena. It meant the Socceroos were still in with a chance heading into their final group match against Peru.

Daniel Arzani and Mathew Leckie had chances to grab a winner in the dying minutes of the game, but in the end, the Socceroos had to settle for the draw in what was an entertaining match.

The Socceroos finished the first half strongly and really built on that momentum in the second. Aaron Mooy, Tom Rogic and Mat Leckie were a constant threat. There was a lift when Arzani replaced Robbie Kruse. While Arzani made an impact, Andrew Nabbout was forced off the field with 20 minutes remaining after appearing to painfully dislocate his shoulder and he was replaced by Tomi Juric.

The Danes started brightly, and it was little surprise that Christian Eriksen was first on the scoresheet. Being aware of the threat of Eriksen made it no easier for the Socceroos to stop him. A reverse flick from Jorgensen found the Spurs' star just inside the box and he powered home a great volley just seven minutes into the game.

Minutes before Denmark's opener, a counterattack led to a corner for the Socceroos. Aaron Mooy took it, Leckie leapt, but his free header went over the crossbar. Leckie remained a constant threat and Tom Rogic was finding pockets of space. The Socceroos then became the beneficiaries of a VAR decision. Replays showed a deliberate handball in the box by Poulsen, and the referee pointed to the spot. Jedinak stepped up and scored. He became the only player in World Cup history to score three or more goals from the penalty spot.

Aaron Mooy went close from distance for Australia soon after before Denmark's Pione Sisto was left holding his head after a curling shot from outside the area flashed just wide. Jorgensen then couldn't find the target with a free header after sneaking behind Australia's defence, while Sisto wasted a further two chances.

Australia was the better side in the second stanza, and van Marwijk was clearly disappointed after the match: 'I feel we should have won. It's like against France. I'm disappointed and proud, and feel we deserved more. I honestly think we've deserved four points from these two games. So, I'm very disappointed. It is just the last piece of the puzzle we are missing. Now we must concentrate on Peru.'

It would be 'do or die' for the Socceroos against Peru and they would also need some luck with the result of the game between Denmark and France.

Australia 0, Peru 2
(*Halftime*: 0–1)
26 June 2018
Referee: Sergei Karasev (Russia)
Crowd: 44,073
Fisht Stadium, Sochi, Russia

Australia: Mat Ryan, Josh Risdon, Aziz Behich, Trent Sainsbury, Mark Milligan, Mile Jedinak, Mathew Leckie, Aaron Mooy, Robbie Kruse (Daniel Arzani 58), Tomi Juric (Tim Cahill 53), Tom Rogic (Jackson Irvine 72)
Peru: Pedro Gallese, Luis Advincula, Miguel Trauco, Christian Ramos, Anderson Santamaria, Yoshimar Yotun (Pedro Aquino 46), Andre Carrillo

(Wilder Cartagena 79), Renato Tapia (Paolo Hurtado 63), Christian Cueva, Edison Flores, Paolo Guerrero

It was an agonising experience for the Socceroo supporters in Sochi. Australia was still hoping for a place in the last 16 following the performances against France and Denmark, but it all ended with a whimper. Goals in each half from André Carrillo and Paolo Guerrero gave Peru a consolation win, leaving Australia at the bottom of the group. Even if Australia had won, their fate had been sealed, with Denmark drawing against France to secure second place in the group.

Outgoing Socceroos' coach Bert van Marwijk praised the Australian team but lamented its lack of goals throughout the group stage: 'It is not a success but also not a failure. Everyone saw the way we performed, and we have got lots of compliments. But compliments don't win you games, goals do… Against France in football terms, we were at least the equal, and against Denmark we were better. Today I have the same feeling but in all three games we couldn't make the difference with goals.'

Australia knew they faced a delicate balancing act against Peru. They had to avoid leaving themselves open while pushing for the win they needed. An early shot from Mile Jedinak was a statement of intent. But Jedinak's desire also got him into trouble when he was booked for a head-high tackle on Christian Cueva.

As if Lima's Estadio Nacional had been transplanted to Russia, the roar of support for the Peruvian team was deafening, especially when their team took the lead. In a match of shadow boxing, Peru suddenly found a perfect punch. A ball over the top of the Australian defence was gathered in the corner by captain Paolo Guerrero, who looked up and curled a deep cross towards André Carrillo. Arriving unheralded at the far corner of the box, Carrillo struck a perfect volley back across Mat Ryan and into the bottom corner. Replays appeared to show Peru was offside, and van Marwijk agreed: 'We had lots of chances and shots, but Peru had maybe two shots and scored. Their first goal I think was offside, so we didn't have luck.'

Australia desperately tried to respond, but chances went begging. Tom Rogic, playing like a man on a mission, ran at the Peruvians and beat four players, but saw his shot beaten away by Pedro Gallese. Then Rogic freed Robbie Kruse into the box for a cutback, but as the goal gaped for Mathew Leckie, Anderson Santamaria somehow scooped the ball away.

By halftime, Australia had mustered six shots, but only one on target. Peru seized the moment in the 50th minute. A move opened space for Cueva to charge down the left and he struck a cross that deflected off Jedinak into the path of Guerrero. The captain struck it at goal and a slight deflection off Mark Milligan helped it past Mat Ryan.

Finally, van Marwijk produced his trump cards, sending on Tim Cahill and Daniel Arzani. Immediately, there was a flurry of chances—Aziz Behich's shot brushing the post on its way wide and Cahill's goal-bound effort hitting his own man. Arzani hit the top of the net with a daring volley from the edge of the box, and then Behich side-footed a low cross just a fraction beyond Cahill's run.

As both the game and the World Cup drifted away, the Australian fans were denied the consolation of Cahill scoring at a fourth World Cup. A day of such hope ended in bitter disappointment. It was a long trip back to Moscow for the disappointed Socceroos' support base.

On reflection, there was so much to like and admire about the Socceroos in Russia, but a real desire to go at opponents was missing. I honestly believe had Ange Postecoglou remained in charge, the team would have performed better. I am not blaming van Marwijk, but Postecoglou's knowledge of the team going back over four years (and knowing his players 'inside out') would have made a difference. I think he would have made greater use of Tim Cahill as an impact player. Cahill still carried an X-factor and a fear element. Certainly, the Socceroos' supporters in Russia were all unanimous in screaming for him to be brought on throughout the three games.

The Socceroos now had to look forward and start planning for Qatar in four years' time—when some of the younger players like Daniel Arzani, Jackson Irvine, Aziz Behich, and Josh Risdon should be at their peak. Graham Arnold would take over as coach to lead us on that journey. 'Arnie' was a top player for the Socceroos and had already built up an impressive CV as a coach. He had been assistant to the master Guus Hiddink in 2006 and had a short spell as interim coach before Pim Verbeek was appointed coach. Arnold also had a top record in the A-League with the Central Coast Mariners and Sydney FC.

The World Cup Finals in 2018 would be memorable on several accounts, including the much-debated introduction of the VAR system. Highlighting the quality of Australia's performance was the fact that the eventual winner of the tournament was France. There were some shocks along the way—Brazil was knocked out in the quarter-finals 2–1 by Belgium. The aura surrounding Brazil seemed to have faded following the German 7-1 annihilation four years before. Croatia, led by the little maestro, Luca Modrić, was a Finals' revelation and would go on to dispatch England 2-1 in the semi-final. France overcame Belgium 1-0 in the other semi-final.

The French, with their stars on show, deservedly took the Final 4-2 with goals from Griezmann, Pogba, Mbappe and an own goal from Mandzukic. I was in Paris for the Final—a very exciting place to be and I watched the game on a big screen at a local watering hole.

WORLD CUP QUALIFICATION AND FINALS 2022-QATAR

The Intervening Years— The Australian team, 2018-2022

The campaign to qualify for Russia had been arduous and draining. The realisation was very clear: Asia was now a very different qualifying route to the World Cup Finals and no games were guaranteed. Like Russia, the journey to Qatar would likely prove another marathon excursion.

I had made the decision to boycott the 2022 World Cup Finals following the FIFA decision to award the tournament to Qatar. FIFA has always been synonymous with skulduggery, backroom deals, shonky decisions, and corruption, but nothing in the past comes even remotely close to this decision—and the money involved to ensure it was made. I had experienced three wonderful World Cup Finals and would love to have attended another, but Qatar also had an appalling human rights record that made it impossible for me to consider going to support the Socceroos there.

Four months after their exit from the World Cup in Russia and under new supremo Graham Arnold, the Socceroos had an impressive 4-0 win over Kuwait in Kuwait City. A month later, Australia went up against fellow Asian heavyweight, South Korea, in Brisbane in a friendly game that ended 1-1. Another friendly followed in Sydney against Lebanon; the game was used as a farewell match for Socceroo legend Tim Cahill who came on for the last ten minutes to soak up the accolades of an appreciative crowd—Australia won 3-0. The Socceroos had an end-of-year friendly against Oman as a preparation game for the Asian Cup Finals in 2019. They won the match 5-0 in what had been an impressive four-game run to start Graham Arnold's reign.

The Socceroos opened their Asian Cup Finals match in the United Arab Emirates with an unexpected 1-0 defeat to Jordan. Australia then regrouped and downed Palestine 3-0 before overcoming Syria 3-2 to progress to the last 16. The Socceroos next overcame Uzbekistan 4-2 on penalties in another below-par performance. Australia then faced the hosts the United Arab Emirates in the quarter-final and despite having the better of the play and chances, they were beaten 1-0 and eliminated. Nevertheless, the tournament was a good preparation for the World Cup qualifiers.

It would be six months before the Socceroos took the field again. They were beaten 1-0 by South Korea in a friendly game in Busan. Australia's 2022 World Cup campaign would commence against Kuwait, who historically had given the Socceroos some real problems in the past.

Australia 3, Kuwait 0
(*Halftime*: 3–0)
Scorers: Leckie (2) Mooy
10 September 2019
Referee: Muhammad Taqi Aljaafari Bin Jahari (Singapore)
Crowd: 11,852
Al Kuwait Sports Club Stadium, Kuwait City

Australia: Mathew Ryan, Rhyan Grant, Aziz Behich, Trent Sainsbury, Milos Degenek, James Jeggo, Aaron Mooy, Jackson Irvine (Mustafa Amini 82), Adam Taggart (Apostolos Giannou 68), Mathew Leckie (Awer Mabil 69), Brandon Borrello
Kuwait: Sulaiman Abdulghafoor, Hamad Al Harbi, Fahad Al Hajeri, Fahad Hammoud Al Reshidi, Amer Al Fadhel, Ahmad Al Dhufairi, Shereedah Al Shereedah (Bader Al Mutawa 46), Sultan Al Enezi, Hussain Al-Musawi (Faisal Al Azemi 77), Abdullah Al Mutairi (Yousef Naser 46), Faisal Zayed

Australia beat Kuwait 3-0 and made a solid opening to start their qualifying campaign for the 2022 World Cup. The away game was played in sweltering conditions. It was billed as a tough test for a young Socceroos side that included 12 players who had 10 caps or less, but captain Mathew Leckie's brace and Aaron Mooy's beautiful shot easily secured all three points in the first half at Al Kuwait Sports Club Stadium.

The hosts frantically tried to force themselves back into the game after the break, but they couldn't find the net and Australia took control as the clock ticked down. Coach Graham Arnold said: 'It was a fantastic win; you know a very positive start to the campaign and a lot of younger fresh faces that we've brought in over the last six months really stood up tonight. We're very proud of them.'

Mat Leckie, who wore the captain's armband after Mark Milligan was injured in the lead-up to the game, thought it was always going to be tough with the temperature at 36 degrees, but he knew the Socceroos could get the result they wanted if they stayed vigilant: 'As I said to the boys before the game, concentration and clarity is going to be the biggest thing and we did it well tonight. I think we were really composed, scored the goals we needed to and saw the game out. Big one for me also to captain my country with Milligan out, but the most important thing was the win, and we did it.'

The Socceroos looked a class above their opponents, but it took a lucky deflection from Leckie to open the scoring after just six minutes. Australia broke the deadlock when playmaker Jackson Irvine's low drive from just inside the box bounced through a sea of legs, including Adam Taggart's, to Leckie who poked it across Kuwaiti goalkeeper Sulaiman Abdulghafoor and into the bottom right corner.

The visitors doubled their lead in the 30th minute when Jackson Irvine rose to nod Mooy's corner over the defence to the waiting Leckie, who stabbed the ball into the bottom right corner. Leckie, the most experienced man in the Socceroos squad, was making his 62nd appearance for the national team.

Kuwait worked hard to deny their opponents ball time, but the deft passes and surging runs of Irvine, Mooy, Leckie, Brandon Borrello and Aziz Behich couldn't be contained. A fluffed clearance from Kuwait's goalkeeper fell to Adam Taggart and he helped Australia put the result beyond doubt in the 38th minute by teeing up Mooy for a cracking shot from outside the box.

Australia sat back in the second half, content to hit the hosts on the counterattack. Kuwait was desperately searching for a way into the game. Al-Musawi had two chances in the 53rd and 59th minutes, but only the later shot required the outstretched Mat Ryan to tip it over the crossbar. Yousef Nasser had an opportunity after Trent Sainsbury's awkward clearance, but Ryan parried his shot past the post.

On a hot evening in Kuwait City, the game slowly petered out as the visitors happily claimed the three points. Right on fulltime, Awer Mabil found himself one-on-one with the Kuwaiti keeper, but the stumbling Abdulghafoor got a hand to the winger's lob.

The win moved Australia into equal first in qualifying Group B with Kuwait, with their next match at home against Nepal.

A month later, Australia was back at home to take on Nepal, a game they were expected to win easily. The Socceroos revealed their new giant centre-back Harry Souttar from Stoke City. Souttar revealed in this match that he would be an enormous problem in the air for his Asian opponents. He is a veritable Goliath and presented a towering menace in the box.

Australia 5, Nepal 0
(*Halftime*: 3–0)
Scorers: Maclaren (3) Souttar (2)
10 October 2019
Referee: Thoriq Munir Alkatiri (Indonesia)
Crowd: 18,563
Bruce Stadium, Canberra

Australia: Mathew Ryan, Rhyan Grant, Aziz Behich, Bailey Wright, Harry Souttar, Mark Milligan, Aaron Mooy (Apostolos Giannou 62), Jackson Irvine, Jamie Maclaren, Mathew Leckie (Awer Mabil 77), Craig Goodwin (Ajdin Hrustic 71)
Nepal: Kiran Chemjong, Dinesh Rajbansi, Ranjit Dhimal, Ananta Tamang, Devendra Tamang, Rohit Chand, Ravi Paswan, Bishal Rai (Santosh Tamang 86), Anjan Bista (Tej Tamang 79), Sujal Shrestha, Abishek Rijal (Bimal Magar 66)

A Jamie Maclaren hat-trick helped the Socceroos to a 5–0 win over Nepal in a largely frustrating performance in Canberra to remain unbeaten in 2022 World Cup qualifying.

Maclaren had a brace inside the opening 20 minutes which, along with a debut Harry Souttar goal just before the half-hour mark, set the tone for a dominant first-half performance. The Socceroos mustered 16 shots to one from 73 per cent of possession.

An own goal off another towering Souttar header got Australia their fourth early in the second half, before Maclaren completed his hat-trick in the dying seconds of the contest.

Despite the mismatch and margin of victory, the Socceroos would have been disappointed not to have scored more. Coach Graham Arnold was happy with the win but echoed his pre-match demand for more ruthlessness from his side: 'We have a lot of work to do. We created plenty of chances, but we have to be more ruthless when it counts.'

From the start, it looked as though Nepal were going to be in for a rough night. The visitors were charitably credited with a solitary off-target shot in a hopeless mismatch between the teams ranked 44th and 161st in FIFA world rankings.

Desperate Nepalese defending resulted in 11 of the 33 goal-bound shots deflecting wide of the target. The midfield trio for the Socceroos looked in great touch, with Jackson Irvine displaying a full array of flicks and tricks to link with the lively Aaron Mooy, while Mark Milligan dictated play masterfully in front of the back four.

In an at-times frustrating encounter, the Socceroos would be thankful that Maclaren was in such good touch in front of goal. The Melbourne City striker had been in sublime form, scoring six goals in four FFA Cup matches, and the 26-year-old continued when wearing the gold of Australia. Having only scored once in 13 previous games, Maclaren had faced questions over his viability as an international goal scorer. Those questions were unlikely to be silenced in light of the opposition, but his hat-trick highlighted his poaching instincts.

All three of Maclaren's goals were scored in and around the six-yard box. After just five minutes, the striker pounced on a fumble by Kiran Chemjong in the Nepal goalmouth after Craig Goodwin's powerful drive from the edge of the penalty area. His second was simplicity itself as both fullbacks combined. Aziz Behich's cross was headed back across goal by Rhyan Grant to the unmarked Maclaren, who ghosted behind the centre-backs to net his second inside 20 minutes. He scored his third after latching on a through ball before slamming a shot past Chemjong from close range. Maclaren said it was his 'proudest moment in a football jersey. Representing my country in Canberra, scoring a hat-trick as a striker is the best feeling. You question are you good enough at this level and I had belief in the tough years.'

Maclaren alluded to the frustration in the second half but argued that the three points was the most important factor in the performance: 'You could see they were wasting time a bit and parking the bus, as you say. At the end of the day, we scored five, didn't concede. Happy with the three points but know it could have been more.'

Giant, Scottish-born Souttar (whose Australian ancestry had been seized upon by Arnold) had a comfortable outing in his maiden international. He was born in Aberdeen, but Australia-qualified by virtue of his WA-born mother. He had nothing to do in his own penalty area but was a constant threat in attack, leveraging his towering, 198-centimetre frame above the fragile Nepalese defenders.

Souttar netted the Socceroos' third with a stooping header as the Nepal defence abandoned its earlier tactic of crowding him. He was left free to run onto Mooy's pinpoint corner. His second goal came after his goal-bound header was unfortunately turned past Chemjong by Dinesh Rajbanshi.

However, any judgement of Souttar as an international quality centre-back would have to be adjourned until after a more stringent examination than Nepal could provide. He at least had family bragging rights—his brother John was yet to find the back of the net in his three senior appearances for Scotland at the time.

The Socceroos only had five days between games as they headed to Kaohsiung to take on Chinese Taipei, who were winless in the group. But they were expected to continue on their winning way.

Australia 7, Chinese Taipei 1
(*Halftime*: 4–0)
Scorers: Taggart (2), Irvine (2) Souttar (2) Maclaren
15 October 2019
Referee: Mongkolchai Pechsri (Thailand)
Crowd: 3,251
Kaohsiung National Stadium, Taiwan

Australia: Mathew Ryan, Rhyan Grant, Brad Smith, Harry Souttar, Milos Degenek, James Jeggo, Aaron Mooy (Mustafa Amini 62), Jackson Irvine, Adam Taggart (Jamie Maclaren 79), Brandon Borrello (Ajdin Hrustic 69), Awer Mabil
Taiwan: Wen-Chieh Pan, Ting-yang Chen, Ruei Wang, Wei-Chuan Chen, Tzu-Kuei Hung, Hao-Wei Chen, Chih-Hao Wen (Hsiangwei Lee 70), Po-Liang Chen (Yenshu Wu 61), Chen Yi-wei, Emilio Estevez (Will Donkin 68), En-Le Chu

Australia continued their perfect start to World Cup qualifying with a 7–1 hammering of a spirited Chinese Taipei side in Kaohsiung. Adam Taggart, Jackson Irvine, and Harry Souttar each scored twice, with Jamie Maclaren also finding the net with his fourth goal in a week for the national team. The win kept Australia comfortably on top of Group B with three victories in as many matches ahead of November's clash with Jordan in Amman.

Graham Arnold made six changes to the team that defeated Nepal 5–0, with Taggart given the nod ahead of hat-trick hero Maclaren. Taggart repaid Arnold's faith with a first-half double—just as he did the last time Australia played Taiwan back in 2012. He opened the scoring after 12 minutes with a diving header from a Rhyan Grant cross for his first international goal in six years.

Awer Mabil and Brad Smith then combined well on the left with a slick one-two before Taggart tapped home a Smith cross in the 19th minute. However, rather than roll over, Taipei showed their skill with a fine goal two minutes later when Chen Yi-wei ghosted between central defenders Milos Degenek and Souttar to send a bullet header past Mat Ryan. It was the first goal conceded in the qualifying campaign by the Australian goalkeeper who was captaining his nation for the first time.

The Socceroos restored their two-goal advantage in the 33rd minute when a great cross-field ball by Aaron Mooy found Grant in space and his right-wing centre pass was smashed home by Irvine. Irvine added his second three minutes later when he headed home a teasing Mabil cross in the 36th minute, ensuring Australia went in at halftime with a healthy 4–1 lead. He had a chance to claim a hat-trick after the restart following more good work by Smith and Mabil, but blazed his shot over the bar from inside the box.

Arnold's decision to replace Brandon Borrello with Ajdin Hrustic proved the source of a late flurry by the Socceroos. Hrustic twice found the head of Souttar—who now had three goals from his first two international appearances. Hrustic also set up Maclaren's second-half strike as Australia delivered the ruthless edge Arnold had been demanding all campaign. The unearthing of Harry Souttar and Ajdin Hrustic had added to Australia's stocks for the future.

A month later, Australia headed to Jordan for their biggest test of the campaign so far. Jordan had proven a difficult team for the Socceroos to overcome in recent years, and this away clash could well be telling on who held top spot in the group.

Australia 1, Jordan 0
(*Halftime*: 1–0)
Scorer: Taggart
14 November 2019
Referee: Fu Ming (China)
Crowd: 9,712
King Abdullah II Stadium, Amman

Australia: Mathew Ryan, Rhyan Grant, Brad Smith, Trent Sainsbury, Milos Degenek, James Jeggo, Awer Mabil (Martin Boyle 73), Aaron Mooy, Jackson Irvine, Adam Taggart (Mitchell Duke 70), Tom Rogic
Jordan: Amer Shafi Sabbah, Ehsan Manel Haddad, Mohammad Al Dumeiri (Salem Al Ajalin 80), Tareq Khattab, Yazan Abou Al Arab, Baha Abdel-Rahman, Ahmad Ersan, Noor Al Din Rawabdeh, Ahmed Samir (Mousa Suleiman Tamari 46), Yaseen Al-Bakhit, Baha Seif Faisal (Hamza Al-Dardoor 62)

Graham Arnold challenged Australia to win every remaining 2022 World Cup qualifier after they held on for an historic but gritty 1–0 win over Jordan in Amman. Before the victory, Australia had never beaten the hosts away. But the win was narrow with Jordan coming close to snatching a point several times in the closing stages of the match.

Jordan started aggressively, pressing the visitors, particularly down the left where playmaker Jackson Irvine was deployed to make way for the returning Tom Rogic in the middle. But Australia was the first to strike with Irvine setting up Taggart with a neat through ball threaded between the opposing centre-backs, and Taggart finished past goalkeeper Amer Shafi.

Jackson Irvine fluffed a glorious chance to double the lead off Aaron Mooy's corner in the 29th minute when the ball rebounded to his feet just outside the six-yard box, only for him to smash it over the crossbar.

After the break, Jordan coach Vital Borkelmans brought on dangerous forward Mousa Mohammad Suleiman for midfielder Ahmed Sameer Saleh. And the change nearly worked five minutes later when he rifled a shot over the top left corner of goal from just inside the box. Tareq Khattab then missed a golden opportunity to level when the unmarked defender headed wide from less than five yards out. The hosts again went close with 10 minutes remaining when Hamza Aldaradreh rose to meet Mousa's free kick, but Ryan made an unbelievable save to deny his header. The hosts continued to push, going close twice more, including when Aldaradreh rose to meet Yaseen Al-Bakhit's cross with only Ryan to beat, but he sent his header over.

Arnold believed his side had proved themselves in their toughest qualifier yet, but he demanded they maintain focus. He declared: 'We're going for 24 (points), you know I want, I expect the boys to build a winning mentality. That's what we talk a lot about, and we want to go through this whole phase undefeated and getting eight wins and getting 24 points and with a great goal difference. It's about improving every time we catch up, and every time we get into camp, it's about building what we've been building, and you can see our attacking players getting better and better and the mentality of the boys working-wise is fantastic.'

The Socceroos had suffered selection issues due to injuries and fatigue caused by long-distance travel during the campaign, but Arnold was optimistic he would soon be able field a full-strength side and that his squad wouldn't lose the cohesion they had developed over the four-month break. He added: 'They'll be fine. Like I said when I first turned up, it was 23–25 strangers and now, I've got 23 great mates that want to fight for each other and work for each other.'

Striker Adam Taggart, who scored the winner, said it had been a 'quality' campaign and that it would be a frustrating wait until the next match at home against Kuwait. However, he also added that 'it would be nice to freshen up and it was nice to end the year on a high.'

No-one could have foreseen that the game against Jordan would be the Australian team's last international game for 18 months as the world was thrown into confusion, fear, and disbelief with the onset of COVID-19. It will forever remain a historic moment as millions of people lost their lives in a pandemic that swept the globe. The virus first came to notice with an outbreak in Wuhan, China, in December 2019. Attempts to contain the outbreak failed, allowing the virus to spread to other areas of Asia and later, worldwide. The World Health Organization (WHO) declared the outbreak a public health emergency and a pandemic on 11 March 2020. The massive loss of life made it one of the deadliest in history. Sport and exercise suffered greatly as the global outbreak resulted in the closure of gyms, stadiums, pools, dance and fitness studios, physiotherapy centres, parks, playgrounds, and team activities.

When the COVID-19 restrictions and lockdowns began to lift, the football World Cup qualifications resumed in mid-2021. However, the Socceroos' qualification chances faced a huge hurdle in that they could not play any of their home games in Australia as the borders were still firmly locked. It would be a compact and hectic schedule to make up for the lost games over 18 months. The first game against Kuwait was originally scheduled for early 2020 but the Socceroos would now go up against Kuwait in Kuwait in June of 2021, despite the match first being designated as an Australian home game.

Australia 3, Kuwait 0
(*Halftime*: 2–0)
Scorers: Irvine, Leckie, Hrustic
3 June 2021
Referee: Jumpei Iida (Japan)
Crowd: The game was played behind closed doors due to COVID 19
Jaber Al-Ahmad International Stadium, Kuwait City, Kuwait

Australia: Mathew Ryan, Milos Degenek, Ryan McGowan, Aziz Behich, Fran Karacic, James Holland (Kenneth Dougall 64), Ajdin Hrustic (Riley McGree 83), Jackson Irvine, Awer Mabil (Chris Ikonomidis 74), Martin Boyle, Mathew Leckie (Mitchell Duke 78)
Kuwait: Sulaiman Abdulghafoor, Fahad Al Hajeri, Ahmad Ebraheem, Fahad Hammoud (Hamad Al Harbi 75), Hamad Al Qallaf, Fahad Al Ebrahim (Mohammad Al Huwaidi 83), Mobarck Al Faneeni (Yousef Naser 74), Shabaib Al Khaldi, Fawaz Ayedh (Bader Al Motawaa 62), Ahmad Al Dhafeeri, Bandar Al Salamah (Eid Al Rasheedi 62)

The Socceroos cruised to a 3–0 victory over Kuwait in stifling conditions at an empty Jaber Al-Ahmad International Stadium in Kuwait City. First-half goals to Mathew Leckie and Jackson Irvine (who slammed home after Hibernian teammate Martin Boyle missed from the spot), sent the Socceroos on their way. Ajdin Hrustic scored Australia's third with a wicked, curling free kick in the only real highlight of a sluggish second half, as Australia consolidated their position in the Middle Eastern heat.

The win took the Socceroos five points clear of Kuwait at the top of qualifying

Group B after a fifth win in five games. Although Australia were expected to comfortably beat a team 107 places beneath them in the world rankings, Graham Arnold would have been pleased with his side's fluidity going forward. In baking-hot conditions, with temperatures cooling to 38 degrees at kick-off from a high of 45 earlier in the day, the Socceroos knew they had to start quickly, and they did.

Despite not playing an international for 567 days —the longest stretch without a match for Australia since the mid-70s—Arnold's side were dominant from the start. Martin Boyle in particular was impressive, bursting forward down the left throughout a first half in which the Socceroos dominated territory to the tune of 72 per cent, managing 15 shots to three.

Both fullbacks also pressed forward at every opportunity, with debutant Fran Karačić and Aziz Behich both posing questions for an increasingly disorganised Kuwait defence. Skipper Leckie, who scored twice the last time these two sides met, gave the Socceroos a crucial early goal inside the opening minute, rising highest in the penalty area after Kuwait failed to clear a corner.

The Socceroos' second came after Hrustic earned a highly debatable penalty after whizzing into the penalty area and theatrically falling to the ground, much to the chagrin of the Kuwaiti defenders. One of them, Bandar Al Salamah, was booked for his enthusiastic protests. Boyle's initial spot kick was saved, but his Hibernian teammate Jackson Irvine reacted fastest to slam the loose ball past stricken keeper Abdulghafoor, whose kicking of the post in frustration appeared entirely justified based on the replay.

Boyle should have scored in open play shortly after, having been beautifully played in by Irvine, but he poked his shot wide of the goal—one of 11 of Australia's 15 shots that were either blocked or off target in the first half.

Kuwait, who posed little threat aside from long-range efforts in the first half, were slightly better after the break, but never mounted a serious challenge on the Australian defence, with Mat Ryan needing to make just one save from their six shots.

As play understandably slowed in the oppressive heat, clear-cut chances also dried up, despite Arnold handing debuts to Blackpool's two-goal, play-off hero Kenny Dougall and Riley McGree. However, Hrustic capped a superb individual performance by lighting up the second half with a peach of a free kick from 25 yards out to further extend the Socceroos' lead.

The Socceroos did not have long to recover and would next take on Chinese Taipei. The games would now come thick and fast. The fact that Australia was forced to play their home games away added to the difficulties. Five days after the victory over Kuwait, Australia had travelled to another international venue: Taiwan.

Australia 5, Chinese Taipei 1
(*Halftime*: 3–0)
Scorers: Souttar, Maclaren, Sainsbury, Duke (2)
8 June 2021
Referee: Al-Abda (Qatar)
Crowd: The game was played behind closed doors due to COVID 19
Jaber Al-Ahmad International Stadium, Kuwait City, Kuwait

Australia: Danny Vukovic, Rhyan Grant, Curtis Good, Harry Souttar, Trent Sainsbury, Kenneth Dougall (Connor Metcalfe 62), Riley McGree (Ajdin Hrustic 74), Denis Genreau (Ruon Tongyik 84), Brandon Borrello (Chris Ikonomidis 62), Mitchell Duke, Jamie Maclaren (Nikita Rukavytsya 75)
Chinese Taipei: Shih Shin-An, Pai Shao-Yu, Chen Chao-An, Chen Ting-Yang, Chen Wei-Chuan, Cheng Hao, Gao Wei-Jie (Li Mao 67), Wu Chun-Ching (Liang Meng Hsin 80), Yoshitaka Komori (Tu Shao-Chieh 47), Emilio Estevez (Lin Ming-Wei 67), Chen Jui-Chieh (Hsu Hsing-Pin 80)

The Socceroos booked their place in the third stage of World Cup qualifying with two games to spare following a dominant 5–1 victory over minnows, Chinese Taipei. Australia had now won six straight games either side of an 18-month lay-off for the first time since Frank Farina's side in 2001.

In 38-degree heat, Arnold named an entirely different starting XI from the 3–0 win over Kuwait, including handing a debut to Denis Genreau in the heart of the midfield. He was joined by two more debutants off the bench (Connor Metcalfe and Ruon Tongyik), adding to the three players who debuted against Kuwait. Kenny Dougall and Riley McGree made their first starts in the green and gold in this match against Chinese Taipei, while defender Curtis Good started at left-back for his first cap since his 2014 debut.

A resolute Chinese Taipei, exactly 100 places below the Socceroos in the world rankings, made things somewhat tough for the Australians on a poor-quality pitch. In what was becoming a regular feature, Harry Souttar headed Australia in front in the 11th minute, with Jamie Maclaren and Trent Sainsbury also scoring in the first half before Mitch Duke added a second-half brace.

The Socceroos were busy early and took the lead when McGree picked out Souttar from a corner and the Stoke City defender powered home a back-post header. Maclaren was later hacked down as he streaked towards goal in the 26th minute and he blasted the penalty down the middle to double Australia's lead. Three minutes later, Brandon Borrello spurned a golden opportunity when he put a tap-in onto the post. In the 41st minute, McGree floated in a corner to the far post where Sainsbury, wearing the captain's armband, comfortably headed home.

Less than a minute into the second half, Genreau burst forward and found Borrello, whose clever cross was well met by Duke at the near post for his first Socceroos' goal since 2013.

The Aussies would have been disappointed after conceding off the back of sloppy defending in the 62nd minute. Tu Shao-Chieh burst forward and cut the ball back for the inexplicably unmarked Wei-Jie Gao, who smacked a first-time shot past Danny Vukovic.

Striker Nikita Rukavytsya made his first appearance since November 2017 in the 74th minute. Ten minutes later, substitute Ajdin Hrustic dropped a clever ball to Rukavytsya who held his ground and cut the ball back for Duke to bury his second and round out the result.

Australia now had a maximum 18 points from six games to sit top of Group B, and with matches against Nepal and Jordan remaining, a top-two finish was guaranteed.

Only three days later, the Socceroos would take the field again against Nepal in a game Australia would be expected to win by a big margin. Graham Arnold, attempting to keep his side fresh, again rotated players for this match.

Australia 3, Nepal 0
(*Halftime*: 2–0)
Scorers: Leckie, Karacic, Boyle
11 June 2021
Referee: Ahmed Abu Bakar Said Al Kaf (Oman)
Crowd: The game was played behind closed doors due to COVID 19
Jaber Al-Ahmad International Stadium, Kuwait City, Kuwait

Australia: Andrew Redmayne (Lawrence Thomas 83), Fran Karacic, Aziz Behich, Milos Degenek, Harry Souttar, Jackson Irvine, Ajdin Hrustic (Ruon Tongyik 83), Connor Metcalfe, Martin Boyle (Awer Mabil 72), Mitchell Duke (Nikita Rukavytsya 62), Mathew Leckie (Jamie Maclaren 62)
Nepal: Kiran Chemjong, Goutham Shrestha, Suman Aryal, Ananta Tamang, Rohit Chand, Pujan Uparkoti, Bishal Rai (Kamal Thapa 90+1), Arik Bista (Suraj Jeu Thakuri (90+2), Nawayung Shrestha (Manish Dangi 61), Sunil Bai (Anjan Bista 46), Suman Lama (Ayush Ghalan 90+1)
Coach: Abdullah Mejeid Farea Matar Sahl Al Mutairi

The Socceroos recorded their seventh successive World Cup qualifying victory with a 3-0 win over a plucky Nepal. Having already secured progression to the next stage of the Asian Football Confederation qualifiers for the 2022 World Cup, the Australians sealed top spot in Group B with their win. It took them to 21 points from seven Group B matches, and it was the first time the Socceroos had won seven straight matches in 24 years.

Captain Mat Leckie, right-back Fran Karačić and attacking weapon Martin Boyle all scored in steamy conditions in Kuwait City against a brave Nepali side that was reduced to 10 men on the stroke of halftime when Rohit Chand was sent off. The Socceroos' win would have been greater if not for some impressive work from Nepali goalkeeper Kiran Chemjong, who foiled the Australians on several occasions, particularly in the second half.

Coach Graham Arnold made nine changes to the side that started in Australia's 5-1 thrashing of Chinese Taipei. Signs were ominous early for Nepal, with the Socceroos needing just six minutes to take the lead. Left-back Aziz Behich provided an inch-perfect cross that was met by Leckie, who headed the ball home for Australia. Scorer turned provider in the 38th minute when the impressive Leckie cut the ball back into the path of Karačić, who in just his second appearance for the Socceroos, scored his first international goal.

Already down 2-0, Nepal's task became even tougher in the 45th minute when they were reduced to 10 men with the dismissal of Chand. The 29-year-old defender was shown a straight red card for a last-man foul on Boyle, who had been found with a sublime flick from Leckie. The Socceroos were in no mood to show their opponents any mercy, and their dominance was rewarded with a third goal in the

57th minute from Boyle. The Scotland-born attacking weapon netted from close range after being found at the far post with a perfectly timed pass from his Hibernian teammate, Jackson Irvine.

But try as they might, the Socceroos couldn't increase their lead any further against a Nepali side that defended desperately. Australia started with their third different goalkeeper in three games, with Sydney FC gloveman Andrew Redmayne earning just his second national team cap, having debuted for Australia in June 2019. Redmayne, behind Mat Ryan and Danny Vukovic in the custodian pecking order, had little to do as Nepal failed to mount any significant attacks. He was replaced in the 83rd minute by the fourth keeper in the current Australian squad, former Melbourne Victory gloveman Lawrence Thomas, who made his international debut.

Australia would have their final Group B game against Jordan again in Kuwait City only five days later. They had already secured top spot for the final round of qualification, but Jordan would be a major test.

Australia 1, Jordan 0
(*Halftime*: 0–0)
Scorer: Souttar
16 June 2021
Referee: Woo-Sung Kim (South Korea)
Crowd: The game was played behind closed doors due to COVID 19.
Jaber Al-Ahmad International Stadium, Kuwait City, Kuwait

Australia: Mathew Ryan, Milos Degenek, Harry Souttar, Trent Sainsbury, Rhyan Grant (Fran Karacic 90+3), Aziz Behich, Jackson Irvine, Kenneth Dougall (James Holland 70), Jamie Maclaren (Adam Taggert 70), Ajdin Hrustic (Riley McGree 83), Martin Boyle (Awer Mabil 83)
Jordan: Mutaz Yasin, Ehsan Manel Haddad, Salem Al-Ajalin (Ali Olwan 86), Mohannad Khairullah, Yazin Al-Arab, Baha Abdel-Rahman (Ibrahim Sadeh 85), Mousa Al-Tamari, Noor Al-Rawabdeh (Odai Al Saify 85), Ahmed Samir (Hamza Al-Dardoor 72), Yousef Al-Rawshdeh (Ahmad Ersan 72), Baha Seif

The Socceroos completed a perfect first phase of 2022 World Cup qualification, defeating Jordan 1–0 to make it eight wins from eight games. Eight straight wins also set a new record for the men's team. Australia now advanced to the next stage with 28 goals scored and just two conceded.

The victory in stifling conditions at Jaber Al-Ahmad International Stadium in Kuwait also represented the first time Australia had recorded back-to-back wins over Jordan, who were knocked out of qualifying as a result.

Coach Graham Arnold said: 'I'm extremely proud. I'm so proud because of what these boys have done with winning seven games away from home, eight straight. The heat was brutal, 47 degrees and these boys played as though it wasn't hot at all.'

It was the stiffest test of the Socceroos' qualification campaign, but they secured the win through a 77th-minute header from defender Harry Souttar, his sixth goal in green and gold. As he has done throughout the qualifiers, Arnold swung several changes to the side that last defeated Nepal 3–0, with captain Mat Ryan, Trent Sainsbury, Rhyan Grant, Jamie Maclaren and Kenny Dougall all coming into the starting XI.

But it was one of those players holding their place that almost gave the Socceroos an early lead when Jackson Irvine advanced into the Jordanian penalty area and hammered a third-minute effort just over the bar. Seeking to keep their dreams of a maiden World Cup appearance alive, Jordan went close three minutes later when Baha'Abdel-Rahman bent a free kick just wide of the goal.

After a turnover in the 76th minute, Aziz Behich almost set Australia up to take the lead. He burst forward and delivered a cross that eventually fell for substitute James Holland to hammer a shot, but it took a deflection and hit the post before being scrambled out for a corner. However, the Jordanians were unable to prevent Souttar from rising up with his almost two-metre-tall frame and heading home the resulting delivery from Martin Boyle.

Jordan's comeback efforts were dealt a hammer blow in the 87th minute when they were reduced to 10 men after a frustrated Mousa Al-Tamari was shown a red card for striking Behich's face as the latter clashed with Ihsan Haddad over a stiff challenge.

In concluding remarks, Arnold reflected: 'Where are we at [as a team]? I reckon we're at about 25 per cent of where we'll end up.' The Socceroos would next return to action when the third phase of Asian World Cup Qualifying began in September.

In a world still gripped firmly in the 'tentacles' of COVID-19, the final qualifying round would kick off in September. Australia was grouped with China, Vietnam, Oman, Japan, and Saudi Arabia. This clearly would be a tougher assignment, but on the recent results, the Socceroos would go in confident of securing a place at their fifth straight World Cup Finals. In the beginning, they would have to continue playing their home games overseas.

Australia 3, China 0
(*Halftime*: 2–0)
Scorers: Mabil, Boyle, Duke
3 September 2021
Referee: Hyung Jin-Ko (South Korea)
Crowd: The game was played behind closed doors due to COVID 19.
Khalifa International Stadium, Doha, Qatar

Australia: Mathew Ryan, Rhyan Grant, Aziz Behich (Callum Elder 79), Trent Sainsbury, Harry Souttar, Ajdin Hrustic, Martin Boyle (Aaron Mooy 69), Jackson Irvine (James Jeggo 79), Tom Rogic (Riley McGree 87), Awer Mabil, Adam Taggart (Mitchell Duke 69)
China: Yan Junling, Zhang Linpeng, Wang Shenchao, Yu Dabao (Wang Gang 46), Jiang Guangtai, Wu Xi, Wu Lei, Jin Jingdao (Yin Hongbo 63), Wu Xinghan (Wei Shihao 60), Ai Kesen (Zhang Yuning 82), Zhang Xizhe (Hao Junmin 46)

The Socceroos notched up a comfortable 3-0 win over China in their World Cup qualifier in Doha. Awer Mabil, Martin Boyle and Mitchell Duke all scored as the Socceroos ran rampant against a Chinese team that failed to muster a single shot on target. Playing in Qatar due to issues with travelling back to Australia related to COVID quarantine requirements, the Socceroos got their third phase of Asian qualifying off to the best possible start within the air-conditioned confines of the Khalifa International Stadium.

Coach Graham Arnold was 'very proud' of his team's performance: 'There is a lot more improvement left ... I thought we were fantastic tonight.'

After group heavyweights Japan had suffered a shock home defeat to Oman earlier in the day, Australia would have taken nothing for granted, and were initially forced to defend deep by China's forward press. However, aside from that brief spell at the start of the contest, China was hopelessly outmatched and outclassed by the Socceroos, who would only have been disappointed that they didn't score more.

Two first half goals from lively front men Mabil and Boyle broke the spirit of China, who then offered very little resistance. Awer Mabil opened the scoring with a brave finish midway through the first half, before a dominant Martin Boyle doubled the advantage minutes later with a sizzling strike. Although wasteful in front of goal, the Socceroos were able to add some flourish to the scoreline thanks to substitute Mitch Duke. He chipped home with just his second touch after coming on, pouncing on a rebound from a Mabil shot following a brilliant piece of build-up from the Socceroos.

This Socceroos victory was their ninth in a row, something an Australian team had only achieved once before, and it was the first time they had done so in World Cup qualifying. It included seven clean sheets.

Graham Arnold had picked an attacking line-up with no natural defensive midfielder. Jackson Irvine and Ajdin Hrustic were his midfield pairing. In the final analysis, this was a top victory given that the team only had four days and just one-and-a-half training sessions to prepare.

The team moved on to Hanoi to face Vietnam. The opportunity to spend more time together was expected to be reflected in an even better performance. The only injury concern was with Martin Boyle who appeared to have tweaked his left hamstring before being substituted late in the game against China.

Australia 1, Vietnam 0
(*Halftime*: 1–0)
Scorer: Grant
7 September 2021
Referee: Abdulrahman Al Jassim (Qatar)
Crowd: The game was played behind closed doors due to COVID 19.
My Dihn Stadium, Hanoi, Vietnam

Australia: Mathew Ryan, Rhyan Grant, Brad Smith (Aziz Behich 56), Trent Sainsbury, Harry Souttar, Ajdin Hrustic (James Jeggo 78), Riley McGree (Aaron Mooy 56), Jackson Irvine, Tom Rogic, Awer Mabil, Adam Taggart (Mitchell Duke 66)
Vietnam: Dang Van Lam, Nguyen Trong Hoang, Phong Hong Duy Nguyen, Bui Tien Dung I (Ho Tan Tai 80), Que Ngoc Hai, Nguyen Thanh Chung (Nguyen Binh Thanh 76), Nguyen Quang Hai, Nguyen Tuan Anh (Nguyen Van Toan 46), Nguyen Hoang Duc, Phan Van Duc (Pham Duc Huy 63), Nguyen Tien Linh (Ha Duc Chinh 76)

Fullback Rhyan Grant's first goal for his country secured the Socceroos a hard-fought 1-0 World Cup qualifying win over Vietnam. On a hot and humid evening at the My Dinh National Stadium in Hanoi, Grant's headed finish just before halftime was enough to extend Australia's winning streak to 10 matches.

With an organised and resolute Vietnam providing stiff resistance, Australia 'huffed and puffed' for large parts of the first half without creating a clear chance. The Socceroos controlled possession early in the match before Vietnamese star Nguyen Quang Hai botched an early chance at goal, his attempt in the seventh minute sailing over the crossbar.

The Australians held their breath following a VAR review for a potential Grant handball in the 30th minute after a shot by Phong Hong Duy Nguyen hit his right arm, but a penalty kick wasn't awarded. The Socceroos had 75 per cent of possession in the opening 30 minutes yet could only manage two shots at goal. Just when it appeared the teams would go into the break level, Ajdin Hrustic's curled cross to the back post in the 43rd minute was allowed to bounce in the box before Grant headed past Dang Van Lam.

Hrustic was arguably Australia's most influential attacking player despite the presence of Celtic star, Tom Rogic. In-form winger Martin Boyle wasn't selected due to the hamstring niggle picked up in the 3-0 win over China in Qatar.

There were several nervy moments for Graham Arnold's men against the Group B minnows who ended the match with more shots than Australia—despite the Socceroos having over 70 per cent possession. Second-half substitute Mitch Duke thought he'd wrapped up the win with a tidy finish in the dying minutes, but his strike was ruled out for offside. It was the second time an Australian goal was chalked off, with Adam Taggart bundling home an effort in the first half which was called back with Brad Smith unable to keep the ball in play before he cut it back across the six-yard box.

The win, coupled with the victory over China, meant Australia had two wins from their opening two matches in the third stage of qualifying. Vietnam were still waiting for their first point in their first appearance at this stage of qualification.

Australia's next fixtures would be against Oman and old rivals Japan in October, with Football Australia pushing to have the game against Oman played in Sydney in what would be the Socceroos' first home fixture since 2019.

In summing up, coach Graham Arnold stated: 'It's the sign of a good team when you don't play at your best, but you can still win.'

A month later, Australia was back in the Middle East to take on Oman and hopefully stretch this incredible run to eleven straight victories.

Australia 3, Oman 1
(*Halftime*: 1–1)
Scorers: Mabil, Boyle, Duke
8 October 2021
Referee: Nawaf Shukralla (Bahrain)
Crowd: The game was played behind closed doors due to COVID 19.
Khalifa International Stadium, Doha, Qatar

Australia: Mathew Ryan, Rhyan Grant (Fran Karacic 80), Aziz Behich, Trent Sainsbury, Harry Souttar, Ajdin Hrustic, Martin Boyle (Chris Ikonomidis 86), Jackson Irvine (James Jeggo 80), Tom Rogic (Aaron Mooy 63), Awer Mabil, Adam Taggart (Mitchell Duke 63)
Oman: Faiyz Al Rusheidi, Abdulaziz Al Gheilani, Ali Al-Busaidi, Ahmed Al-Khamisi, Mohammed Al-Maslami, Harib Al-Saadi, Abdullah Fawaz (Omer Al-Fazari 65), Salaah Al-Yahyaei, Zahir Sulaiman Al Aghbari (Arshad Al-Alawi 35 (Mohsin Al-Khaldi 82)), Khalid Al-Hajri (Abdulaziz Al-Muqbali 65), Al Mandhar Al Alawi (Issam Al Sabhi 65)

The Socceroos overcame arguably the trickiest test of their World Cup 2022 qualification campaign so far to clinch a record-breaking 3–1 win over Oman. It was far from a comfortable win, but the result extended the Socceroos' streak to a remarkable eleven straight victories, a world record run in World Cup qualification. And with Asian heavyweights Japan stunned for the second time in this final round of qualifying in suffering a 1–0 loss away to Saudi Arabia, Australia's win took on extra significance before their looming clash with the 'Blue Samurai'.

Coach Graham Arnold made two changes to his line-up from the clash with Vietnam, bringing Martin Boyle back into the starting XI as well as fullback Aziz Behich replacing Brad Smith after the US-based star contracted COVID-19.

Australia claimed an early lead through a superb Awer Mabil half-volley in the ninth minute. But they failed to control the ball or assert any real grip on proceedings in an often-frustrating night in Doha. But less than a minute later, Socceroos' gloveman Mat

Ryan was forced to pull off a miraculous save as Oman showed their counterattacking threat with a raid on the Australian box, with Ryan tipping a driven Zahir Al-Aghbari shot from the edge of the box over his bar. The dangerous Al-Aghbari unleashed two more vicious shots in the opening 20 minutes which both tested Ryan, as the Socceroos were sometimes sloppy in possession.

Oman claimed a deserved equaliser through Rabia Al-Mandhar in the 28th minute but were struck a major blow when midfielder Zahir Al-Aghbari, their best player of the opening half-hour, was carted from the field soon after. Jackson Irvine executed an exceptional tackle to poach the ball from him, sending the Omani player crashing to the turf in severe discomfort. He was substituted immediately and taken from the field on a medi-cab with what appeared to be a dislocated shoulder—it was a massive blow to Oman's chances.

Both teams had chances in the dying embers of the half, with Trent Sainsbury shutting down a dangerous opportunity by outmuscling the Omani striker and shielding the ball for Ryan to collect. Graham Arnold cut a frustrated figure on the touchline in the first half. He spoke about his halftime speech in his post-game interview: 'We got dragged into an erratic game at times. Oman threw a lot at us. We were a bit erratic, but once we got the boys in at halftime and calmed them down and we focused more on keeping the ball and moving them side-ways and making them chase the ball, and I felt that we took over the game.'

Australia started the second half on the front foot, scoring just four minutes into the period through a Martin Boyle diving header. The in-form Hibernian striker reacted the fastest to bury an Adam Taggart rebound. Boyle was denied a penalty shortly afterwards before Australia's substitutions began to take control of the game. Mitch Duke and Aaron Mooy were introduced in the 63rd minute for Adam Taggart and Tom Rogic. It was a trio of substitutes who put the result beyond doubt, with Chris Ikonomidis playing fullback Fran Karačić into space, who then cut the ball back to Mitch Duke to pass into the net in the 89th minute.

The midfield was heavily congested in the Socceroos' clash with Oman, with passes breaking down and free-flowing attacking play a scarcity. Australia's typical strategy of flooding down the wing and using the fullbacks to stretch the opposition was frustrated by the Oman defence, as they hustled and constantly harried the Socceroos in possession. Australia was also poor from set pieces, an issue which had reared its head in recent matches. They failed to make seven corners and a number of wide free kicks count in any meaningful fashion.

Oman were tough and physical rivals, winning duels both in the air and on the ground. Revitalised Celtic star Tom Rogic made his 50th appearance for the Socceroos at the air-conditioned Khalifa International Stadium, in Doha, Qatar.

Australia now sat equal top of Group B with three wins from three games in this stage of qualifying. The top-two teams would claim automatic entry into the World Cup Finals. Saudi Arabia were also on nine points but with a worse goal difference, while Oman and the so-far disappointing Japan were in third and fourth respectively with one win and two losses—the same as China's record.

Australia headed to Japan full of confidence having secured themselves a place in history following eleven straight World Cup qualifying wins. They eclipsed the ten straight victories by Germany (2018), Spain (2010) and Mexico (2006). Our oldest foes, the Japanese 'Blue Samurai', appeared in a heap of trouble having lost two of their opening three games of the qualifying stage. Australia on the other hand were in the box seat having won three straight and sitting on top of the group. Graham Arnold stated: 'We go to Japan now, the Japanese no doubt have all the pressure on them because they've only won one game out of three.' On setting the record of eleven straight wins, Arnold said: 'It's obviously something that I'll reflect on in the future. It's obviously a great achievement, but for today it's all about recovery and getting players ready for the Japan game and (going) for 12 straight.'

Australia 1, Japan 2
(*Halftime*: 0–1)
Scorer: Hrustic
12 October 2021
Referee: Abdulrahman Al Jassim (Qatar)
Crowd: 14,437
Saitama Stadium 2002, Saitama, Japan

Australia: Mathew Ryan, Fran Karacic (Rhyan Grant 89), Aziz Behich, Trent Sainsbury, Harry Souttar, Ajdin Hrustic, Jackson Irvine, Tom Rogic (James Jeggo 82), Aaron Mooy (Awer Mabil 61), Martin Boyle (Chris Ikonomidis 89), Adam Taggart (Mitchell Duke 62)
Japan: Shuichi Gonda, Hiroki Sakai, Yuto Nagatomo (Yuta Nakayama 85),

Maya Yoshida, Takehiro Tomiyasu, Wataru Endo, Ao Tanaka, Hidemasa Morita (Gaku Shibasaki 85), Yuya Osako (Kyogo Furuhashi 61), Junya Ito, Takumi Minamino (Takuma Asano 78)

This match had a tough ending for the Socceroos after they battled back to level terms late in the second half. Japan needed the win so much, and looked more desperate, always striving to get to those second balls and just having that little bit more quality in the end. The Socceroos really battled, but the better chances did fall to the home side, and they probably deserved the three points.

Australia's spectacular 11-match winning run had come to an end, and in the process, they handed Japan a World Cup qualification lifeline. The heartbreaking 2-1 defeat extended a winless run against the hosts that stretched back to 2009.

After a nervous start, Australia conceded inside the opening ten minutes as fullback Aziz Behich hopelessly misread a deflected cross which was belted home by Ao Tanaka.

Japan had the best of the chances throughout the game and were denied again and again by sublime keeping from Socceroos' captain Ryan. Despite a much-improved second half from the visitors, Australia was repeatedly cut open through the middle and were disjointed in defence while repeatedly giving up possession, particularly in the first half.

A stunning second-half free kick from midfield revelation Ajdin Hrustic following a controversial overturned penalty had the Socceroos on the brink of a hard-fought draw at Saitama Stadium. Hrustic charged forward but was collected by a sliding challenge from Hidemasa Morita on the very brink of the box. It was initially deemed a penalty by the referee, and Boyle lined up the ball on the 12-yard-dot. But after a lengthy delay, the VAR overturned the decision and deemed it a free kick just outside the 18-yard box instead, awarding a yellow card to Morita. Hrustic hit a sublime strike from the dead ball, smashing it into the crossbar and down into the net.

The game then opened up as both sides chased a winner. But an 85th-minute own goal from fullback Aziz Behich consigned Australia to a cruel defeat.

Coach Graham Arnold said: 'I thought it was a great spectacle to watch. I thought both teams had a go at each other, it was an exciting game... At the end of the day, it wasn't meant to be. We're on nine points from four games. It's one game at a time.'

To qualify for a fifth consecutive World Cup, the Socceroos had to finish in the top two in the six-team Group B. A third-place finish would send the Socceroos to a play-off against the third-placed team from Group A, followed by an intercontinental play-off—the fraught route Australia took in 2018.

Attention now turned to the blockbuster clash in Sydney next against unbeaten Group leader Saudi Arabia. Hrustic said after the match: 'First of all we're devastated. We did drop three points here. I don't think we deserved it... if we would have come off with a one-one draw we would have copped it. We're going to continue; we're going to keep going. I'm 100 per cent sure we'll finish on top if we keep going the way we have been.'

Captain Mat Ryan added: 'With how it played out, obviously it hurts. It always hurts when you lose. We feel a little bit hard done by the amount of bad luck for that second to go in... For sure we'll continue to get better.'

Coach Graham Arnold had made a bold selection call for the clash, trying to overload the midfield with his biggest names. He named veteran Aaron Mooy on the left side in place of winger Awer Mabil, a role the playmaker had sometimes taken on in the Premier League with Brighton. It marked a hugely significant return for Mooy, who had been a Socceroos mainstay for the last half-decade. But Mooy, back in the starting line-up for the first time in 598 days, had struggled to combine with fullback Aziz Behich, the duo repeatedly being caught out in defensive transition.

The move was intended to allow the Socceroos to dominate possession. However, while Mooy was one of the most comfortable Australians with the ball and showed his class with a couple of fine moments, the Socceroos struggled for incision going forward and missed Mabil's pace and ability to beat defenders. Mooy, lacking match fitness with China's league paused, had played a crucial role off the bench in Australia's three previous matches but was hooked after 70 minutes in the Japan loss.

Midfield trio Ajdin Hrustic, Tom Rogic and Jackson Irvine often struggled to maintain possession and were swamped by Japan's midfield, who constantly harassed Australia and regularly poached the ball in dangerous positions, sparking deadly counterattacks that led to both goals.

Japan showed no signs of the sluggishness that had dogged them in recent matches, getting off to a dazzling start with an intensity in defence and attack that left the Socceroos shell-shocked and down an early goal. Australia struggled to get into the game, regularly coughing up the ball cheaply under pressure from Japan's high-pressure defence.

The loss was a wake-up call. From what seemed a cakewalk to automatic World Cup qualification, suddenly Australia was now brought back to the field. The late Japanese winner changed the complexion of the qualifiers completely, and we had no idea at the time by how much. The next big clash would be at home against group leaders, Saudi Arabia. Border restrictions had been eased and after a long 763 days without a home game, Australia would play the important match in Sydney. Mathew Leckie summed up the situation: 'We've been away for so long, and home advantage is a big thing in football. We'll definitely be coming out with a heap of energy and putting them on the back foot early.'

The Saudis were expected to sit back and counterattack, hoping their quick, technical attackers could catch the Socceroos in transition. Both Aaron Mooy and Tom Rogic were ruled out with injury. Australia would also be protecting a very long record: not since a 2–0 loss to New Zealand back in 1981 had Australia lost a World Cup qualifier at home.

Australia 0, Saudi Arabia 0
(*Halftime*: 0–0)
11 November 2021
Referee: Ko Hyung Jin (South Korea)
Crowd: 23,314
Western Sydney Stadium, Parramatta, Sydney

Australia: Mathew Ryan, Rhyan Grant, Aziz Behich, Trent Sainsbury, Harry Souttar (Milos Degenek 78), James Jeggo, Martin Boyle (Riley McGree 87), Jackson Irvine, Awer Mabil (Mitchell Duke 66), Mathew Leckie (Andrew Nabbout 78), Ajdin Hrustic (Kenneth Dougall 87)
Saudi Arabia: Mohammed Al-Yami, Sultan Al-Ghannam, Nasser Al Dawsari, Abdulelah Alamri, Ali Al Bulayhi, Mohamed Kanno, Fahad Al Muwallad, Abdulelah Al Malki, Salman Al Faraj, Salem Al Dawsari, Feras Al-Birakan (Saleh Al-Shehri 73)

The Socceroos drew 0–0 with Saudi Arabia at a sodden Western Sydney Stadium. The team's long-awaited homecoming became something of a damp squib. Playing their first home game in over two years, the Socceroos were unable to stamp their authority over a well-drilled Saudi Arabian team playing their first game outside of the Gulf since the beginning of the pandemic. Frustrated by the incessant rain as well as spoiling tactics from their guests, the Socceroos just could not send their fans home happy.

Saudi Arabia remained at the top of the group, three points ahead of the Socceroos, with a draw neither helping nor hindering either side's chances of finishing in the top two and qualifying for the 2022 World Cup. Coach Graham Arnold said: 'Overall, we played well. We created the chances, but they didn't go in tonight. We're in a great position still, 10 points in five games. If we beat China, we are in a fantastic position.'

In a match of few chances, Awer Mabil's 53rd-minute effort was the first shot on target from either side. The hosts forced stand-in Saudi Arabia goalkeeper Mohammed Al-Yami into three excellent saves in the second half. On the hour mark, Al-Yami denied Mathew Leckie from close range with a strong, one-handed save, although Jackson Irvine should have done better seconds later when he sliced an Awer Mabil cross wide from in front.

Commenting after the game, Leckie said: 'I think the boys, we had a great performance today. It was just the centimetres that stopped us from scoring a couple of goals. They defended well as well. And that double opportunity after the free kick, the keeper pulled off a great save.'

It certainly was. Al-Yami first denied Mabil's dipping effort from 25 yards with a firm, two-handed push before sticking a leg out to thwart Martin Boyle on the follow-up in the 65th minute.

Despite those chances, the Socceroos were forced to hang on for a point later on after a well-disciplined Saudi Arabian side turned the screw in the final 10 minutes, testing Mat Ryan three times in a bid to spoil the homecoming. Salman Al-Faraj and Salem Al-Dawsari both shot straight at the Socceroos skipper from inside the penalty area, before Al-Dawsari forced a brilliant save from Ryan with a long-range effort that he punched clear. Salem Al-Shehri also sent a glancing header just wide of the post as the Socceroos desperately hung on.

As conditions worsened over the course of the match, tempers began to simmer, with Boyle letting his frustrations get the better of him. Arnold reflected: 'I think a little bit of frustration set in with the time-wasting and the tactics from the Saudis. We must learn to be better with that. I think that was when they got a couple of their chances. It is what Matty [Ryan] is there to do, save those goals. I was proud of them.'

One major area of concern for Arnold and the Socceroos was the fitness of centre-back Harry Souttar who was stretchered off after going down holding his knee. He was in serious doubt for the Socceroos' next clash against China in Sharjah in less than a week. He had been the find of these qualifiers—a 'rock' at the heart of the Australian defence and such an aerial threat when moved forwards for corners or free kicks.

Six days later, the Socceroos were back in the Middle East for the game against China. What had been a dream start to these qualifiers was now stuttering along and Australia needed to get back on track. A major blow was announced with the news that defender Harry Souttar had sustained an anterior cruciate ligament (ACL) injury in the game against Saudi Arabia in Sydney. The Stoke City defender returned to the United Kingdom where he would undergo further assessment at his club and commence his rehabilitation. Socceroos' staff would remain in contact with Stoke and Souttar throughout his rehabilitation and offer every possible support and assistance to enable the young defender to return to the pitch as soon as possible. It was feared he could be missing for 12 months and might not even make the World Cup if Australia qualified.

Arnold was devastated with the news on Souttar: 'It's very serious. I'm at this moment really down and devastated for Harry. He's such a great kid. I believe he's the best centre-back in Asia, and if it turns out to be a bad injury it's not only a blow for Harry, it's a big blow for us.' Milos Degenek was brought into the Australian team as a replacement. Arnold would likely bolster his defensive numbers through the inclusion of Sunderland's Bailey Wright and possibly Ryan McGowan as another option.

Australia 1, China 1
(*Halftime*: 1–0)
Scorer: Duke
17 November 2021
Referee: Ko Hyung Jin (South Korea)
Crowd: 1,050
Sharjah Stadium, Sharjah, United Arab Emirates

Australia: Mathew Ryan, Rhyan Grant (Fran Karacic 83), Aziz Behich, Trent Sainsbury, Milos Degenek, Ajdin Hrustic (Riley McGree 76), Jackson Irvine, James Jeggo, Mitchell Duke (Jamie Maclaren 71), Martin Boyle

(Nikita Rukavytsya 83), Mathew Leckie (Awer Mabil 77)
China: Yan Junling, Zhang Linpeng, Wang Shenchao, Zhu Chenjie, Tyias Browning (Wang Gang 46), Xu Xin, Wu Lei (Zhang Yuning 90+3), Wu Xi, Aloisio (Wu Xinghan 80), Ai Kesen, Alan (Ba Dun 80)

The Socceroos' World Cup qualification hopes took another massive blow after slipping to a 1-1 draw with China in the UAE. 16 years and a handful of hours after the Socceroos ended a 32-year wait for qualification to football's biggest stage on that iconic 2005 night against Uruguay, the Australians were now in severe danger of falling short in their bid for a fifth-straight World Cup appearance.

After defeat to Japan and a goal-less draw at home to group leaders Saudi Arabia, the Socceroos looked set to return to their winning ways as they dominated much of the match and scored late in the first half through a Mitch Duke header. Australia maintained control in the second stanza and looked to be cruising to victory as they comfortably held possession, despite rarely threatening the China goal.

Then the match turned on its head in the 70th minute when the VAR intervened, calling on the referee to review a potential Australian handball in the box. A cross from a deep-lying set piece had struck Jimmy Jeggo's raised arm, and Wu Lei made no mistake from the spot as he levelled the scores.

China then had the better chances as both sides desperately hunted victory, while Graham Arnold's raft of substitutes made precious little impact as the match slipped away to a disappointing draw.

With four games to play, the Socceroos were now five points behind unbeaten Saudi Arabia and one behind Japan, who leapfrogged Australia with a 1-0 win over Oman. World Cup qualifying would pause until late January, with Australia to host Vietnam and then play away to Oman a few days later. The deciding matches in late March would see the Socceroos host Japan and play away to Saudi Arabia.

Australian captain Mat Ryan said: 'Disappointing, I don't think we did enough tonight. Didn't create enough clear-cut chances. Obviously, there is probably a controversial talking point (the penalty) but there are other moments throughout the game where we need to be better... It hurts tonight but it's all about the response.'

Goal-scorer Mitch Duke said: 'Yeah frustrating, always, when you go one nil up and you concede and go in with a draw... We have got to brush this off and make sure we focus on the remaining four games and finish strong, maximum points out of the remaining games and feel confident we can get the job done.'

China's trio of naturalised Brazilians started the match for the first time together, and it took just three minutes for Alan to force a Mat Ryan save when he blasted across goal from an extremely tight angle. Martin Boyle responded four minutes later with a beautiful curling cross from the edge of the area, but the runners didn't arrive on the edge of the six-yard area. Just one minute afterwards, Australia had a golden opportunity to open the scoring when Aziz Behich played a square ball from the side of the area to midfielder Jackson Irvine, who couldn't guide his shot on target in a near carbon-copy of the Socceroos' best opportunity against Saudi Arabia.

Soon afterwards Mat Leckie controlled a Boyle cross in the centre of the box and turned and struck quickly, but straight into the palms of China's keeper, Yan Junling. While Australia quickly settled into possession, China was proving dangerous on the counterattack. The 18th minute provided another huge scare in defence as Ai Kesen charged towards goal in pursuit of a long ball. Mat Ryan was caught near the edge of his box and opted to head it, but only found Lu Wei whose volley was sprayed wide of the open net.

The Socceroos were happy to bomb crosses into the box, but like against Saudi Arabia, it was largely ineffectual, until Boyle delightfully dipped a ball to the front post and Duke rose highest to head it down past the keeper in the 38th minute. The advantage was nearly doubled when the Socceroos broke quickly in the 43rd minute and Hrustic crossed well to Leckie, whose first touch gave Chinese gloveman Junling just enough time to close down the resulting strike from close range.

China's defence had shown plenty of desperation with their World Cup dreams on the brink of disappearing beyond reach, but copped a severe blow when centre-back Tyias Browning, who had earlier made a brilliant diving challenge to rob Martin Boyle in the box, was forced off with a pulled hamstring on the brink of halftime.

Australia started the second half somewhat more languidly as the pace of the game slowed. But like the first period, the Socceroos settled after a nervous first quarter of an hour. Early in the second half, Hrustic played Aziz Behich through on goal with a well-weighted ball, but a defender beat him to the mark by a hair. Hrustic's influence was growing, and he shimmied into space in the 58th minute before lobbing a ball through to an onrushing Leckie in the box, but he couldn't control it under pressure.

Then the match turned in a moment as VAR called the referee back to examine a potential penalty incident with 20 minutes remaining. Graham Arnold was stunned, repeatedly asking: 'What? What?' But from a deep China free kick, the ball had struck Jeggo's raised arm as he leapt to head the ball away and the referee called it a penalty. Mat Ryan dove the wrong way as Wu Lei blasted home from the spot.

Former Australian striker Andy Harper was shocked by the decision, saying in commentary: 'They should send the VAR through to the lab to split the atom because they have just split the hair. I'm dumbfounded, to be honest.'

Duke was taken off for Jamie Maclaren after the goal, while wingers Awer Mabil and Riley McGree were introduced six minutes later for Leckie and Hrustic. Fran Karačić replaced Rhyan Grant at right-back in the 83rd minute, with 34-year-old striker Nikita Rukavytsya replacing Martin Boyle. But Arnold's attempts to wrest back momentum had little effect. Mabil was the only other player to make any sort of impact in the final minutes. Australia reverted to launching crosses into the area, which almost inevitably fell to the men in red shirts. There was a late flashpoint as Milos Degenek butted heads literally with China substitute, Zhang Yuning. Degenek fell to the turf and both players were handed yellow cards, which could well have been red cards. But time expired on a disappointing night in Sharjah.

The result against China was a very poor result for the Socceroos and left the team on the outside looking in. Japan and Saudi Arabia were now the favourites to automatically progress to the World Cup in Qatar. The hounds were now out baying for blood, and it was Graham Arnold and his team that they were out to savage. The criticism was ramping up and the recent poor results against Japan (loss away), Saudi Arabia (draw at home) and China (draw away) added fuel to the fire. Arnold went on the offensive through the press: 'They forget what's happened in the past. In 2021, during a pandemic, we've had ten World Cup qualifiers, nine away from home, we've won seven, drawn two and lost one. Considering what we've gone through, we're in a great position.'

Arnold was defending his players, but the major criticism was of himself and his role as the coach. One of his harshest critics was Mark Bosnich who attacked Arnold's remark after the draw with Saudi Arabia that the Socceroos 'had played great'. Speaking on *Stan Sport,* Bosnich was scathing: 'I wonder what not playing great looks like. Playing great for me means you've won 3–0 and it's a Barcelona-esque-from-10-years-ago performance… Come on.' There was no love lost between the old team-mates. Bosnich concluded that Australia would struggle to qualify for Qatar unless there was 'a tweak of tactics'. Arnold fired back: 'When Bozza says a tweak of tactics, I wish it was that easy. A tweak? What's a tweak?' He picked up a glass as part of the interview and moved it on the table moving it a couple of centimetres and chuckled: 'We'll move that from there to there, that's a tweak.'

It had been a complicated 18 months of not being able to play at home, lockdowns, some of his players catching COVID (forcing them to isolate and ruling them out of matches), and some playing little or no football as their competitions were suspended. The game against Saudi Arabia summed up the issues. Only four days before the game, only five of his players were in the country and the team would eventually be confined to just one training session. Arnold fired off a final salvo: 'If some people get their way, they'll chase me out the door like they chased out Ange [Postecoglou]. But I'm not going anywhere. We're building something great.'

Australia would open the World Cup year in late January for their next clash against Vietnam in Melbourne. The constant media attacks were not doing Australia or Graham Arnold any favours at a time when they most needed support.

Australia 4, Vietnam 0
(*Halftime*: 2–0)
Scorers: Maclaren, Rogic, Goodwin, McGree
27 January 2022
Referee: Hyung-Jin Ko (South Korea)
Crowd: 27,740
Melbourne Rectangular Stadium (AAMI Park)

Australia: Mathew Ryan, Fran Karacic, Joel King, Milos Degenek,
Trent Sainsbury, Jackson Irvine, Martin Boyle (Marco Tilio 81),
Aaron Mooy (James Jeggo 81), Tom Rogic (Riley McGree 74), Mathew Leckie
(Craig Goodwin 66), James Maclaren (Mitchell Duke 66)
Vietnam: Bui Tan Tuong, Bui Tien Dung I, Tran Dinh Trong, Pham Xuan Manh
(Nguyen Phuong Hong Duy 61), Vu Van Thanh, Le Van Xuan
(Nguyen Thanh Chung 46), Do Hung Dung (Tran Minh Vuong 71),
Luong Xuan Truong (Nguyen Cong Phuong 46), Tuan Hai Pham,
Nguyen Quang Hai, Phan Van Duc (Nguyen Cong Phuong 46)

A masterful performance from Tom Rogic inspired the Socceroos to a 4–0 win over Vietnam in Melbourne, ensuring Australia stayed in the race for an automatic World

Cup qualifying spot.

Rogic had been in brilliant form at Celtic under Ange Postecoglou, and after missing the November window through injury, he scored one goal and teed up another for Jamie Maclaren. Craig Goodwin and Riley McGree scored their first Socceroos goals off the bench in the second half to ensure Australia snapped a three-game winless run to remain in touch with leaders Saudi Arabia and Japan.

Assistant coach René Meulensteen took the reins in Graham Arnold's COVID-19-enforced absence. Arnold had been due to finish his quarantine period on the Thursday before the match but didn't clear the required protocols to attend. A Football Australia spokesman said he would be assessed daily as to whether he could travel to Oman for the next qualifier five days later.

The change of voice on the sideline seemingly didn't faze Rogic, who was involved in everything in an electrifying first half. He looked to have rifled Australia into the lead inside 20 seconds, sending the AAMI Park crowd of 27,740 into raptures. But after a VAR referral, referee Ko Hyung-jin ruled an offside Jackson Irvine had interfered with Vietnam goalkeeper Bui Tan Truong.

From there, Australia's creative moments were few and far between until the commanding Rogic helped deliver the breakthrough on the half-hour mark. The playmaker lofted a cross towards Maclaren, who in his first start since June, slipped unmarked between two defenders to power home a header. Then two minutes into stoppage time in the first half, Mathew Leckie slipped a pass through to Rogic who coolly doubled Australia's lead.

To the delight of the large and vocal Vietnamese contingent, the visitors burst out of the break with Tuan Hai Pham lashing a shot just wide minutes after the restart. Ryan also made a reflex save to deny Nguyen Cong Phuong in the 62nd, then four minutes later, Nguyen Thanh Chung headed a close-range effort over the bar.

Ryan then turned provider, hoofing a long ball into the path of Goodwin, who, six minutes after entering the fray, coolly chipped Bui Tan Truong to settle Australia's nerves. Four minutes later, Goodwin teed up McGree for the young gun to cut onto his right and lash home, rounding out a successful first Socceroos game in Melbourne since December 2017.

With Aziz Behich unavailable, Sydney FC youngster and Olyroo Joel King started at left-back for his first cap, while Melbourne City sensation Marco Tilio received a late debut off the bench.

The victory over Vietnam gave a temporary reprieve to the coach and players, but realistically Australia still faced a massive hill to climb to qualify automatically. The Socceroos would now head back to the Middle East to tackle Oman in Muscat— another must-win game.

Australia 2, Oman 2
(*Halftime*: 1–0)
Scorers: Maclaren, Mooy
27 February 2022
Referee: Mohammad Abdulla Hassan (UAE)
Crowd: The game was played behind closed doors due to COVID 19.
Sultan Qaboos Sports Complex, Muscat, Oman

Australia: Mathew Ryan, Fran Karačić, Aziz Behich, Milos Degenek, Trent Sainsbury (Ryan McGowan 85), Jackson Irvine, Martin Boyle, Aaron Mooy (James Jeggo 85), Tom Rogic (Ajdin Hrustic 62), Mathew Leckie (Craig Goodwin 73), Jamie Maclaren (Mitchell Duke 62)
Oman: Faiyz Al Rusheidi, Amjad Al Harthi (Aiman Dhahi 71), Abdulaziz Al Ghellani (Mahmoud Al-Mushaifi 46), Ahmed Al-Khamisi, Fahmi Said, Abdullah Fawaz, Munzer Al-Alawi (Mohammad Al Amri 90+2), Arshad Al-Alawi, Mataz Saleh, Khalid Al-Hajri (Marwan Awlad Wadi 81), Omar Al-Fazari (Muhsen Al Ghassani 46)

The Socceroos suffered a heavy blow to their hopes of automatic World Cup qualification with a 2–2 draw against Oman in Muscat. The draw meant that Australia was now three points behind Japan and four adrift of Group B leaders, Saudi Arabia.

The Socceroos twice led the match, first through a 15th-minute penalty to Jamie Maclaren and later through an Aaron Mooy strike. But those goals were both cancelled out by a brace from midfielder Abdullah Fawaz.

Fawaz first scored with a beautiful curling strike into the top corner of Mat Ryan's goal to make it 1–1, but Mooy would later send his thunderbolt of a volley into the Oman net to give Australia what could have been a winning 2–1 lead.

However, Oman had other ideas and when Australia defender Fran Karačić gave up a penalty with a clumsy challenge, Fawaz made no mistake from the penalty spot to secure a draw in the 89th minute.

The draw meant Australia faced a must-win match against an in-form Japan to avoid having to reach Qatar via the play-offs. If Graham Arnold's team could achieve that win, they would then have to travel to face the group leaders, Saudi Arabia, needing a result to have any chance of avoiding a play-off.

Japan had beaten the Socceroos 2–1 earlier in the campaign. Earlier, the 'Samurai Blue' beat Saudi Arabia 2–0 in Saitama. The victory brought Japan within a point of Saudi Arabia in Group B.

In my new role as a member of Football Australia's National Indigenous Advisory Group, I was invited to attend the critical match against Japan in Sydney. A great crowd turned out in support of the Socceroos at Stadium Australia in drizzling rain.

Australia 0, Japan 2
(*Halftime*: 0–0)
24 March 2022
Referee: Nawaf Shukralla (Bahrain)
Crowd: 41,852
Stadium Australia, Sydney, Australia

Australia: Mathew Ryan, Rhyan Grant, Joel King, Trent Sainsbury, Milos Degenek, Gianni Stensness (Ben Folami 90), Martin Boyle (Jamie Maclaren 84), Connor Metcalfe (James Jeggo 46), Awer Mabil (Marco Tilio 68), Mitchell Duke (Bruno Fornaroli 68), Ajdin Hrustic
Japan: Shuichi Gonda, Miki Yamarie, Yuto Nagatamo (Yuta Nakayame 63), Ko Itakura, Maya Yoshida, Wataru Endo, Junya Ito, Ao Tanaka (Genki Haraguchi 84), Hidemasa Morita, Takumi Minamino (Kaoru Mitoma 84), Takuma Asano (Ayase Ueda 63)

I confess I was overwhelmed with disappointment after this game; it clearly demonstrated the higher skill level and technical ability of Japan over our side.

Australia last failed to qualify for the World Cup in 2002 but the Socceroos now faced a play-off against the third-placed team from the other Asian qualifying group for the right to face the fifth-ranked team from South America for World Cup qualification.

Substitute Kaoru Mitoma scored twice in the final few minutes to give Japan a 2–0 win over Australia at a rain-soaked Olympic Stadium in Sydney. The win sent his country through to a seventh successive edition of the World Cup Finals. Japan's first victory over the Socceroos in Australia since 1998 also secured Saudi Arabia's passage to Qatar.

An entertaining qualifier looked to be heading towards a scoreless stalemate in the 89th minute when the ball was cut back from the by-line and Mitoma pounced to fire it past Australian goalkeeper Mat Ryan. Winger Mitoma put the result beyond doubt five minutes later when he skipped through the tiring Australia defence and found the net again under Ryan's despairing dive.

With Wataru Endo running midfield and Takumi Minamino a constant threat up front, Japan deserved the win against an Australia side missing almost an entire team of regulars because of COVID-19 infections and injury. Minamino hit the woodwork twice inside five minutes towards the end of the opening half, the first from a rocket of a header that crashed down off the bar and post but stayed out of the goal.

The Socceroos also had their chances, most notably a Miki Yamane own goal that was ruled out for a foul on the goalkeeper. Australia gave away too much possession in midfield and struggled to deal with Japan's pace on the break. Forward Ajdin Hrustic, the only Australian with the skill to match the Japanese, fashioned a couple of chances at the start of the second half but his long-range free kick was parried away, and he screwed a shot wide.

Japan looked like making the breakthrough in the 80th minute when Hidemasa Morita's pass found Minamino on the six-yard line, but Trent Sainsbury stood tall to clear the shot. Junya Ito had another chance saved seven minutes later, leaving the way clear for Mitoma to perform his late heroics.

On such a dreary night for Australian football, perfectly matching the drizzling rain at Stadium Australia, the Socceroos were thoroughly outplayed and outclassed by the 'Blue Samurai'. The defeat extended a winless run against Japan to nine matches over 13 years and was the first loss in a 'live' World Cup qualifier at home (i.e. where the result mattered to Australia's qualification hopes) in over four decades.

The Socceroos would now face a sudden-death match against Asia's other third-placed team, potentially the UAE at that stage, with the victor progressing to a final do-or-die battle with South America's fifth-placed team, potentially Uruguay.

The Socceroos had to continue on to their final group game against Saudi Arabia in Jeddah knowing it was already a dead rubber—the Saudis and Japan had secured

Group B's top-two spots and Australia were now facing a two-game play-off: the first would be against the third-placed team from Group A. It was confirmed that this opponent would be the United Arab Emirates. Coach Graham Arnold was weathering a blistering array of attacks and there were repeated calls to have him replaced.

Australia 0, Saudi Arabia 1
(*Halftime*: 0–0)
30 March 2022
Referee: Abraham Mohammad Makhadmeh (Jordan)
Crowd: 51,433
King Abdullah Sports City, Jeddah, Saudi Arabia

Australia: Mathew Ryan, Nathaniel Atkinson, Aziz Behich, Gianni Stensness, Trent Sainsbury, James Jeggo, Martin Boyle, Denis Genreau (Mitchell Duke 82), Awer Mabil (Marco Tilio 73), Bruno Fornaroli (Nicholas D'Agostino 46), Ajdin Hrustic
Saudi Arabia: Mohammed Al Owais, Mohammed Al Burayk (Saud Abdulhamid 88), Yasser Al Shahrani, Hassan Al Tambakti, Abdullah Madu (Ahmed Sharahili 66), Sami Al-Najei (Abdulaziz Al-Bishi 66), Hattan Bahebri (Saleh Al Shehri 66), Mohammed Kanno, Salman Al Faraj, Salem Al-Dawsari, Feras Al-Birakan (Ziyad Al Sahafi 88)

Australia lost 1–0 to Saudi Arabia as the third stage of Asian World Cup qualifying came to a disappointing end for the Socceroos, and it piled even more pressure on Graham Arnold.

The Socceroos were undone by a Salem Al-Dawsari penalty in the second half to suffer a third defeat in the group. It meant Australia had won just one of their past seven qualifiers heading into June's play-off match against the UAE. Speculation continued to build that Arnold was unlikely to be in charge for that game.

The 'Green Falcons' had already been confirmed as finalists at Qatar 2022 when Australia lost 2–0 at home to Japan, and with this win they topped the group on 23 points with their first World Cup qualifying win over the Socceroos. They were eight points clear of Australia.

Despite missing several key players including Tom Rogic, Aaron Mooy, Mathew

Leckie, Jackson Irvine, Jamie Maclaren and Harry Souttar, Australia created the better chances in the first half. Nathanial Atkinson debuted at right-back, and Arnold also handed starts to midfielder Denis Genreau and striker Bruno Fornaroli, while Gianni Stensness moved to central defence in the absence of Milos Degenek.

Awer Mabil and Martin Boyle came close to opening the scoring and it was Scottish-born winger Boyle who thought he had found the opener in the 36th minute. A defence-splitting pass by Ajdin Hrustic released Boyle who sprinted clear and rounded the Saudi goalkeeper before slotting home, but his celebrations were cut short as the assistant referee flagged for offside. After a four-minute VAR review, the decision was upheld despite replays suggesting Boyle was very close to being onside as he started his run.

Mabil fired a dangerous shot that had to be tipped over the bar in the second half, but Australia's enterprise came unstuck when James Jeggo was penalised for a clumsy trip on Sami Al-Najei inside the box in the 62nd minute. Al-Dawsari stepped up to send Mathew Ryan the wrong way and give the hosts the lead. Encouraged, the hosts finished the game the stronger, and it was only a couple of smart saves from Ryan that denied Saudi Arabia a second goal.

The Socceroos' nightmare slump had continued with this 1–0 defeat to Saudi Arabia in Jeddah. Hoping to rebound from their 2–0 defeat to Japan, the Socceroos instead continued their worrying downward spiral. Australia had now lost back-to-back qualifiers for the first time since 1977. The result left coach Graham Arnold on the verge of losing his job ahead of two must-win play-offs in June.

Forced to field another new-look side, Arnold was pleased at the way some youngsters performed but was forced to rue another soft penalty decision conceded by Jimmy Jeggo—a needless foul on the hour mark. Attention now turned to the sudden-death play-off against the UAE.

It was probably fortunate that the Socceroos would not go into battle again for three months to allow the team time to get over the disappointment and also time for so many injuries to heal. Football Australia, against a surge of demands to sack coach Graham Arnold, stood with the coach to see out the two crucial sudden-death qualifiers. In the end, it was announced that Peru would be the fifth-placed South American team that Australia must get past provided they beat the UAE. At least the Socceroos had met them in the last World Cup in Russia and were well aware of the talent and skill they possessed. In a plus, both play-off games against the United

Arab Emirates and Peru would be played in Qatar, which had become something of a home away from home for Australia during these qualifiers.

Australia 2, United Arab Emirates 1
(*Halftime*: 0–0)
Scorers: Irvine, Hrustic
8 June 2022
Referee: Ilgiz Tantashev (Uzbekistan)
Crowd: 6,500
Ahmed Bin Ali Stadium, Al-Rayyan, Qatar

Australia: Mathew Ryan, Nathaniel Atkinson, Aziz Behich, Bailey Wright, Kye Rowles, Aaron Mooy, Martin Boyle, Ajdin Hrustic (Milos Degenek 90+1), Jackson Irvine, Craig Goodwin (Jamie Maclaren 72), Mathew Leckie (Awer Mabil 90+1)
United Arab Emirates: Khalid Eisa, Khaled Ebraheim Aldhanhani, Walid Abbas, Khalifa Al Hammadi, Mohammed Al Attas, Ali Salmeen (Majed Hassan 88), Caio Canedo (Sebastian Tagliabue 89), Abdullah Salmeen (Omar Abdulrahman 88), Abdalla Ramadan (Yahya Nader 75), Harib Abdullah Suhail, Ali Mabkhout (Ali Saleh 74)

The Socceroos were a step closer to qualifying for the 2022 World Cup after securing a must-win 2–1 victory over the United Arab Emirates. Rising star Ajdin Hrustic, who won the Europa League with Eintracht Frankfurt the previous month, scored a late volley to lift Australia to a 2–1 win in their do-or-die play-off match in Doha.

Australia was on the back foot after a tentative, conservative performance in the first half that saw both sides struggle to create serious chances. The Socceroos came out firing in the second, with midfielder Jackson Irvine opening the scoring in the 55th minute after a clever series of passes with stand-out winger Martin Boyle. Winning the ball high up the pitch, Martin Boyle danced and weaved past a defender and whipped in a low cross for midfielder Jackson Irvine to poke home at the near post.

But the UAE struck back less than two minutes later through striker Caio Canedo who capitalised on some scrambling Australian defence to equalise in the 57th. Centre-back Bailey Wright was beaten on the flank by dangerous teen winger Harib Abdullah, who whipped in a cross that was deflected into the path of Canedo to slam home. The goal seemed to remind the Socceroos what they were playing for, and as the second half wore on, the side strung together several convincing passing sequences and created more overloads down either wing.

Adelaide United forward Craig Goodwin had a great chance to increase Australia's tally in the 62nd minute, latching onto a deep Boyle cross, but his volley fizzed over the crossbar. A 70th-minute substitution of A-League Golden Boot winner Jamie Maclaren gave Australia some extra movement and energy up front, with the Melbourne City forward finding himself in dangerous pockets in the box within minutes, forcing a fine save from UAE goalkeeper Khalid Eisa in the 80th minute.

Just as the game looked to be edging towards extra time, it was the 25-year-old Ajdin Hrustic who came to the Socceroos' rescue. A corner from Aaron Mooy was initially headed clear by the UAE's defence, only for the ball to fall right into Hrustic's path. With a single, fluid movement, the number 10 met the ball perfectly, the force of the strike ricocheting off a UAE defender and spinning into the net!

The UAE pressed forward desperately as Arnold turned to his bench, bringing on another defender in Milos Degenek and fresh legs in Awer Mabil in stoppage time. The final whistle was heard with great relief—however, despite the crucial win, questions would be asked over Australia's first-half performance, which was flat and conservative when in possession. That passive play could have been punished by the UAE's quick transitional players, especially left winger Harib Abdullah, who snuck in behind Australia's defence several times and forced goalkeeper Mat Ryan into several crucial saves.

After the game, Jackson Irvine said: 'That's how the games go sometimes, you can feel that cagey environment. We picked our moments well and when we had moments of quality were capitalised on them, and in games like this it will come down to fine margins. We obviously gave away a goal which was disappointing, but we knew we had enough in the key moments to win the game and obviously pleased with taking one of them myself. Obviously, it's a great feeling, but you have that moment of elation when the final whistle goes… We have a great squad with a good energy about us and I'm excited for next week already.'

Hrustic declared: 'We have put so much work in and we have been working our ass off so to say. And we conceded a goal, and we shouldn't have. We kept going, kept fighting and we took our chance, and the goal for Australia was for all the boys, for the staff, because we have been through a lot, and it hasn't been easy. I don't think everyone realises how much work we put in, so I'm happy, really happy.'

Martin Boyle said: 'It was a tough one. It was a tough one but the most disappointing thing, when we scored, we conceded straightaway. But we showed good character, I think we dominated the majority of the game. Matty made a few good saves at the near post, but I thought we were really good, and we took the chances when they came.'

The Socceroos had fielded a surprise starting XI featuring two youngsters with just a single appearance each in defensive duo Kye Rowles and Nathaniel Atkinson, while veteran winger Mat Leckie started at centre-forward. That came after the Socceroos suffered three injury blows in the lead-up to the match with Jason Davidson, Trent Sainsbury and Adam Taggart all missing the match. Tom Rogic had previously withdrawn from the squad due to personal reasons. Coach Graham Arnold opted to reward players who had featured regularly for their clubs this season, with two key exceptions to the rule in veteran duo Mat Ryan and Aaron Mooy.

The Socceroos would now play Peru, also in Doha, for a place in the World Cup proper. Victory would ensure qualification to a fifth-straight World Cup and a $15 million qualification prize from FIFA. But against a deadly Peruvian side, the Socceroos still faced the very real possibility of missing out on football's premiere competition for the first time in two decades.

Six days later, Australia would battle with Peru for the coveted World Cup qualifying spot. The win over the UAE had ensured that coach Graham Arnold would retain his position as coach, despite the howling and baying for the axe to fall on him. Probably not since the game against Uruguay back in 2005 had Australia faced such a daunting opponent in a final World Cup qualifier. For Australia to have even reached this final stage was a massive achievement. They had been dealt a very tough 'hand' for what was unquestionably the longest and most taxing qualifying series in Socceroos' World Cup history. They had faced and were forced to overcome the impact of the COVID-19 pandemic, including being denied the opportunity to play games at home. Additionally, there had been COVID-19 sickness, confinement, and a crippling run of injuries to key players at crucial times. In the face of all this, instead of constant criticism, both Arnold and his team deserved long-overdue accolades.

Australia 0, Peru 0
(*Halftime*: 0–0)
Australia won 5-4 on penalties

4 June 2022
Referee: Slavko Vincic (Slovenia)
Crowd: 6,500
Ahmed Bin Ali Stadium, Al-Rayyan, Qatar

Australia: Mathew Ryan (Andrew Redmayne 120), Nathaniel Atkinson (Fran Karacic 90), Aziz Behich (Craig Goodwin 120), Bailey Wright, Kye Rowles, Aaron Mooy, Martin Boyle, Ajdin Hrustic, Jackson Irvine, Mathew Leckie (Jamie Maclaren 87), Mitchell Duke (Awer Mabil 69)
Peru: Pedro Gallese, Luis Advincula, Miguel Trauco, Carlos Zambrano, Alexander Callens, Renato Tapia, Andre Carrillo (Edison Flores 65) Sergio Pena (Pedro Aquino 80), Christofer Gonzales, Christian Cueva (Alex Valera 116), Gianluca Lapadula

For sheer excitement, emotion, and elation, this game is up there with the 2005 clash with Uruguay. The Socceroos had now qualified for a fifth-straight World Cup after a penalty shoot-out win over Peru in their intercontinental play-off in Qatar. Substitute goalkeeper Andrew Redmayne was the hero, making the winning save as Australia won the shoot-out 5-4 after the match finished 0-0 after extra time.

Redmayne declared: 'I'm no hero. I just played my role like everyone else did tonight. Not even the 11 on the pitch, it was much more than that, it is a team effort. I can't thank the team enough, the staff enough. You know, I'm not going to take credit. The boys ran out 120 minutes, and it not only takes 11 on the field but the boys on the bench, the boys in the stands.'

Redmayne will now forever be known as the 'grey Wiggle' for his goal-line antics. Mat Ryan was the man to make way for Redmayne after putting in a stellar performance to keep Peru off the board for 120 minutes. Mitch Duke summed up the situation after the game: 'I'm sure Matty would have been disappointed, but everyone played their part. I can't explain this feeling, it is just complete ecstasy, and I can't wait to celebrate with the boys. Thank you for believing in us. We are going to a World Cup, five in a row!'

Coach Graham Arnold had been under enormous pressure heading into the match after some underwhelming performances in the lead-up, and after the match he paid tribute to the players for their efforts under trying conditions. He said: 'So proud of the players, you know? No one knows what those boys have been through to get to here. It was so hard, the whole campaign, and the way they've stuck at it and committed themselves to it, incredible.'

After 120 goal-less minutes, Aaron Mooy, Craig Goodwin, Ajdin Hrustic, Jamie Maclaren and Awer Mabil all scored from the spot to make up for Martin Boyle's miss, before Redmayne denied Peru's Alex Valera to spark joyous Australian celebrations at the Ahmad bin Ali Stadium. Redmayne had dived to his right, stopped Alex Valera's shot, and then stood up and pulled a grinning face that sent Australian supporters wild. In that incredible moment, he not only saved the penalty, but also Arnold's career to complete a 1008-day qualification program that came down to the blink of an eye.

The victory was a triumph for Arnold, who would now lead the country to the World Cup Finals after fighting to save his job when he missed out on automatic qualification in March. His decision to bring on Redmayne in place of Ryan just before fulltime will go down as a masterstroke, with the Sydney FC goalkeeper joining Mark Schwarzer and John Aloisi as World Cup penalty shoot-out heroes.

Arnold explained his decision: 'Look, Andrew Redmayne is a very good penalty saver, and to try to get into the mind … to add that little bit of uncertainty in their brains. That's the reason why.' Peru would have studied Mat Ryan inside out, but in bringing on Redmayne that all went out the window. Adding to this was the antics of Redmayne on the goal line, with some comparing him to the 'Wiggles Hot Potato', and he was reminiscent of the great Liverpool goalkeeper, Bruce Grobbelaar.

The dramatic finish came after a goal-less 120 minutes, with Peru going closest to breaking the deadlock when substitute Edison Flores hit the post with a header in the second period of extra time. Earlier, Australia made the early running in a stadium dominated by Peruvian fans, with Duke flashing a couple of early efforts past the goal, while Scottish-born winger Boyle was dangerous out on the right.

The first shot on target for either team came via Hrustic in the 81st minute, but his long-range free kick was easily claimed by Peru captain Pedro Gallese. Four minutes later, Aziz Behich just failed to bend a skidding effort on target after the left-back picked up a loose ball and beat two Peruvians before having a shot from outside the box.

Hrustic nearly stole the win for Australia in the 88th minute when he was found by substitute Mabil's cutback, but Gallese just managed to keep the midfielder's shot from squirming in. Flores had Peru's first shot on target in the game in the first period of extra time before his header hit the post.

Arnold then turned to Redmayne moments before the final whistle in a decision that will go down in Australian sporting folklore. Arnold later declared: 'The doubters don't bother me. It's these boys that I care for. I called out to Anthony Albanese the other day, to give everyone, give the fans a day off to celebrate this because I believe this is one of the greatest achievements ever, to qualify for this World Cup the way we've had to go through things. Twenty World Cup qualifiers and we've played 16 away from home. It's been tough, but we did it.'

Redmayne summed up the connection between the players and their coach: 'It's hard to put into words how big this is. It's a massive achievement. That's down to Arnie. That's down to the belief he puts into the players. The respect he gives the players. All the little one-per-cent-ers. The man management. The people external to this group don't see the work and love and passion that Arnie puts into every single player that comes into camp and puts on that green and gold shirt.'

In the aftermath, it was revealed that the plan to substitute captain and first-choice goalkeeper Mat Ryan with Andrew Redmayne for a penalty shoot-out scenario was a tight secret and not even Ryan was aware of it. However, Redmayne had been made aware of the possibility a month before the game by goalkeeper coach John Crawley, who had informed him to prepare along those lines. Australia could now look forward to Group D in Qatar, facing current world champions France, Tunisia, and Denmark.

The Socceroos would now set about preparing for Qatar. There would be two games against New Zealand in late September as a farewell and also to celebrate 100 years of international games between Australia and the Kiwis. Teen sensation Garang Kuol, who was still yet to play a senior game other than an appearance off the bench for the Central Coast Mariners, was amongst the squad named for the two-game series against New Zealand. Kuol, as a 17-year-old, had come off the bench in the A-League All Stars' game against Barcelona and put in an eye-catching performance. At the time of his selection, Premier League club Newcastle United were on the verge of signing the young star.

The games against New Zealand would be the last matches before Arnold named his 26-man World Cup squad in late November. Super coach, the legendary Guus Hiddink, was enticed out of retirement to return to Australia and take an active role on the Socceroos' support team for the New Zealand matches. Arnold and Hiddink had formed a strong relationship when Arnold was Hiddink's assistant during the 2006 qualifiers and World Cup Finals' appearances. There was a mutual bond of respect between the two men. The presence of Hiddink in the camp would be an enormous boost to morale and to the players.

The first game in Brisbane saw Australia win the match 1–0 through an Awer Mabil cracker, though the match overall was a lacklustre effort after the incredible high of the victory over Peru. Arnold admitted that his team was a bit flat through little preparation time and they were surprisingly outmuscled at Suncorp. He stated that he expected better for the return game in New Zealand; Australia duly won the second rubber 2–0 and were a far better side. Garang Kuol came on and his introduction inspired the Socceroos into action. He made an amazing run down the right before teeing up his Mariner's teammate Jason Cummings to add Australia's second to follow a 54-minute goal by Mitch Duke.

Two weeks later, it was announced in the press that Kuol had signed for Newcastle United in the Premier League. Young Kuol looked an exceptional talent and despite his young age, he may have already been featuring in Arnold's plans for the World Cup. Another young and future Australian star Alex Robertson was coming into notice with Manchester City as the 19-year-old was called into the 'sky blues' senior team training by manager, Pep Guardiola. Robertson was yet to decide on where his international allegiance lies—his grandfather Alex and his father Mark had played for Australia, but he was born in Scotland and his father played there, and his mother was from Peru. What a dilemma for the young man to ponder!

However, worrying news came through only a month out from the Socceroos' World Cup squad announcement that star player Ajdin Hrustic had been injured while playing for his Italian Serie A team, Hellas Verona. Hrustic had rolled his ankle in a game and suffered ligament injury. This was a real blow as Hrustic had developed into one of the Socceroos' key players and there was a real possibility that he would not recover in time for the World Cup.

In late October, the Socceroos took a human rights' stance and called out Qatar over their treatment of migrant workers in the construction of the World Cup stadiums. They also called for the decriminalisation of same sex relationships. FIFA responded in typical fashion by sending a letter to all participating countries to 'focus on football' and stop dragging the sport 'into every ideological or political battle that exists'.

There was another blow for the Australian team when news came through that Martin Boyle had suffered a knee injury in Hibernian's Scottish Cup win over St

Mirren. However, reports filtered through later that Boyle had been sent to a specialist in Manchester and the news was a bit more positive: the injury was not as bad as first thought and that he should be fine for Qatar. Boyle had been a revelation since bursting into the Australian team and his loss would have been huge for the Socceroos. There were similar concerns for centre-backs Harry Souttar and Kye Rowles who were still recovering from injuries.

Graham Arnold, who had copped so much criticism throughout the qualifying period, announced that his 'contract is over with the last kick of the ball at the end of the tournament. For the first time in four-and-a-half years, I have my own future back in my own hands.' On 8 November, he announced his World Cup squad of 26 players:

Goalkeepers: Mathew Ryan, Danny Vukovic, Andrew Redmayne
Defenders: Harry Souttar, Kye Rowles, Milos Degenek, Bailey Wright, Thomas Deng, Nathaniel Atkinson, Fran Karačić, Aziz Behich, Joel King
Midfielders: Aaron Mooy, Jackson Irvine, Cameron Devlin, Ajdin Hrustic, Riley McGree, Keanu Baccus
Forwards: Jamie Maclaren, Mitchell Duke, Jason Cummings, Mathew Leckie, Garang Kuol, Craig Goodwin, Awer Mabil, Martin Boyle

There was great joy for those picked, and despair for those missing out. Criticism was not long in coming, particularly over the goalkeeping choices with Mitch Langerak overlooked. It was later announced that goalkeeping coach John Crawley had selected the three goalkeepers. Similarly, the omission of Tom Rogic and Adam Taggart raised some eyebrows. However, there was much praise in the selection of young Garang Kuol.

Arnold advised that he had left the door open until the last minute for young Australian star Cristian Volpato to join the squad, but the 18-year-old prodigy turned down the chance to be a part of the Socceroos' World Cup squad for Qatar. Volpato had been getting rave reviews at AS Roma and had scored a goal and provided an assist in his most recent outing. He was held in very high regard by his team manager Jose Mourinho and his manager Francesco Totti. Volpato stated that he wanted to concentrate on his club AS Roma and would make no decision on his national choice until later.

Arnold had additionally taken the brave step to leave his son-in-law Trent Sainsbury out of the squad. However, Sainsbury, a former captain who had played in two World Cups, had not had much game time and his form had been indifferent.

2022 World Cup Finals

The bulk of the Australian squad arrived in Qatar a week before the tournament began. Martin Boyle and Harry Souttar could not start full training with the squad at their base because of their injury concerns. In the case of Boyle, a replacement standby in Marco Tilio was flown over just in case. Boyle would have a week to prove he was fit. The week leading up to the World Cup kick-off was full of excitement, intrigue, and shock. Socceroo legend Tim Cahill was appointed Head of Delegation with the Socceroos for the tournament and his knowledge and inspiration was visible among the players who got to train with and converse with him daily.

Former FIFA President, Sepp Blatter repeated a statement from a few years earlier that awarding Qatar the World Cup was a mistake. Reaction to the decision had been festering ever since it was announced, and in the years since, the majority of the 22 FIFA Executive Committee members who had awarded the rights to Qatar had been implicated in some form of corruption. The human rights' record of the host nation was also being questioned as was the illegality of homosexuality in the nation. There were also estimates of over 6,500 deaths amongst the workforce to build the World Cup infrastructure, although Qatari officials counter-claimed that there were only three deaths.

In good news for the Australian camp, Kye Rowles, Harry Souttar and Ajdin Hrustic were all cleared to take part in the Cup, but a question mark still hovered over Martin Boyle.

Only days out from the World Cup start, Qatar officials announced that beer would not be sold at the stadiums. They could only be procured at the Fan Fest site. This was a complete backflip on their original agreement. Budweiser, the major beer sponsor, was infuriated and FIFA again severely embarrassed.

Meanwhile, the Australian team had given Martin Boyle every chance to overcome his injury, but the flying winger was ruled out. He would be a massive loss for Australia. As if in compensation, first-game opponents (and reigning World Cup Champions) France had their central striker Karim Benzema also ruled out with a thigh injury.

Despite the misgivings and consternation of many, the World Cup kicked off with a glittering launch. Qatar became the first ever host nation in the history of the tournament to lose their opening game when beaten easily by Ecuador 2-0. England started with a bang, smacking Iran 6-2 and Saudi Arabia achieved one of the greatest upsets in the history of the game by downing the Messi-led Argentina, 2-1.

Australia 1, France 4
(*Halftime*: 2–1)
Scorer: Goodwin
23 November 2022
Referee: Victor Gomes (South Africa)
Crowd: 40,875

Australia: Mathew Ryan, Nathaniel Atkinson (Milos Degenek 85), Aziz Behich, Harry Souttar, Kye Rowles, Aaron Mooy, Mathew Leckie, Jackson Irvine (Keanu Baccus 85), Riley McGree (Awer Mabil 73), Craig Goodwin (Garang Kuol 73), Mitchell Duke (Jason Cummings 56)
France: Hugo Lloris, Benjamin Pavard (Jules Kounde 89), Lucas Hernandez (Theo Hernandez 13), Ibrahima Konate, Dayot Upamecano, Adrien Rabiot, Ousmane Dembele (Kingsley Coman 77), Aurelien Tchouameni (Youssouf Fofana 77), Antoine Griezmann, Kylian Mbappe, Olivier Giroud (Marcus Thuram 89)

All Socceroo fans went into this game with a degree of hope against the reigning World Cup champions. We had qualified against all the odds. Four years ago in Russia, Australia had gone down to France 2-1 in their opening match, with the winning goal only coming with ten minutes to go.

The French had traditionally been slow beginners in major tournaments. A draw with them would have been a great result and start in Qatar. The target for the Socceroos was four points with a win over Tunisia and a draw against either France or Denmark. However, a draw with France was not to be. Despite the Socceroos taking the lead in the ninth minute, we were eventually blown away by the French. Mbappe and Dembele simply tore us apart on the flanks.

The usual armchair critics were immediately slamming the team and the coach. I did not see it that way at all. We had Harry Souttar and Kye Rowles returning from long injury lay-offs. Ajdin Hrustic was still on the bench and a major player for us in Martin Boyle had been ruled out. The reality is that France were the current world champions and a realistic chance of retaining the trophy.

Graham Arnold announced before the game that he wanted Australia to play like eleven boxing kangaroos. In the beginning, they did hold their own with the world champions. However, France unquestionably could have won the game by a wider margin. Nathaniel Atkinson, the young right-back, was given the impossible task of shackling Mbappe.

After being forced on to the back foot by France from the kick-off, Australia hit back and scored a stunning goal. Harry Souttar sent a pinpoint ball to Mathew Leckie on the right wing. Leckie cut inside Lucas Hernandez, with the French left-back twisting his knee in trying to stop Leckie. Leckie then raced inside and sent the ball to the far post for the oncoming Craig Goodwin to smash into the roof of the net. We were living the dream!

However, France was shocked into action and applied mounting pressure with a flurry of attacking raids, only to be blocked by desperate Australian defence with some crunching tackles. In the 21st minute, the Socceroos were inches from going two up. Striker Mitch Duke let fly from long range after pouncing on a loose ball. His strike rocketed goalward, but it flew just wide of the post.

In the 27th minute, a French corner was initially cleared but it fell to Theo Hernandez who delivered a pinpoint cross to Adrien Rabiot in space to nod home.

Only six minutes later, the Socceroos' defence was again under pressure; Mat Ryan played out from a goal kick to Jackson Irvine, and on to Nathaniel Atkinson, who was pressured immediately by the French. Rabiot pounced and cut the ball back to Olivier Giroud, 2–1.

The Socceroos were lucky not to buckle completely and were under immense pressure to stay in the game. Mbappe should have scored France's third in the 45th minute when he blasted Antoine Griezmann's cross over the bar from close range.

Then against the run of play, Australia nearly equalised when Riley McGree floated a ball into the penalty area from the by-line, and Jackson Irvine rose to meet it. His header had Lloris beaten, but it hit the left post and bounced away.

There was no respite after the break. Giroud nearly had France's third goal with a scissor kick that flashed just wide. Behich cleared an attempt from Griezmann off the line. But the sheer weight of attack and possession cut Australia open. Dembele crossed and Mbappe headed home. Three minutes later, Mbappe was free to cross, and there was Giroud to head home the fourth for France.

Graham Arnold went to his bench, sending on Jason Cummings, Garang Kuol (who became Australia's youngest ever World Cup player), and Awer Mabil. After the match, Arnold reflected: 'Yeah look at the end of the day they're a quality side. They're world champions for a reason. I was happy with the first half. Second half we ran out of legs a bit, but that's the type of level these (French) players play at. We'll pick the boys up for sure. They should be proud of their effort, the commitment they gave. But again, they are the world champions for a reason.'

Goal-scorer Craig Goodwin told the media he was overjoyed to score, despite the disappointment of the loss: 'It's almost an indescribable feeling. To score at a World Cup against the champions is something I'll remember forever.'

The Socceroos would have to regroup and learn from this match. The return from injury of Rowles, Souttar and a cameo by Hrustic would be welcome additions for the next match. Our hopes were helped when Tunisia and Denmark fought out a scoreless draw in the other match in the group.

In summing up, the Socceroos were beaten by the current world champions and a galaxy of stars, including arguably the world's greatest player, Kylian Mbappe. The next game against Tunisia was a must-win match. Australia would be facing a mountain of Tunisian support as over 30,000 Tunisians live and work in Qatar, and another 20,000 had come in for the Cup. Arnold spoke of the importance of the match in the lead-up: 'We've got to be ready for that war. Fight fire with fire.'

There were very quick turnarounds between games in Qatar, leaving limited time for recuperation. Arnold was informed of criticism of the team's performance back home after the France game, most notably from Craig Foster and John Aloisi, and responded: 'I don't know what they are saying. And it's not for me, it's for the nation. Two wins (at World Cups) in 17 games. I want to put a smile on Australian faces.' Arnold was not dwelling on the French result but looking to the next two games and lifting his players: 'They were down, they were disappointed, of course. But I grabbed them and told them how proud I was of the work ethic and their commitment. All the stats showed that they put in 100 per cent plus. But it's those little mistakes that turn into big mistakes. You've got to look at the positives, and what our kids are going to learn out of it.'

Despite the loss to France, there had been an enormous turn out in Melbourne's

Federation Square for the game and the place 'went off' when Craig Goodwin gave Australia the early lead. Arnold said he showed the players some footage of the crowd in Melbourne and 'the energy of the fans back at home when Goody scored'. This was already shaping as the World Cup of boilovers: Iran beat Wales, Saudi Arabia beat Argentina, Japan beat Germany—the reality was the global gap in class had closed considerably and anybody at this level was capable of winning.

Australia 1, Tunisia 0
(*Halftime*: 1–0)
Scorer: Duke
26 November 2022
Referee: Daniel Siebert (Germany)
Crowd: 41,823

Australia: Mathew Ryan, Fran Karacic (Milos Degenek 75), Aziz Behich, Harry Souttar, Kye Rowles, Jackson Irvine, Mathew Leckie (Keanu Baccus 85), Aaron Mooy, Craig Goodwin (Awer Mabil 85), Riley McGree (Ajdin Hrustic 64), Mitchell Duke (Jamie Maclaren 64)
Tunisia: Aymen Dahmen, Montessar Talbi, Yassine Meriah, Dylan Bronn (Wajdi Kechrida 73), Mohamed Drager (Ferjani Sassi 46), Ali Abdi, Ellyes Skhiri, Alissa Laidouni (Wahbi Khazri 67), Issam Jebali (Taha Khenissi 73), Naim Sliti, Youssef Msakni

The Socceroos won a World Cup game for only the third time in their history and for the first time in 12 years with a dogged 1–0 victory over Tunisia to revive their final-16 hopes. Striker Mitch Duke scored the only goal of a tight game with a clever header in the first half and Australia then desperately held on to silence Tunisia's vociferous fans.

It was Australia's first World Cup clean sheet since 1974 and gave the nation a chance to reach the last 16 for only the second time. Socceroos' legend Harry Kewell. commentating on SBS, said: 'This was the best performance I have seen Australia play for a very long time. I hope they continue this.'

Australia now sat second in Group D with three points from two games, having been well-beaten 4–1 by holders France in their tournament-opener. The Socceroos would next face Denmark, who lost to France 2–1 later that same day.

After the Tunisian win, Arnold warned that the job was not done: 'I felt our performance, our fight, our grit, our determination... The old Aussie way was very important tonight. And I'm very proud of the boys.' He added: 'What I said to the boys when I got them in the circle after the game was I'm very proud. But we've achieved nothing. This moment, yes, we will talk about after. We've got one win, and it hasn't been done for 12 years and all that stuff, but we're here to go as far as we can go. It's about getting their sleeping right, recover well and the mindset ready for Denmark. I don't want any celebration. Just enjoy these couple of minutes with the fans here in the stadium. Get yourself in the dressing room, ice baths, recover and get ready for the next one.'

Captain Mat Ryan said: 'Just super proud. It was a collective effort from the get-go, we just left it all out there on the park and that's the objective every game we play but somehow, we took it to another level today and I can't fault the effort today. It's what dreams are made of what occurred here this afternoon.'

Australia's best World Cup performance had come in 2006 when they reached the last 16, in the days of Tim Cahill, Harry Kewell and Mark Viduka. Graham Arnold's Australian team did not have players of that ilk, but they had lots of heart and kicked off to deafening whistles in front of 42,000 at Al Janoub Stadium, where their fans were heavily outnumbered.

Each Australian touch was met with whistles from the throbbing ranks of Tunisia's bouncing, bellowing and flag-waving supporters. Australia had only ever won two matches at the World Cup before this match, and they had only squeezed into this edition via a play-off. But they started the better team against a Tunisia team who had held Denmark 0–0 in their opener and who were looking to reach the knockout stage for the first time.

The match was shown on prime-time Saturday night television in Australia and viewers saw their gritty side dominate the first 15 minutes to leave Tunisia unable to get out of their own half. However, Tunisia had the first sniff of goal in the 19th minute, but skipper Youssef Msakni was squeezed out and then defender Mohamed Dräger blazed his shot over the bar.

In the 23rd minute, Australia took the lead that their domination of possession deserved. Craig Goodwin, who scored the opener in the loss to France, crossed from the left and the ball ricocheted for Mitch Duke to glance his header back over his own shoulder and into the net. Commentator Harry Kewell marvelled at Duke's finish: 'Wow, what a start. Unbelievable! That is unbelievable. You know how difficult that is? That is the perfect header for us.' Duke later dedicated his match-winning goal to his son and said it is 'a moment I will hold very dear for the rest of my life'. His goal sparked an outburst of jubilation from the small contingent of Australia fans behind the goal, and momentarily silenced the hostile and unwavering support for Tunisia.

Harry Souttar made a heroic last-ditch block from the dangerous Msakni as halftime approached. Tunisia's fans had their heads in their hands in injury time when Msakni finally escaped Souttar, only to side foot wide from close range.

Coach Jalel Kadri brought off Drager at the break and replaced him with a midfielder, Ferjani Sassi, and a match that had simmered up to that point threatened to boil over. Australia was playing on the break and were inches away from a second, but Mathew Leckie couldn't connect on a low cross as he slid in front of goal.

The Socceroos survived a desperate onslaught from Tunisia in the second half, with Youssef Msakni forcing goalkeeper Mat Ryan into a save at his near post. The anxiety was palpable in the stadium when Tunisian substitute Wahbi Khazri almost poked in a late equaliser, before six added minutes were signalled by the fourth official. But Australia, who had to come through two play-offs to qualify for the tournament in Qatar, held on for a significant victory, and they would go into their final group match with everything to play for.

After the whistle, Arnold reminded his players: 'At the end of the day, it's just one game. Nothing will change for us. I told the players I am very proud, but we have achieved nothing at this moment. We are here and want to go as far as we can go. I don't want emotion from the players staying up all night looking at social media and all that stuff, I want them to recover and refocus.'

This was such an exciting game to watch, and it was great for Graham Arnold and his team. They put in an outstanding performance. Harry Souttar's bone-crunching and perfectly timed tackle on Taha Yassine Khenissi when he was clear was a game-saving moment that clearly lifted the Australian team. When informed again of television critics back home before this game, Graham Arnold was philosophical: 'Who cares? They've never coached. I haven't seen who was critical. Some of them have never even been to a World Cup. So, I don't listen to them. They have no effect on me.'

In a great result for Australia, France beat Denmark, meaning Australia only needed a draw against Denmark to progress, unless Tunisia somehow upset France. Injured Socceroo Martin Boyle was installed as the team's 'Official Vibes Manager.' The incredible and growing support back home was lifting the squad and on seeing the euphoria, Jackson Irvine remarked: 'Jesus Christ. It's hard to even to… I wish I was there as well. I wish I could do both. That just looks absolutely incredible. And I hope every single one of them has had a night they'll remember for the rest of their lives.'

The victory galvanised national support in Australia that only the Socceroos can deliver. The upsets just kept happening: Morocco beat Belgium 2-0. Graham Arnold analysed what lay ahead in tackling the Danes: 'We can't control what they (Denmark) do, we can help control, but we can't control everything. We respect them. But it's all about us, getting our game plan right and making sure we make it very hard for the Danes.' He was all about keeping his players focused and advised them to stay off social media.

Australia 1, Denmark 0
(*Halftime*: 0–0)
Scorer: Leckie
1 December 2022
Referee: Mustapha Ghorbal (Algeria)
Crowd: 41,232

Australia: Mathew Ryan, Milos Degenek, Aziz Behich, Harry Souttar, Kye Rowles, Aaron Mooy, Mathew Leckie (Ajdin Hrustic 89), Jackson Irvine, Craig Goodwin (Keanu Baccus 46), Riley McGree (Jamie Maclaren)
Denmark: Kasper Schmeichel, Rasmus Kristensen (Alexander Bah 46), Joakim Maehle (Andreas Cornelius 70), Joachim Andersen, Andreas Christensen, Pierre-Emile Hojbjerg, Mathias Iensen (Mikkel Damsgaard 59), Christian Eriksen, Martin Braithwaite (Kasper Dolberg 59), Andreas Skov Olsen (Robert Skov 69), Jesper Lindstrom

What an incredible game, performance—and win. The Socceroos created history on an unforgettable night in Qatar, securing an incredible 1-0 win over world No. 10, Denmark, to secure a place in the World Cup round of 16 for just the second time.

The Danes were considered pre-tournament as one of the Cup's 'dark horses'. They dominated the first half but were repeatedly denied by desperate defending from the Australians. The Socceroos needed at least a draw to have a chance of progressing. Veteran forward Mat Leckie struck his first-ever World Cup goal, clinically finishing a brilliant end-to-end counterattack in the 60th minute to give Australia a shock lead.

The Australians then desperately repelled Danish attack after attack in an excruciatingly tense final half-hour that was made even more dramatic when it was noticed that Tunisia were beating France. This meant that the Socceroos had to beat Denmark (rather than draw) to qualify. However, the Socceroos' victory secured Australia's first appearance in the World Cup knockouts since 2006, a feat only achieved by the 'Golden Generation' who were headlined by legends including Tim Cahill, Harry Kewell, Mark Viduka and Mark Schwarzer. Graham Arnold's youthful side had done something that even that side couldn't: win two matches, having beaten Tunisia 1–0 in the last match.

The win over Denmark prompted a big call from coach Arnold: 'It's the first time ever an Australian team's won two games at a World Cup, in a row, maybe we're talking about a new "Golden Generation". Because I've been listening and hearing about that Golden Generation of 2006, they got four points, and now we've got six, so maybe we're talking about a new generation.'

The win ensured Australia finished second in Group D behind France (who were defeated by Tunisia). The Socceroos would now face the winner of Group C. It was a date with Lionel Messi's Argentina after they downed Poland 2–0.

Arnold was overcome with emotion: 'I'm just so pleased with the players' work ethic, the commitment, the fight they had and the way they played. Denmark is a very good team, they're top 10 in the world for a reason, they've got high quality players who play in top leagues around the world. Defensively I thought we were outstanding tonight … I'm just so proud and happy, it's what World Cups are for, I truly believe that the Socceroos are the team that unites the nation—you don't see this when the cricket World Cup's on … Federation square like it is, pubs like they are, if it's rugby union, rugby league or anything, but the World Cup of football unites the nation, and I'm just so proud we've been able to put smiles on people's faces.'

Australia started brilliantly with Riley McGree finding space on the edge of the area and unleashing a vicious drive in the third minute that unfortunately cannoned into the back of Mitch Duke.

However, Denmark quickly asserted control, capitalising on Socceroos' errors and overrunning the defence. Just four minutes into the match, Socceroos left-back Aziz Behich received a rather harsh yellow card for a tug back on Denmark attacker Skov Olsen. Denmark threatened in the opening minutes, with Mat Ryan forced into a diving save at his near post to snaffle a dangerous, low cross.

Veteran defender Milos Degenek was forced into a desperate lunging block in the 10th minute inside the box to deny Jesper Lindstrom as Denmark continued to find space early and threaten the Australian defence. And less than a minute later, Ryan was forced into a strong save from Mathias Jensen's strike from a tight angle. Ryan was forced into save after save, the most worrying moment coming in the 19th minute when Maehle cut the ball into the six-yard box and Harry Souttar deflected it goalward. But Ryan awkwardly managed to scoop out a clearance. Australia was absorbing enormous pressure.

But the Socceroos managed to survive and get a shot of their own on target in the 22nd minute. Against the run of play, a long ball fell to Riley McGree who struck a long-range half-volley that went straight to Kasper Schmeichel.

Olsen took another tame shot in the 25th minute, but only managed to direct it at Ryan, before Eriksen dragged a long shot wide four minutes later.

Australia began to settle after the half-hour mark, with Duke managing a rare shot in the 41st minute before winger Craig Goodwin delivered one of the best moments of the half in stoppage time when he fizzed a low cross into the six-yard box. But Australian reinforcements hadn't attacked the front post and Christensen cleared well.

Central midfielder Keanu Baccus emerged off the bench at halftime for Craig Goodwin, who had covered 6 kilometres in a lung-bursting first half. Denmark also made a substitute, with Alexander Bah replacing Rasmus Kristensen.

Australia started the second half brightly, with a pair of early corners leading to a wild Behich volley. Three minutes into the half, Riley McGree raced down the left wing and crossed the ball for Jackson Irvine, but it was just behind the midfielder and his shot was wayward.

But once again, Denmark soon settled and resumed their assault on the Australian goal, forcing Kye Rowles and Jackson Irvine into clearances in the box. In the 57th minute, Milos Degenek was turned around by Jesper Lindstrom and copped a yellow card as he dragged back the attacker. Eriksen attempted to catch Ryan out with a curling shot, but overhit the attempt from the extremely thin angle. Denmark made a double substitution soon afterwards, bringing on Mikkel Damsgaard and Kasper

Dolberg for Mathias Jensen and Martin Braithwaite.

But Australia rode out the assault and went from box-to-box in a scintillating counterattack that started with Souttar in a lightning-surge. The Socceroos took the ball the length of the field as Leckie raced onto a Riley McGree ball from the left, before turning Danish defender Joakim Maehle inside out on the edge of the area. Leckie then finished clinically into the bottom corner, igniting raucous celebrations. It was his 14th goal in the green and gold, but first in his three World Cups. Leckie stated how he felt after the game: 'Proud, exhausted, everything. It's hard to describe the emotions right now. We always knew we could do it. We believed.'

Denmark pushed forward after the goal and continued to create chances in the final half-hour. Australian hearts were in mouths when Kasper Dolberg went down in the box in the 71st minute under pressure from Harry Souttar, raising serious fears of a penalty. But Dolberg was called back for a tight offside as he raced to get on the end of a cross. Australia continued to defend with desperation and tenacity as Denmark poured forwards, with even goalkeeper Kasper Schmeichel pushing forward in the dying minutes. Denmark pushed hard for an equaliser, with the Europeans needing to win to qualify for the knockouts.

Arnold turned to his bench, replacing attacking midfielder Riley McGree with defender Bailey Wright, and changing the Socceroos' formation to hold out the European heavyweights. The alteration to a five-man defensive line proved a master stroke. Jamie Maclaren replaced Mitch Duke in the 82nd minute, as the Socceroos defended stoutly until the final whistle. Denmark striker Andreas Cornelius headed over the crossbar in the final minute of stoppage time from a corner kick before Australia exploded in ecstasy at the fulltime whistle. Leckie said: 'That last 15, 20 minutes, we battled to the end. It didn't matter what they threw at us. We weren't conceding.'

The final whistle resulted in an outpouring of euphoria back in Australia as large crowds erupted with joy in Federation Square in Melbourne and around the country. No other Australian sport can generate the scale of this massive support. The Socceroos were through to the last 16 for the second time in their history and would face Argentina, and in Lionel Messi, arguably the greatest player of all time. In assessing the task ahead, it was important to realise that the Argentinian squad was valued at $970 million and the Socceroos at $60 million. Legendary Argentinian skipper Lionel Messi himself was valued at $337 million (or five times the worth of the entire

Australian team). However, this Socceroos' team had achieved so many firsts and overcome so many obstacles in winning two games at a World Cup tournament. They had to weather a storm of Danish attacks for the final 20 minutes knowing that Tunisia was leading France 1–0 and that they simply had to win to progress. Graham Arnold was fully justified for his claim three years before that his team would become 'the greatest Socceroos team ever'.

It was announced that Darling Harbour in Sydney would host a similar turn out to Federation Square in Melbourne to enable Socceroo fans to watch the match against Argentina on a big screen. The Sydney Opera House would also be lit up in the Socceroos' green and gold colours. The big hurdle for Australia now was backing up again for their fourth game in just eleven days. It was a big ask, although Argentina was in the same boat. Despite recognising the danger of Messi, Arnold said: 'The thing is, if you focus too much on Messi, then you're forgetting about the other players.' It would be a case of getting in Messi's face but not neglecting his team-mates.

Australia 1, Argentina 2
(*Halftime*: 0–1)
Scorer: own goal
4 December 2022
Referee: Szymon Maciniak (Poland)
Crowd: 45,032

Australia: Mathew Ryan, Milos Degenek (Fran Karacic 72), Aziz Behich, Harry Souttar, Kye Rowles, Keanu Baccus (Ajdin Hrustic 58), Mathew Leckie (Garang Kuol 72), Aaron Mooy, Riley McGree (Craig Goodwin 58), Jackson Irvine, Mitchell Duke (Jamie Maclaren 72)
Argentina: Emiliano Martinez, Nahuel Molina (Gonzalo Montiel 80), Marcos Acuna (Nicolas Tagliafico 72), Cristian Romero, Nicolas Otamendi, Enzo Fernandez, Rodrigo De Paul, Alexis MacAllister (Exequiel Palacios 80), Lionel Messi, Julian Alvarez (Lautaro Martinez 71), Alejandro Gomez (Lisandro Martinez 50)

Arguably the world's best footballer, Lionel Messi, helped end Australia's best World Cup, scoring the opening goal in Argentina's 2–1 win that eliminated the Socceroos.

The Australians departed Qatar after their best performance at the World Cup, with two wins in a single edition of the tournament for the first time. They replicated the 2006 teams' performance of advancing from the group stage and losing in the round of 16.

Messi's ninth World Cup goal helped to book Argentina a quarter-final against the Netherlands. However, Graham Arnold's men—having already matched the 'Golden Generation' of 2006 in a staggering World Cup campaign, delivered a sensational performance to threaten Argentina until the final minutes.

Arnold made just one change to his starting line-up, despite the brutal turnaround from Australia's win over Denmark just three days ago. Keanu Baccus, who impressed off the bench in all three group matches, replaced winger Craig Goodwin—the same switch that occurred at halftime against Denmark. Argentina also made just one change of their own, with Juventus star Ángel Di Maria benched after a thigh injury in their win over Poland. Alejandro Gómez replaced him in the starting line-up.

The Socceroos started brightly against World Cup giants Argentina, chasing a first-ever place in the quarter-finals and arguably the greatest ever victory in Australian sport. The Australians defended with discipline and structure, while surprisingly having the better attacking chances.

However, the Socceroos copped an early scare inside the first five minutes when Argentina fired a cross into the box that struck the arm of 24-year-old Keanu Baccus right on the edge of the box, but Argentina's penalty shouts were immediately waved away as the ball had bounced off Baccus' body into his hand. And the hard-tackling Baccus, in his first-ever international start, made a statement with a crunching bump on Lionel Messi that flattened the diminutive legend just two minutes later.

Argentina controlled possession from the start (an incredible 83.3% in the first 10 minutes). Midfield star Jackson Irvine copped a disappointing yellow card in the 15th minute for a late tackle, and having picked up a caution against France, he would have been suspended for the next game if Australia had beaten Argentina.

Australia made a rare foray forward in the 19th minute down the left flank, with Aziz Behich playing into the box, but he was muscled off the ball that rolled out for a goal kick. The Socceroos earned the first corner of the game five minutes later after a sustained period of possession, but Aaron Mooy's cross was headed away and his follow-up ball sailed harmlessly long. Another corner handed the Socceroos their first shot of the match when Riley McGree's ball found towering defender Harry Souttar, but his header lacked power.

The Socceroos' exceptional start came undone in the 35th minute as Lionel Messi scored his 94th international goal and his first-ever in the World Cup knockouts. Immediately after a fiery clash with Messi, Socceroos' fullback Aziz Behich fouled Papu Gómez in a dangerous position out wide. Harry Souttar headed the initial cross away, but it fell to Messi on the flanks. Having had limited involvement in the match to that point, Messi played a pinpoint one-two on the edge of the box with Nicolás Otamendi before threading his shot between three defenders and into the net. It was the first on-target shot of the match.

Three minutes later, Socceroos' fullback Milos Degenek earned a yellow card for flattening a rival in a physical, aerial duel. It was emblematic of the hard-fighting Australian approach that conceded eight fouls in the opening half. But the Socceroos responded well after the goal and saw out the remainder of the half.

Argentina substituted Gómez less than five minutes into the second half to bring on striker Lautaro Martinez, and the South Americans sent an early warning shot when they worked the ball into the box. It fell to Messi on the edge of the area, but his strike was deflected straight to keeper Mat Ryan.

Ryan made a terrible mistake to gift Argentina a second goal in the 57th minute: he received a back-pass from a teammate and was quickly closed down by two Argentina forwards. However, instead of immediately clearing the ball up the pitch, Ryan attempted to dribble past his opponents, but soon coughed up the ball for Argentina striker Julian Alvarez to pass into the empty net.

Graham Arnold responded with a double substitution with Ajdin Hrustic and Craig Goodwin coming on for Riley McGree and Keanu Baccus. But Australia's challenge seemed to be fading as Argentina began to step up the pressure, creating chance after chance. Messi in particular ran riot, embarking on a series of marauding runs that nearly delivered another goal.

With 20 minutes to play, Graham Arnold rolled the dice and emptied his bench with a trio of substitutions. Mitch Duke, Milos Degenek, and Mat Leckie all came off, with Jamie Maclaren, teen starlet Garang Kuol, and Fran Karačić brought on. Earlier substitute Craig Goodwin fired the Socceroos back into contention. Aziz Behich raced down the left flank and crossed the ball, which was blocked to Goodwin. Goodwin charged onto the ball and blasted a first-time, long-range shot. It was heading wide before taking a massive deflection off Argentina's Enzo Fernández that sent the ball into the back of the net!

In the 82nd minute, Behich nearly scored the goal of the tournament when he wove past four or five defenders in an incredible run into the box, but his shot from close range was well blocked by a sliding Lisandro Martinez. The Socceroos were pouring on the pressure in a desperate push for an equaliser and Argentina were feeling 'the heat'. Both teams continued to carve out opportunities as the match opened up and players tired. Messi raced into the box and laid the ball off to teammate Lautaro Martinez, but he blasted his shot horribly wide.

In the seventh minute of stoppage time, Mat Ryan was forced into a series of brilliant saves, twice blocking Lautaro Martinez's efforts, while defender Harry Souttar was sent forward as a makeshift striker as Australia went all-out in attack. Messi danced into the box past Aaron Mooy soon after and curled a shot just wide of the top corner. Teen sensation Garang Kuol showed his immense talent with a sublime touch to bring down a cross from Goodwin, leave his defender dead, and fire off a shot in the final seconds, but it was brilliantly saved by Emiliano Martinez.

What a performance. Jackson Irvine was reduced to tears after the game, reflecting: 'We gave it everything. Just like we have every minute of this competition. So proud of all the players and the staff. Just not enough on the day. I think we did everything we could to give ourselves a chance in the game. When Argentina is celebrating like this, victory against Australia, I think it shows what kind of opposition we gave them today. It's difficult to comprehend everything at the moment. It's all quite raw. I hope we made everyone proud.'

Coach Graham Arnold said he was proud of his players: 'I have to be very proud of the players. You know, we played against the number three in the world. And the first goal from Messi was a quality goal. The (Ryan) mistake cost us. I just hope that everyone back in Australia really respects what we've done and are proud of us as well. We took it to them.'

Harry Souttar, who had been one of the defenders of the tournament, said he was gutted to be out of contention: 'Just really gutted for the lads. I think you saw how much it means to us. How much effort we put in. Yeah, we took it right to the end. What can I say, they're a world-class team. Simple as that. They've got world-class players that can turn it on in an instant, like you saw with the first goal. We're gutted. We're so disappointed. But I think we can be proud of ourselves and the journey that we've had.'

Argentina coach Lionel Scaloni was full of praise for the Socceroos: 'It was a very tough opponent to be honest. Tonight's match was very useful for everyone to understand how difficult it is, this competition.'

The ultimate tribute came from one of the true greats, Lionel Messi, who said after the game: 'It was a very strong and difficult match. We knew it was going to be a physical match and they were very strong.' Messi added he would not be celebrating his 1000th match: 'No, truly no. This was a tough game.'

It is unquestioned that the 2022 Socceroos performance in Qatar set a new benchmark and surpassed the 'Golden Generation' of 2006. Winning two must-win games 1-0 in a pressure-cooker environment was a stunning testament to the team's fortitude and belief. The most positive outcome was that this team was a young side and would only get better, and some of the squad would go on to bigger leagues and clubs as well.

Graham Arnold's contract ended immediately when the final whistle was blown, and he confessed: 'I haven't even thought about [my future]. My contract is up. I just want to go away, have a good holiday, have a break, and see what happens.' Arnold had been under intense pressure through the qualifiers, and many had called for his head, but he survived, only just in some estimates, to see Australia qualify and then perform to the highest level on the highest stage. He had silenced the army of doubters. Many had criticised the Socceroos' qualifiers against Japan and Saudi Arabia, but that had been turned on its head through the outstanding results those two teams achieved in Qatar—Saudi Arabia beat Argentina 2-1, Japan beat Germany 2-1, Japan beat Spain 2-1 and Japan drew 1-1 with Croatia in the last 16, only going out on penalties.

Arnold delivered an impassioned plea and a piece of sound advice: 'We need to spend money and get help from the government to put some money into the game to help develop kids. One thing I would really love to see before I finish up completely in football is that the government build us a house. We don't have a home. We have been homeless since I have been involved for 37 years in the national teams. We need a home, a facility like... the AIS [Australian Institute of Sport], something that the government can help fund for the development of the national teams but also for the good of Australian football.'

The 2022 World Cup will be remembered for the amazing run of upsets. They clearly demonstrated that the gap between the top and lower nations has shrunk considerably. Fittingly for Messi (and in another compliment to the Socceroos),

Argentina won the World Cup Final, defeating France 4–2 on penalties after the game had finished 3–3 after extra time. It was the greatest Final in the history of the tournament. Morocco was a standout of the tournament, topping their group and beating both Spain and Portugal before being eliminated by France 2–0 in their semi-final. France defeated England in their quarter-final 2–1 after Harry Kane missed a penalty to equalise. Croatia, following on from their runner-up position in 2018, took third place by defeating Morocco 2–1.

POSTSCRIPT

The incredible support generated by the Socceroos' World Cup run must be capitalised upon. Additionally, the Socceroos must now receive the full backing of Football Australia, and even stronger backing from governments at all levels. The Commonwealth Government must come to the realisation eventually that rugby league and AFL cannot generate the economic, trade or cultural connections with our biggest trading partners in Asia. The Socceroos 'open that door' like no other sporting code in the country. They must be supported to the maximum level and the rewards could be staggering in terms of investment opportunities and advertising.

I strongly endorse Graham Arnold's request after the World Cup for the government to step in and fund a home base for the Socceroos, including training grounds, indoor facilities, gymnasium, and accommodation. This centre could be modelled on the highly successful Australian Institute of Sport (AIS) and Football Australia to provide top coaching staff and administration. It's time to not just *qualify* for a World Cup but actually *prepare* to win the thing. I would even go so far as suggesting a name: the Rale Rasic Australian Football Academy, recognising Rale's role as a coach of the first Australian team to qualify for the World Cup Finals and also the role he played in the establishment of the AIS.

The Government needs to recognise the opportunities arising through potential connections globally—particularly with Asia—that soccer provides. Immense economic and financial benefits can flow through trade that football will inspire. The other codes do not have that influence; the NRL is a game that is almost entirely based in and confined rigidly to New South Wales and Queensland. AFL has a much broader national base, but it is just a game confined to Australia. The government needs to recognise this and make the most of the opportunities available. At this moment, early

2023, we have a young team full of exciting potential for the future. They just need to be nurtured and prepared—Garang Kuol, Alou Kuol, Harry Souttar, Riley McGree, Nathanial Atkinson, and Marco Tilio are some fine examples. I would hope we could persuade top young talent in Cristian Volpato (AS Roma) and Alex Robertson (Manchester City) to decide to throw their weight behind an international career with the Socceroos.

FIFA has made the decision that the 2026 World Cup Finals will be jointly hosted by Canada, the United States and Mexico. It will also be contested by an expanded 48 teams. This to me is driven by nothing more than FIFA-generated greed. I think it will detract from the class of the Finals' series. But I know one thing: I will be there for the next one and I think the Socceroos will most definitely be there too.

In late January 2023, Graham Arnold was announced to be staying on as Socceroos' coach for the 2026 World Cup campaign. This was a massive lift for the team going forward, and Arnold received a justified multimillion-dollar contract to boot. In December, Arnold had been named as the coach of the 2022 World Cup Finals by the widely acclaimed French publication, L'Equipe. Arnold will become the first coach to lead the Socceroos through two entire World Cup campaigns.

The players were totally supportive of their coach, with Socceroos defender Kye Rowles telling *Bein Sports*: 'He's created a great family environment around the Socceroos and has been an awesome head coach. Tactically he set us up perfectly at the World Cup—the substitutions were always on point —and the game plans were spot on. We've struck up a good balance and that's because of "Arnie" creating that culture of "we're all in it together".'

Mathew Leckie added his support that Arnold is the right man for the job: 'He's the main reason why we have such a good culture in the group... I think he proved that he deserves it.'

Arnold reflected that Qatar was a fantastic achievement but enthused 'but there's plenty more to come and I truly believe that, and so I'm really looking forward to what's in front of us.'

We all look forward to the next four years – 'Go you Socceroos'.

REFERENCES

Behrent, S (2011) *History of the Socceroos,* Viking Books, Melbourne.

Blake, H & Calvert, J (2015) *The Ugly Game – The Qatari plot to buy the World Cup,* Simon & Schuster, London.

Cahill, T (2015) *Tim Cahill – Legacy,* Harper Collins Publishers, Sydney.

Cockerill, M (1998) *Australian Soccer's Long Road to the Top,* Lothian Books, Melbourne.

Corrigan, B (2004) *The Life of Brian,* ABC Books, Sydney.

Crouch, T (2006) *The World Cup—The Complete History,* Imprint Books, Adelaide.

Elsey, B & Pugliese S G (2017) *Football and the Boundaries of History,* Palgrave Macmillan, NY, USA.

Farina, F (1998) *Farina My World is Round,* Vox Peritus, Brisbane.

Fink, J (2007) *How Australia Became a Football Nation,* Hardie Grant Books, Melbourne.

Foer, F (2004) *An {Unlikely} Theory of Globalisation—How Soccer Explains the World,* Harper Collins, New York.

Forrest, B (2014) *The Big Fix—A True Story of the Search for the Match-fixers Bringing Down Football,* Harper Sport, London.

Foster, C (2010) *Fozz on Football,* Hardie Grant Books, Melbourne.

Gatt, R (2006) *The Rale Rasic Story,* New Holland Publishers, Sydney.

Glanville, B (2018) *The Story of the World Cup,* Faber & Faber, London.

Goldblatt, D (2006) *The Ball is Round—A Global History of Football,* Viking Books, London.

Goreman, J (2017) *The Death & Life of Australian Soccer,* UQP, Brisbane.

Grant, S (1974) *Jack Pollard's Soccer Records,* Jack Pollard Books, Sydney.

Harper, A (2004) *Mr and Mrs Soccer Les Murray and Johnny Warren,* Random House, Sydney.

Harper, A (2006) *the Socceroos—Voodoo to Destiny,* Limelight Press, Sydney.

Hay, R & Murray, B (2014) *A History of Football in Australia,* Hardie Grant Books, Melbourne.

Hay, R (2016) *Football and War—Australia and Vietnam 1967-1972,* Sports & Editorial Services, Melbourne.

Hill, D (2017) *The Fair and the Foul—Inside Our Sporting Nation,* William Heinemann, Sydney.

Hill, S (2017) *Simon Hill—Just a Gob on a Stick,* New Holland Publishers, Sydney.

Holt, N (2018) *The Mammoth Book of the World Cup,* Constable & Robinson, London.

Howe, A (2018) *Encyclopedia of Socceroos,* Fair Play Publishing, Sydney.

Jennings, A (2015) *The Dirty Game—Uncovering the Scandal AT FIFA,* Century Books, London.

Kuhn, G (2011) *Soccer VS the State—Tackling Football and Radical Politics,* PM Press, Oakland, USA.

Kreider, R (1996) *A Soccer Century—A Chronicle of Western Australian Soccer from 1896 to 1996,* Sports West Media, Perth.

Lenahan, A & Burnett, A (2022) *Socceroos: 100 Years of Camaraderie and Courage,* Media Books, Sydney.

Lusetich, R (1992) *Frank Arok—My Beloved Socceroos,* ABC Books, Sydney.

Meijer, M (2006) *Guus Hiddink—Going Dutch,* Random House, Sydney.

Mersiades, B (2018) *Whatever It Takes - the Inside Story of the FIFA Way*, Powderhouse Press, USA

Micallef, P (1994) *The World Cup Story—An Australian View,* Phillip Micallef Publishing, Sydney.

Miller, D (1986) *England's Last Glory,* Pavilion Books, London.

Mosely, P (2014) *Soccer in New South Wales 1880-1980,* Sports and Editorial Services Australia, Melbourne.

Murray, B (1998) *The World's Game—A History of Soccer,* University of Illinois Press, Chicago.

Murray, B & Hay, R (2006) *The World Game Downunder,* Australian Society for Sports History, ASSH Studies 19, Melbourne.

Murray, L (2011) *The World Game—The Story of How Football went Global,* SBS Books, Sydney.

Murray, L (2006) *By the Balls—Memoir of a Football Tragic,* Random House, Sydney,

Murray, L (2014) *The World (Game) According to Les Murray,* Hardie Grant Books, Melbourne.

O'Hara, J (1994) *Ethnicity and Soccer in Australia,* ASSH Studies in Sports History No. 10, Melbourne.

O'Neil, J (2007) *It's Only a Game—A Life in Sport,* Random House, Sydney.

Peacock, A (2015) *That Night,* Ebury Press, Sydney.

Postecoglou, A (2016) *Changing the Game—Football in Australia Through My Eyes,* Michael Joseph, Melbourne.

Radbourne, L (2022) *The Immortals of Australian Soccer,* Rockpool Publishing, Summer Hill.

Oliver-Scerri, GE (1988) *Encyclopaedia of Australian Soccer 1922-88,* Showcase Publications, Sydney.

Schwab, L (1979) *The Socceroos and Their Opponents,* Newspress, Melbourne.

Schwarzer, M (2006) *World Cup Destiny from Sydney to Stuttgart,* ABC Books, Sydney.

Slater, R (1999) *Robbie Slater—The Hard Way,* Harper Collins, Sydney.

Solly, R (2004) *Shoot Out—The Passion and the Politics of Soccer's Fight for Survival,* John Wiley & Sons, Brisbane.

Spragg, I (2017) *The World Cup in 100 Objects—A history of the World's Greatest Football Tournament,* Andrew Deutsch Publishers, London.

Stensholt, J & Mooney, S (2015) *A-League—The Inside Story of the Tumultuous First Decade,* Nero Books, Melbourne.

Taylor, M (2011) *Football: A Short History,* Shire Publications, Oxford.

Thompson, T (2006) *One Fantastic Goal—A Complete History of Football in Australia,* ABC Books, Sydney.

Trifonas, P. P (2001) *Umberto Eco and Football,* Icon Books, Cambridge.

Wade, P (1995) *Captain Socceroo—The Paul Wade Story,* Harper Sports, Sydney.

Wagg, S (1995) *Giving the Game Away - Football, Politics & Culture on Five Continents,* Leicester University Press, London.

Wallace, NM (2004) *Our Socceroos,* Random House, Sydney.

Warren, J (1980) *Johnny Warren's World of Australian Soccer,* Liahona Books, Hong Kong.

Warren, J & Dettre, A (1974) *Soccer in Australia,* Paul Hamlyn, Sydney.

Warren, J & Dettre, A (1977) *Soccer the Australian Way,* Summit Books, Sydney.

Warren, J (2002) *Sheilas, Wogs and Poofters—Johnny Warren and Soccer in Australia,* Random House, Sydney.

Wilson, T (2006) *Australia United—Adventures at the 2006 World Cup, Germany,* GSP Publishing, Melbourne.

ABOUT THE AUTHOR

Emeritus Professor John Maynard is a Worimi Aboriginal man from the Port Stephens region of New South Wales.

He has held several major positions and served on numerous prominent organisations and committees including, Deputy Chairperson of the Australian Institute of Aboriginal and Torres Strait Islander Studies (AIATSIS) and the Executive Committee of the Australian Historical Association. He was the recipient of the Aboriginal History (Australian National University) Stanner Fellowship in 1996, the New South Wales Premiers Indigenous History Fellow 2003, Australian Research Council Postdoctoral Fellow 2004, University of Newcastle Researcher of the Year 2008 and 2012.

In 2014 he was elected a member of the prestigious Australian Social Sciences Academy and in 2020 made a Fellow of the Australian Academy of the Humanities. He gained his PhD in 2003, examining the rise of early Aboriginal political activism.

He has worked with and within many Aboriginal communities, urban, rural, and remote. Professor Maynard's publications have concentrated on the intersections of Aboriginal political and social history, and the history of Australian race relations.

He is the author of several books, including *Aboriginal Stars of the Turf, Fight for Liberty and Freedom, Aborigines and the Sport of Kings, True Light and Shade, Living with the Locals* and *The Aboriginal Soccer Tribe* (Second Edition, Fair Play Publishing, 2019).

More really good football books from Fair Play Publishing

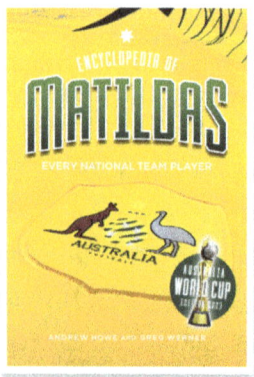

Encyclopedia of Matildas
World Cup Edition 2023
by Andrew Howe and Greg Werner

Burning Ambition
by Nick Guoth and
Trevor Thompson

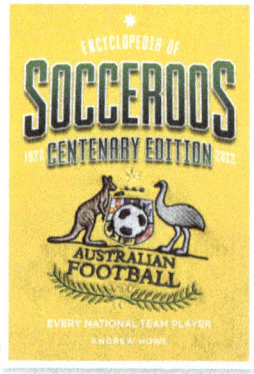

Encyclopedia of Socceroos
Centenary Edition 1922-2022
by Andrew Howe

Hear Us Roar
Compiled by Bonita Mersiades

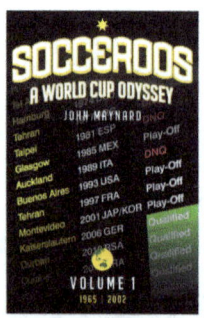

Socceroos
A World Cup Odyssey
Volume 1, 1965-2002
by John Maynard

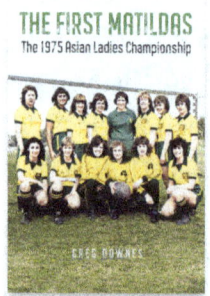

The First Matildas
by Greg Downes

Available from fairplaypublishing.com.au
and all good bookstores

www.ingramcontent.com/pod-product-compliance
Lightning Source LLC
Chambersburg PA
CBHW072049110526
44590CB00018B/3100